HORIZON
ZERO DAWN

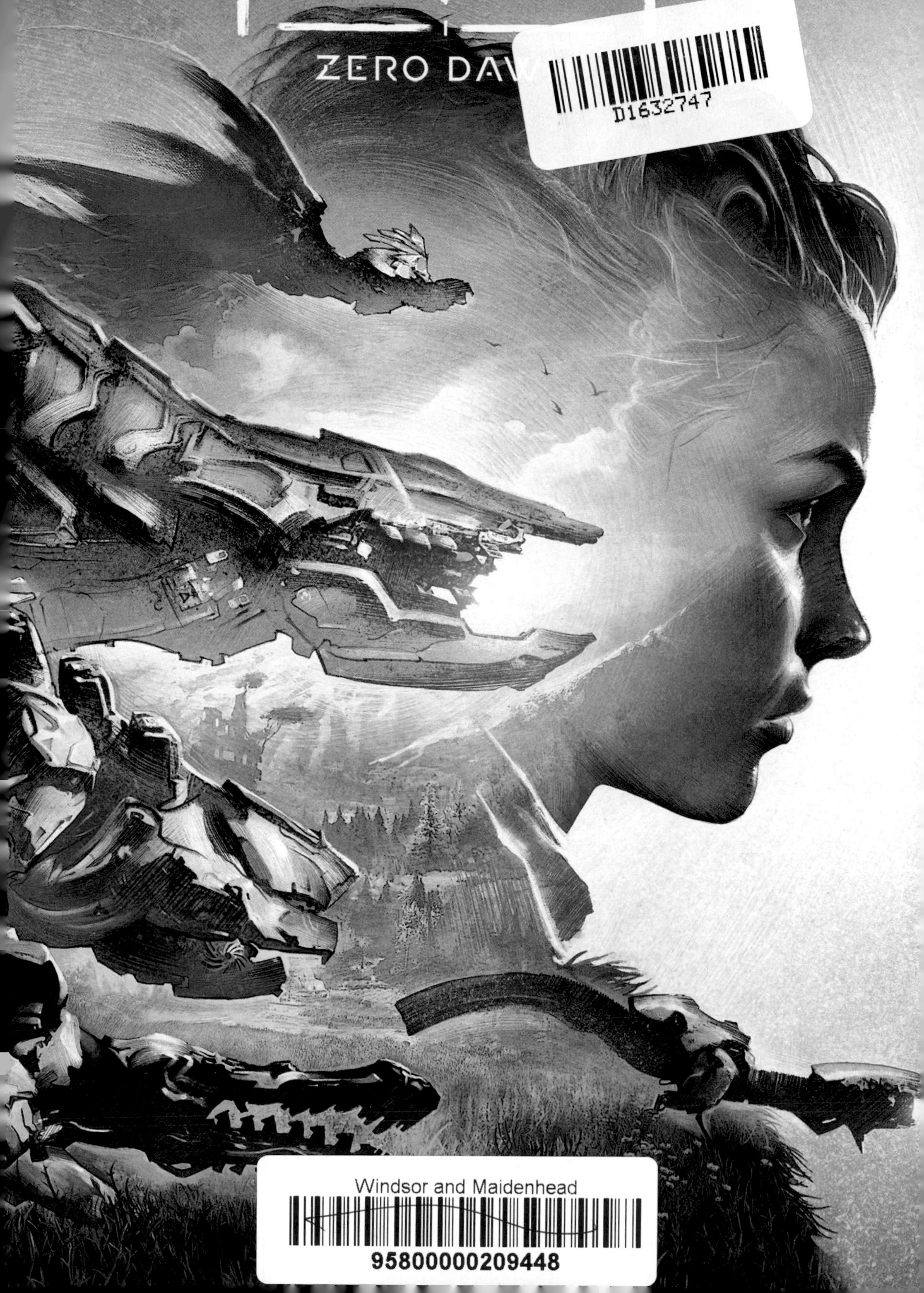

HORIZON ZERO DAWN

Group Editor
Jake Devine

Designer
Dan Bura

TITAN COMICS

Editorial Assistant
Calum Collins

Production Manager
Jackie Flook

Publicist
Phoebe Trillo

Publishing Director
Ricky Claydon

Editor
Phoebe Hedges

Art Director
Oz Browne

Digital & Marketing Manager
Jo Teather

Publishing Director
John Dziewiatkowski

Senior Creative Editor
David Leach

Sales & Circulation Manager
Steve Tothill

Head of Rights
Jenny Boyce

Operations Director
Leigh Baulch

Production Controllers
Caterina Falqui & Kelly Fenlon

Marketing Coordinator
Lauren Noding

Acquisitions Editor
Duncan Baizley

Publishers
Vivian Cheung & Nick Landau

GUERRILLA GAMES

Narrative Director / Benjamin McCaw Contributing Writers / Ariadna Martinez, Annie Kitain

Art Direction / Jan-Bart van Beek, Gilbert Sanders, Craig Stuart, Roland Ijzermans, Misja Baas, Ilya Golitsyn

Producers / Tim Symons, Lamine Outeldait Executive Producer / Angie Smets

Special Thanks / Hermen Hulst, Michiel van der Leeuw

Published by Titan Comics, a division of Titan Publishing Group, Ltd. 144 Southwark Street, London SE1 0UP
Titan Comics is a registered trademark of Titan Publishing Group, Ltd. All rights reserved.

Horizon Zero Dawn™ ©2022 Sony Interactive Entertainment Europe. Published by Sony Interactive Entertainment Europe Ltd.
Developed by Guerrilla. "Horizon Zero Dawn" is a trademark of Sony Interactive Entertainment Europe. All rights reserved.

A CIP catalogue record for this title is available from the British Library.

STANDARD EDITION ISBN: 9781787734104
SONY GEAR STORE EXCLUSIVE ISBN: 9781787739178
First edition: February 2022
10 9 8 7 6 5 4 3 2 1

Printed in Canada.

For rights information contact jenny.boyce@titanemail.com

WWW.TITAN-COMICS.COM
Become a fan on Facebook.com/comicstitan
Follow us on Twitter @ComicsTitan

HORIZON ZERO DAWN™

WRITER
ANNE TOOLE

STORY
BEN MCCAW

SCRIPT EDITOR
ANNIE KITAIN

ARTIST
ELMER DAMASO

COLORS
BRYAN VALENZA & STELLADIA

LETTERS
JIM CAMPBELL

GUERRILLA

TITAN COMICS

FOREWORD

What is it about Erend?

Is it the big shiny hammer? The muttonchops? The mohawk? His unique blend of oafish strength and emotional vulnerability? The way he looks up to Aloy, respectfully aware that she is out of his league?

Whatever it is, with the success of *Horizon Zero Dawn*, he quickly became a fan-favorite. (He was always a favorite of the writing team at Guerrilla!)

Which is why, when we embarked upon a second four-issue series of the *Horizon Zero Dawn* comic book, it felt like Erend should take the spotlight. And what better way to embellish his legend than to set it against the backdrop of one of Horizon's most epic backstory events – the siege and liberation of Meridian? By doing so, we could simultaneously feature one of our favorite characters and show off a compelling, never-before-seen moment in our timeline.

You hold the result in your hands, and we very much want you to enjoy the action – but also the heart of the story: Erend's ever-evolving tumult over his dear departed sister, Ersa. Above all, we hope you feel for the big guy as much as we do.

Comics are a collaborative medium, and this book would have been impossible without the invaluable talents of writer Anne Toole, artist Elmer Damaso, colorist Bryan Velenza, letterer Jim Campbell, and the teams at Guerrilla and Titan Comics. Thanks to all for their hard work and inspiring creativity!

As Erend would say: Enough talk. By the forge, let's get to the fight!

Ben McCaw

Studio Narrative Director

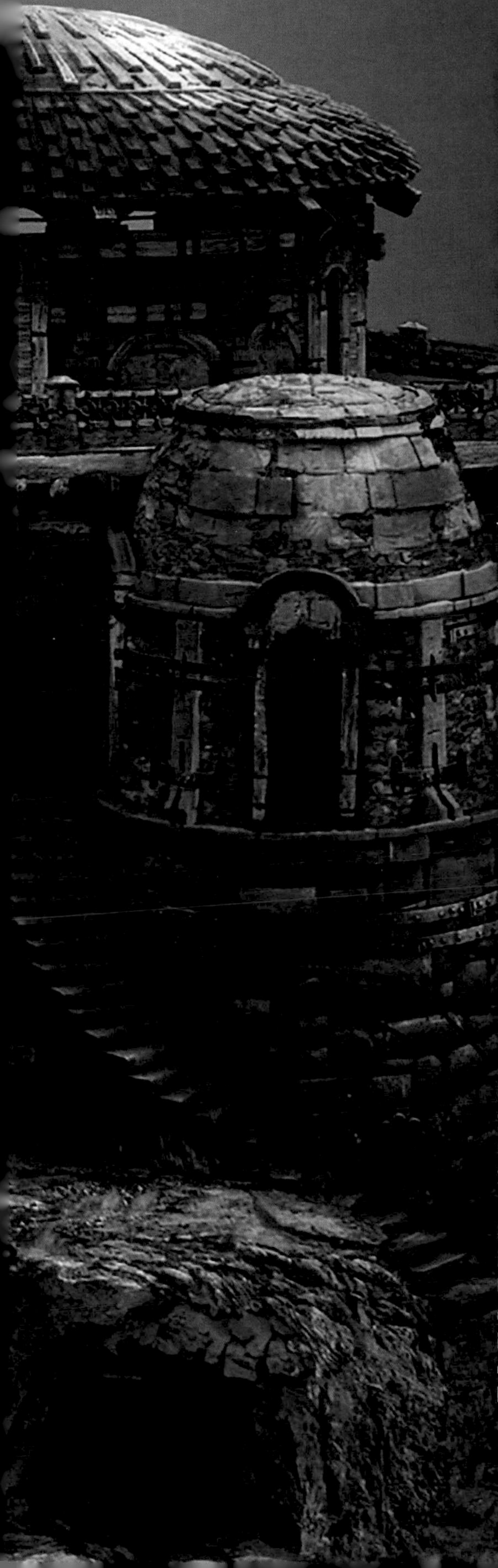

THE WORLD OF HORIZON

Our story takes place a thousand years after a global cataclysm. Earth has been remade into a lush, thriving ecosystem, but with a new dominant species: the machines.

These massive, animal-like robots fill the lands, oceans, and skies, serving as the guardians and enforcers of the revived natural order.

New generations of humans formed into pre-industrial tribes, without knowledge of the doomed civilization that preceded them, that of the "Old Ones" – us.

This story is set during the events of *Horizon Zero Dawn*. Aloy's search for answers led her to Meridian, where she helped Erend bring Dervahl to justice for the death of his sister, Ersa. Soon after, she learned that the Eclipse cult had a base in the northern ruins of Maker's End. But just as she set out to find it, Erend requested her aid yet again.

An Oseram trader has been murdered near Pitchcliff. And Korl, an old associate of Dervahl's, was spotted near the scene. Erend is determined to bring this dangerous fugitive to justice...

NOTEBOOK

Meridian – The City of the Sun, populated by the Carja people. Ruled by Sun-King Avad.

Hunter's Lodge – Based in Meridian, the Hunter's lodge employs the greatest machine hunters in the land to complete contracts and hunt bounties.

Sunhawk – Leader of the Hunter's Lodge. The title is earned by the hunter who takes down the most dangerous known machine.

Hawk – One who has proven themselves worthy of the hunt, Hawks take on contracts and train up the next generation of hunters.

Thrush – A Hawk-in-training, every Hawk is assigned one thrush to train.

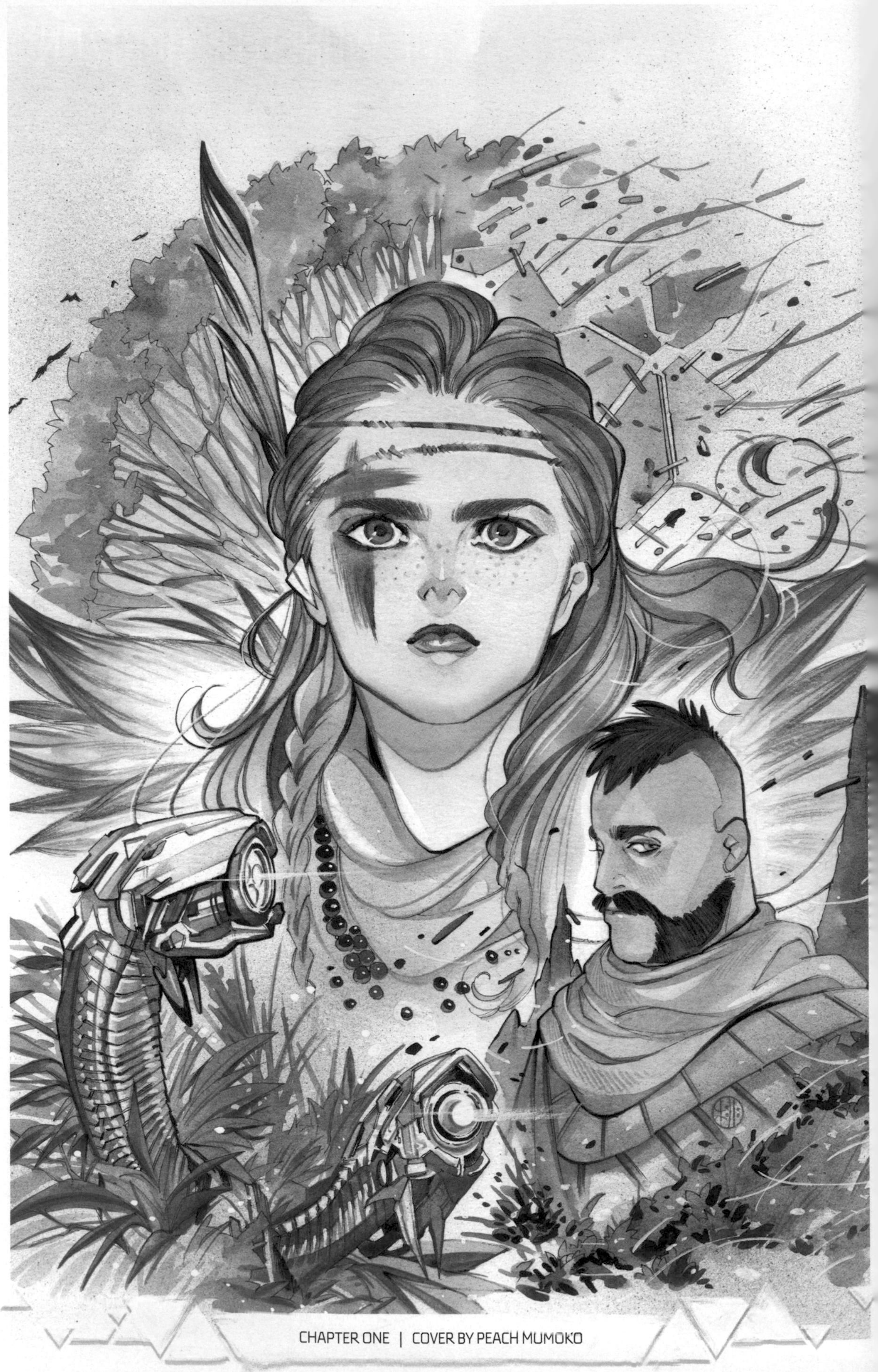

CHAPTER ONE | COVER BY PEACH MUMOKO

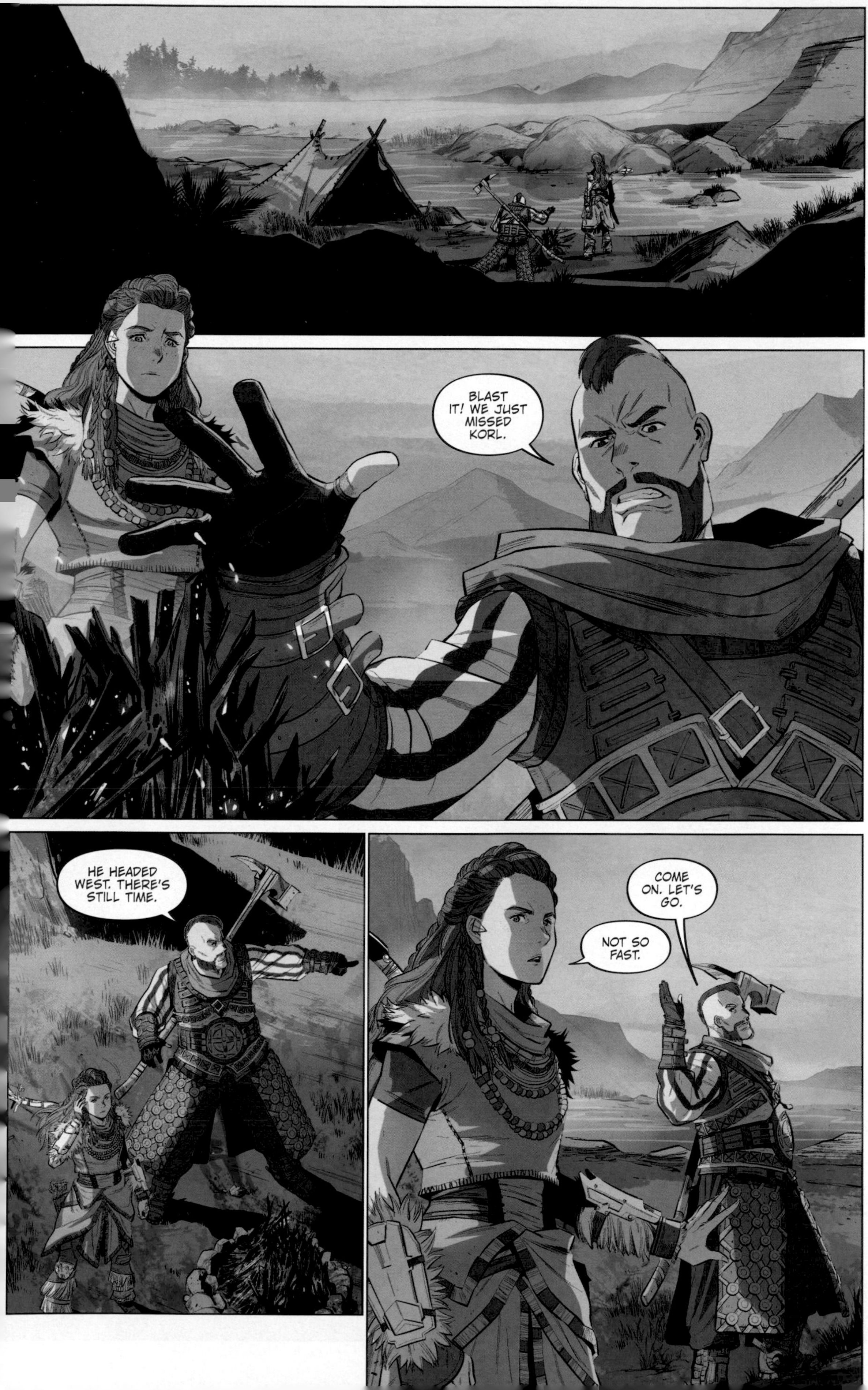
BLAST IT! WE JUST MISSED KORL.
HE HEADED WEST. THERE'S STILL TIME.
COME ON. LET'S GO.
NOT SO FAST.

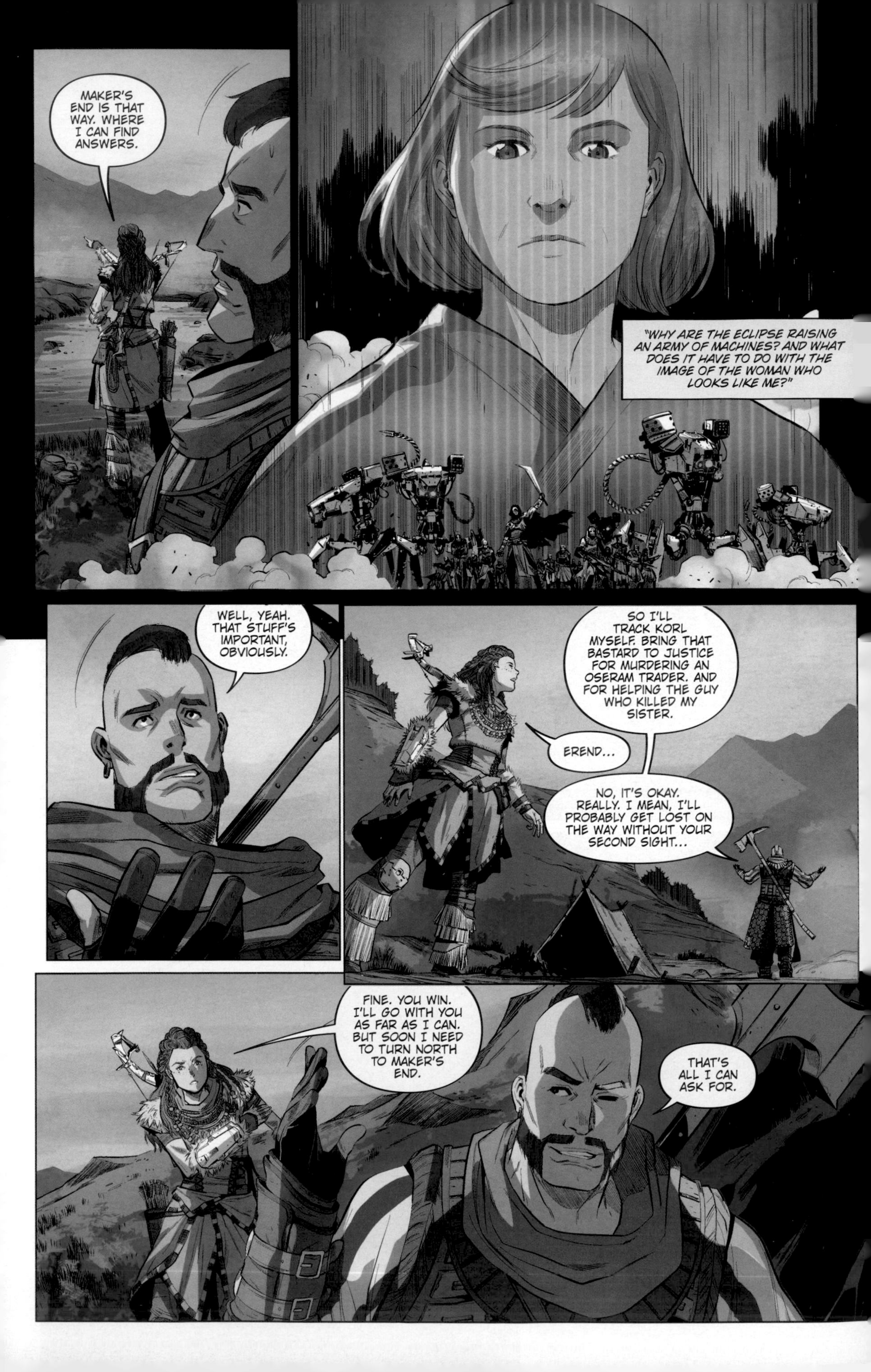
MAKER'S END IS THAT WAY. WHERE I CAN FIND ANSWERS.
"WHY ARE THE ECLIPSE RAISING AN ARMY OF MACHINES? AND WHAT DOES IT HAVE TO DO WITH THE IMAGE OF THE WOMAN WHO LOOKS LIKE ME?"
WELL, YEAH. THAT STUFF'S IMPORTANT, OBVIOUSLY.
SO I'LL TRACK KORL MYSELF. BRING THAT BASTARD TO JUSTICE FOR MURDERING AN OSERAM TRADER. AND FOR HELPING THE GUY WHO KILLED MY SISTER.
EREND...
NO, IT'S OKAY. REALLY. I MEAN, I'LL PROBABLY GET LOST ON THE WAY WITHOUT YOUR SECOND SIGHT...
FINE. YOU WIN. I'LL GO WITH YOU AS FAR AS I CAN. BUT SOON I NEED TO TURN NORTH TO MAKER'S END.
THAT'S ALL I CAN ASK FOR.

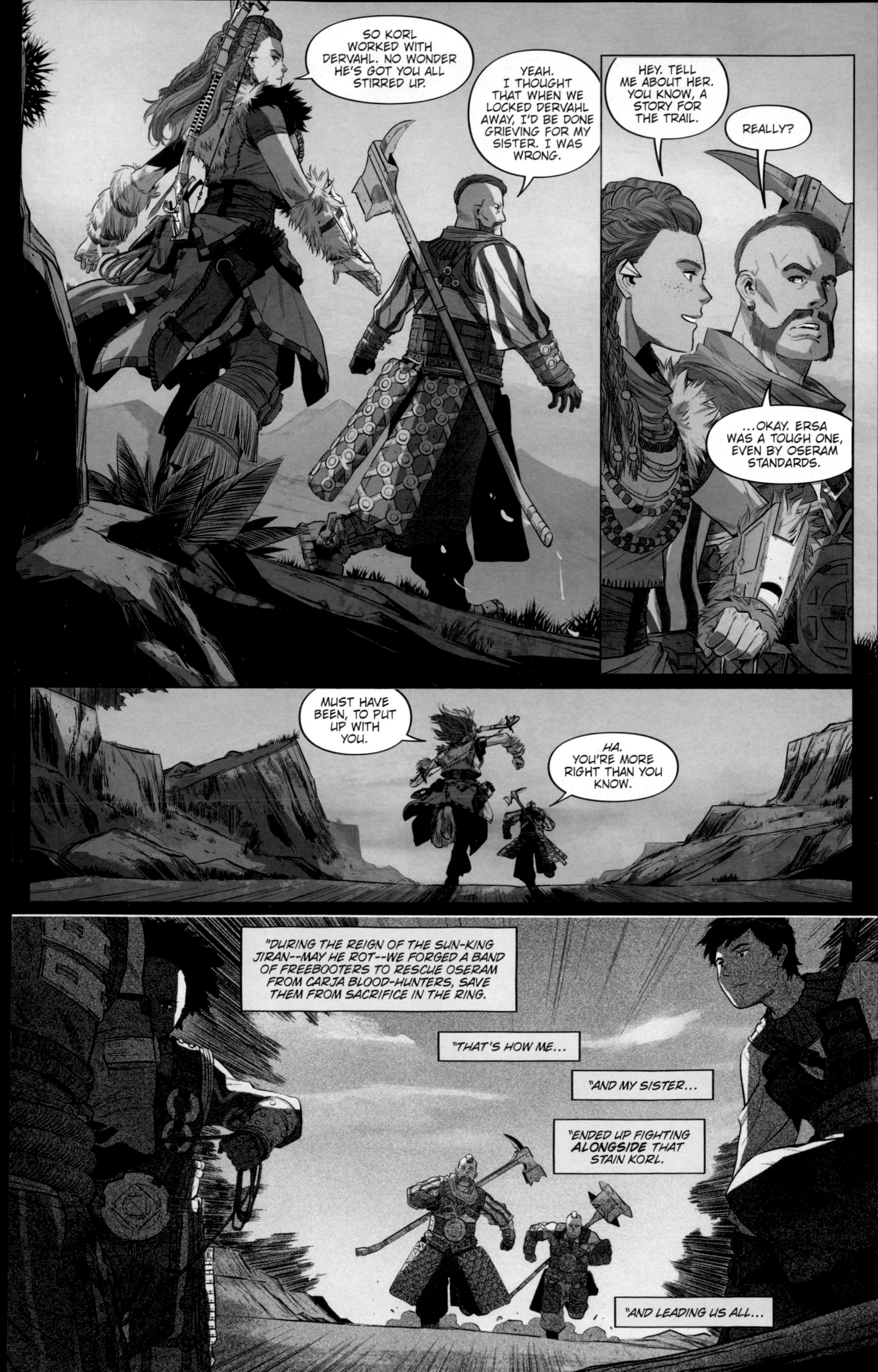
SO KORL WORKED WITH DERVAHL. NO WONDER HE'S GOT YOU ALL STIRRED UP.
YEAH. I THOUGHT THAT WHEN WE LOCKED DERVAHL AWAY, I'D BE DONE GRIEVING FOR MY SISTER. I WAS WRONG.
HEY. TELL ME ABOUT HER. YOU KNOW, A STORY FOR THE TRAIL.
REALLY?
...OKAY. ERSA WAS A TOUGH ONE, EVEN BY OSERAM STANDARDS.
MUST HAVE BEEN, TO PUT UP WITH YOU.
HA. YOU'RE MORE RIGHT THAN YOU KNOW.
"DURING THE REIGN OF THE SUN-KING JIRAN--MAY HE ROT--WE FORGED A BAND OF FREEBOOTERS TO RESCUE OSERAM FROM CARJA BLOOD-HUNTERS, SAVE THEM FROM SACRIFICE IN THE RING.
"THAT'S HOW ME...
"AND MY SISTER...
"ENDED UP FIGHTING ALONGSIDE THAT STAIN KORL.
"AND LEADING US ALL...

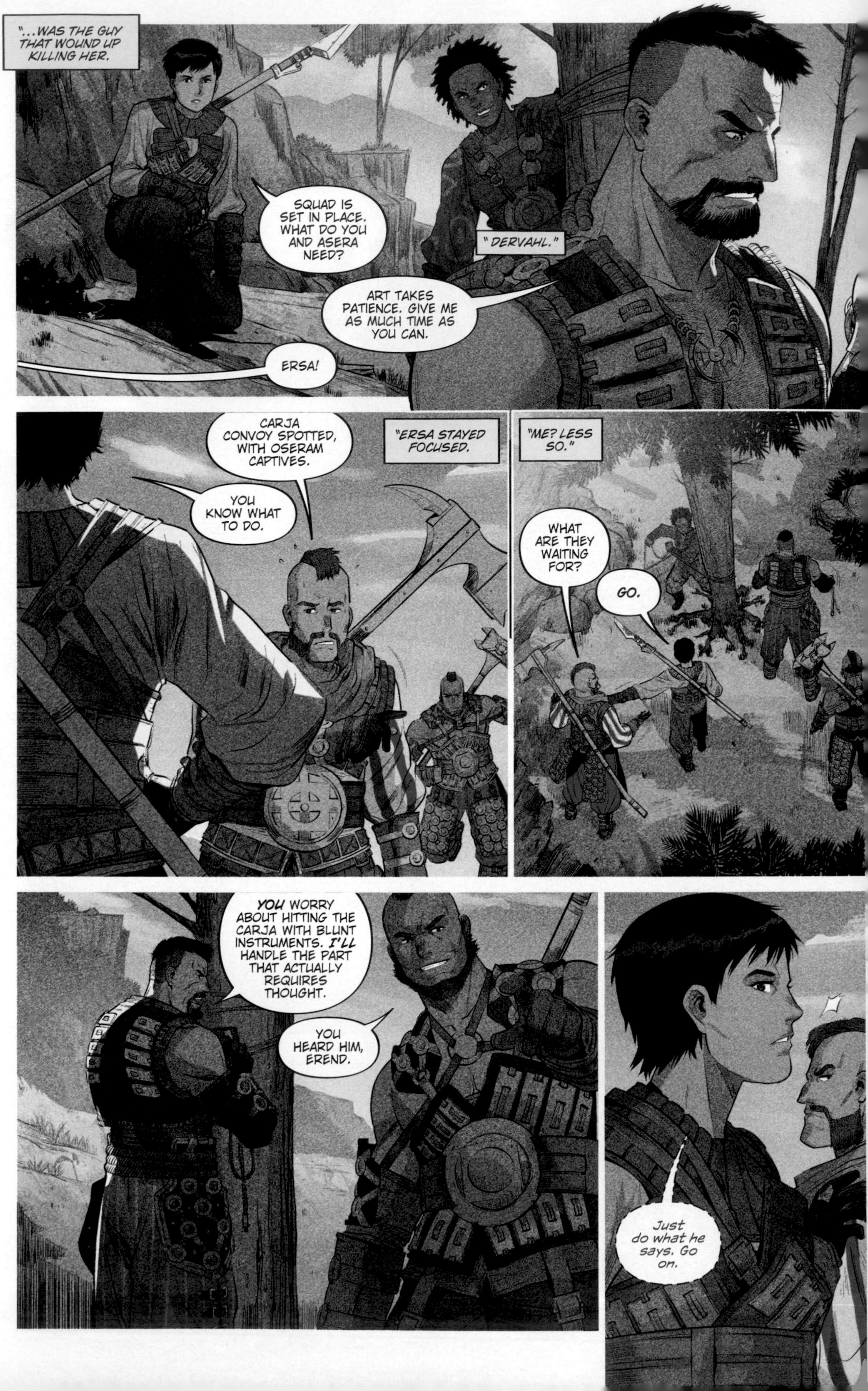
"...WAS THE GUY THAT WOUND UP KILLING HER.
SQUAD IS SET IN PLACE. WHAT DO YOU AND ASERA NEED?
" DERVAHL."
ART TAKES PATIENCE. GIVE ME AS MUCH TIME AS YOU CAN.
ERSA!
CARJA CONVOY SPOTTED, WITH OSERAM CAPTIVES.
YOU KNOW WHAT TO DO.
"ERSA STAYED FOCUSED.
"ME? LESS SO."
WHAT ARE THEY WAITING FOR?
GO.
YOU WORRY ABOUT HITTING THE CARJA WITH BLUNT INSTRUMENTS. I'LL HANDLE THE PART THAT ACTUALLY REQUIRES THOUGHT.
YOU HEARD HIM, EREND.
Just do what he says. Go on.

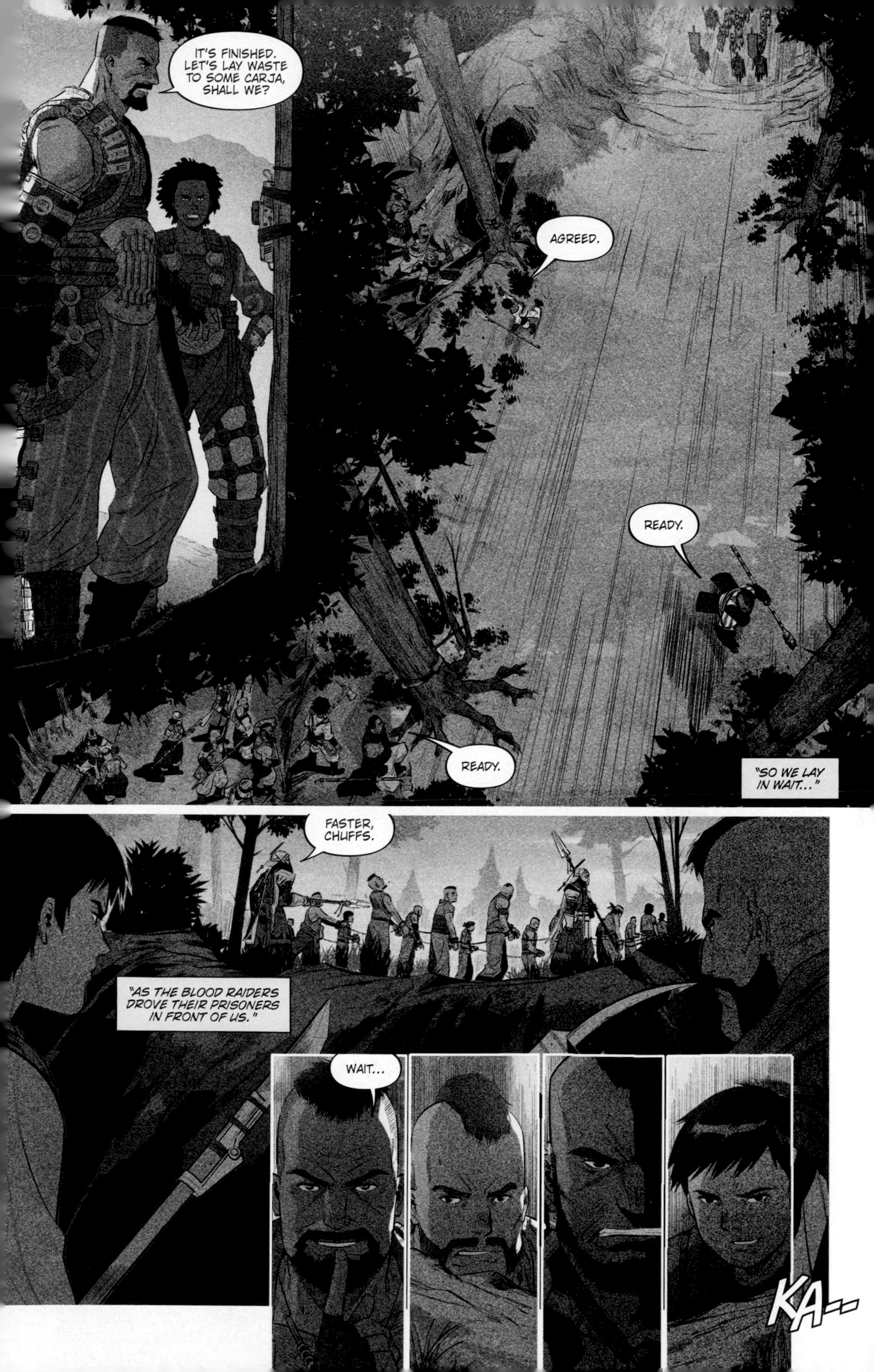

IT'S FINISHED. LET'S LAY WASTE TO SOME CARJA, SHALL WE?
AGREED.
READY.
READY.
"SO WE LAY IN WAIT..."
FASTER, CHUFFS.
"AS THE BLOOD RAIDERS DROVE THEIR PRISONERS IN FRONT OF US."
WAIT...
KA--

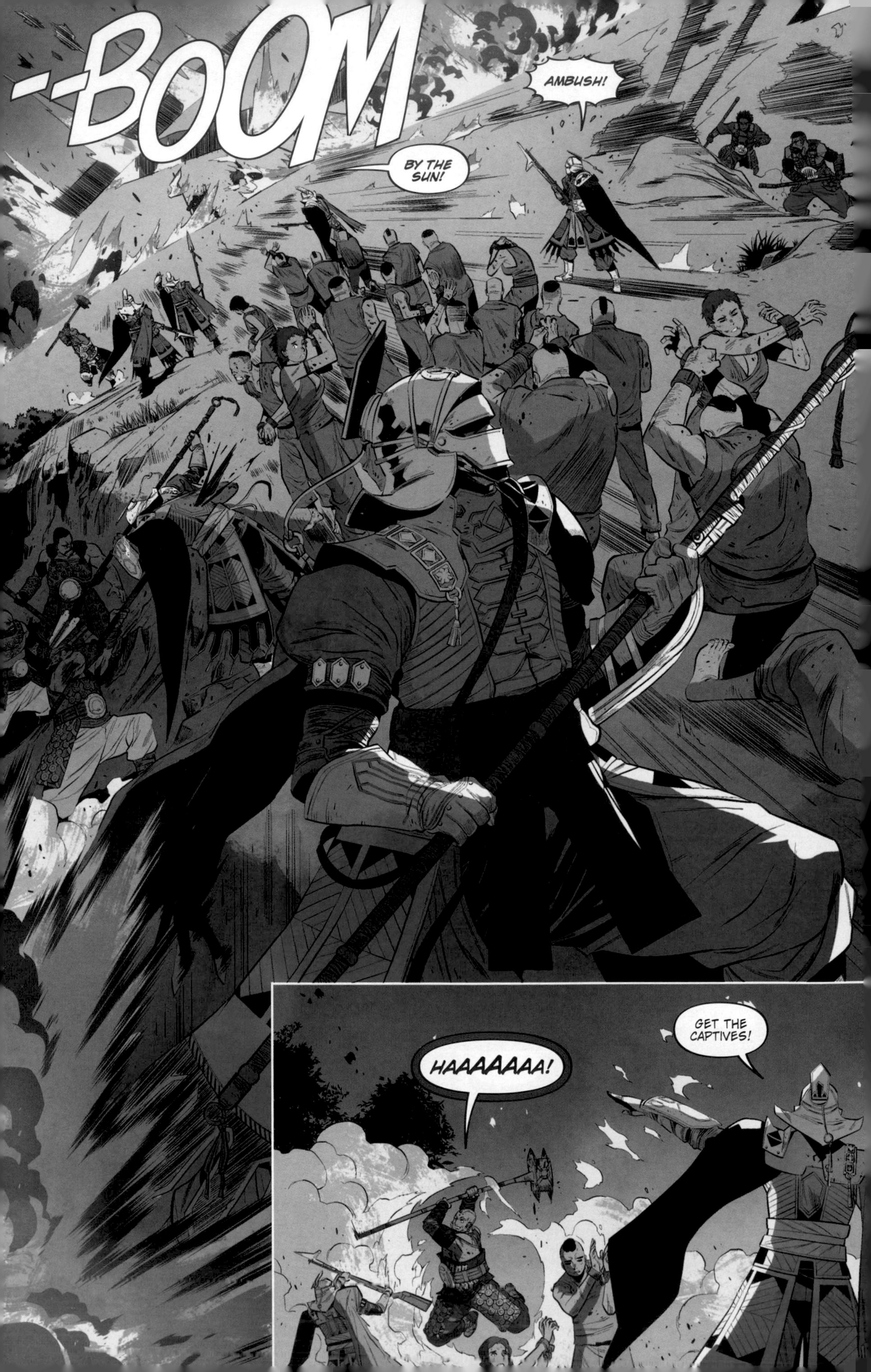
--BOOM
AMBUSH!
BY THE SUN!
GET THE CAPTIVES!
HAAAAAAA!

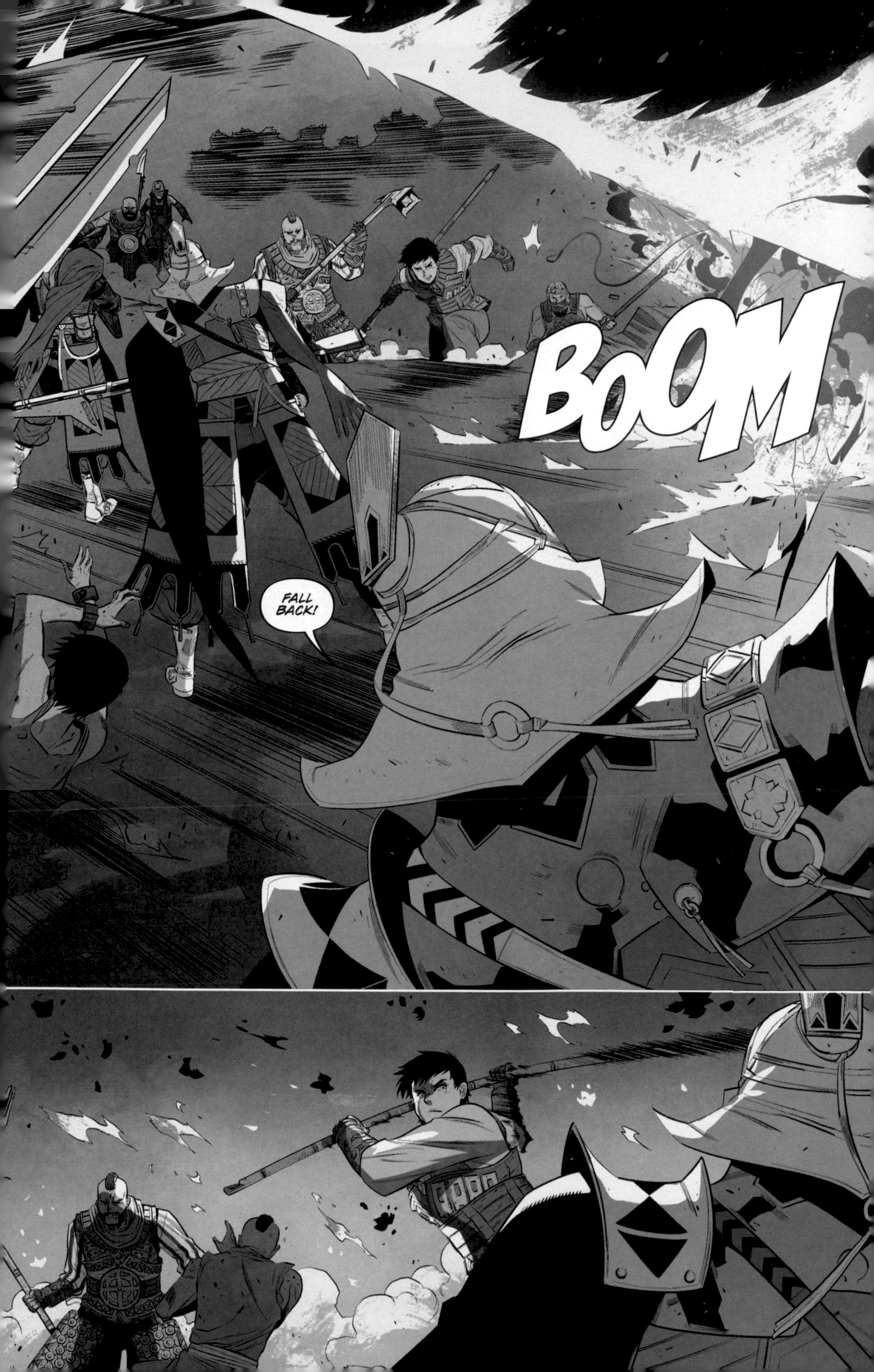
BOOM
FALL BACK!

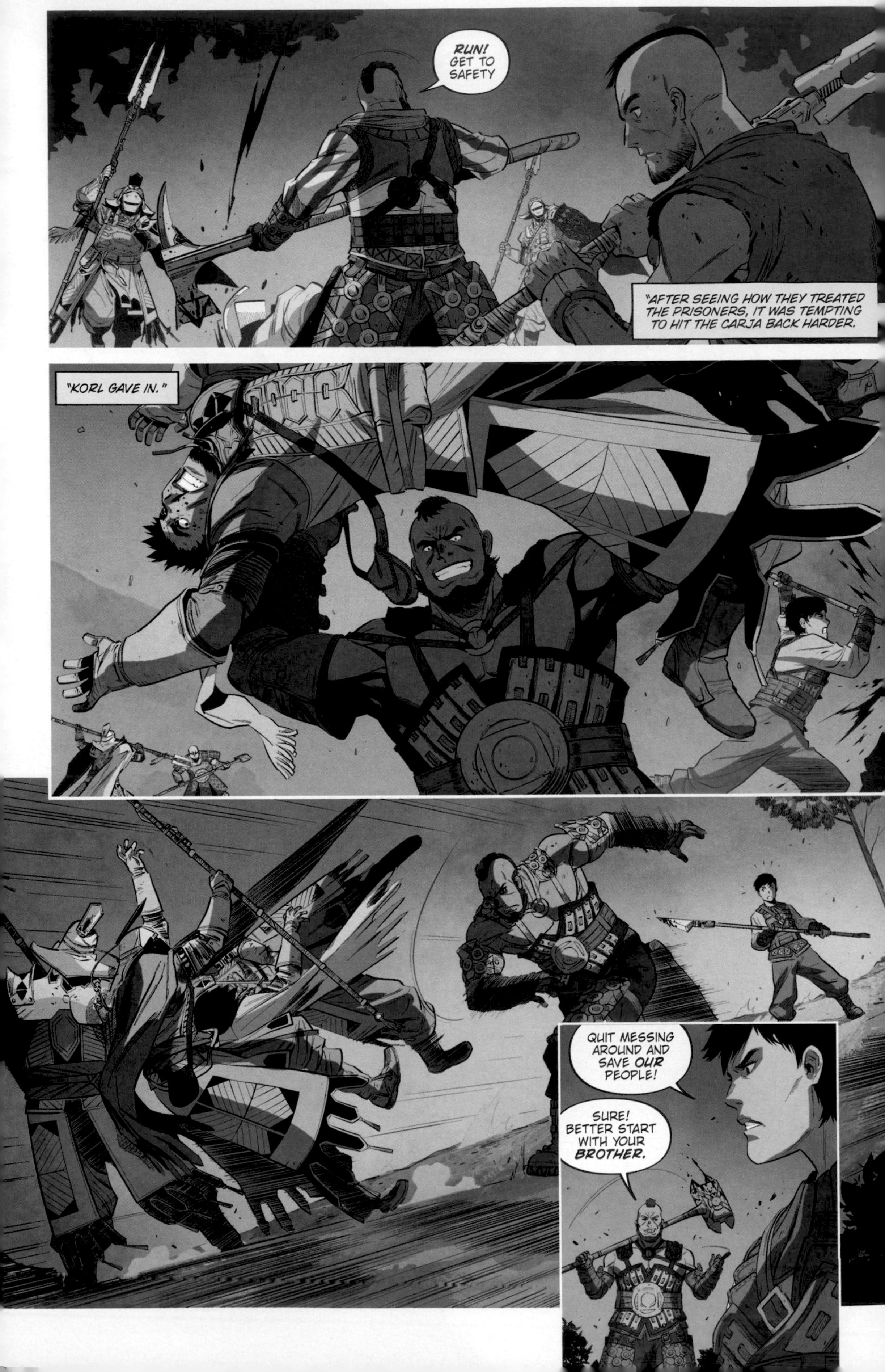

RUN! GET TO SAFETY
"AFTER SEEING HOW THEY TREATED THE PRISONERS, IT WAS TEMPTING TO HIT THE CARJA BACK HARDER.
"KORL GAVE IN."
QUIT MESSING AROUND AND SAVE OUR PEOPLE!
SURE! BETTER START WITH YOUR BROTHER.

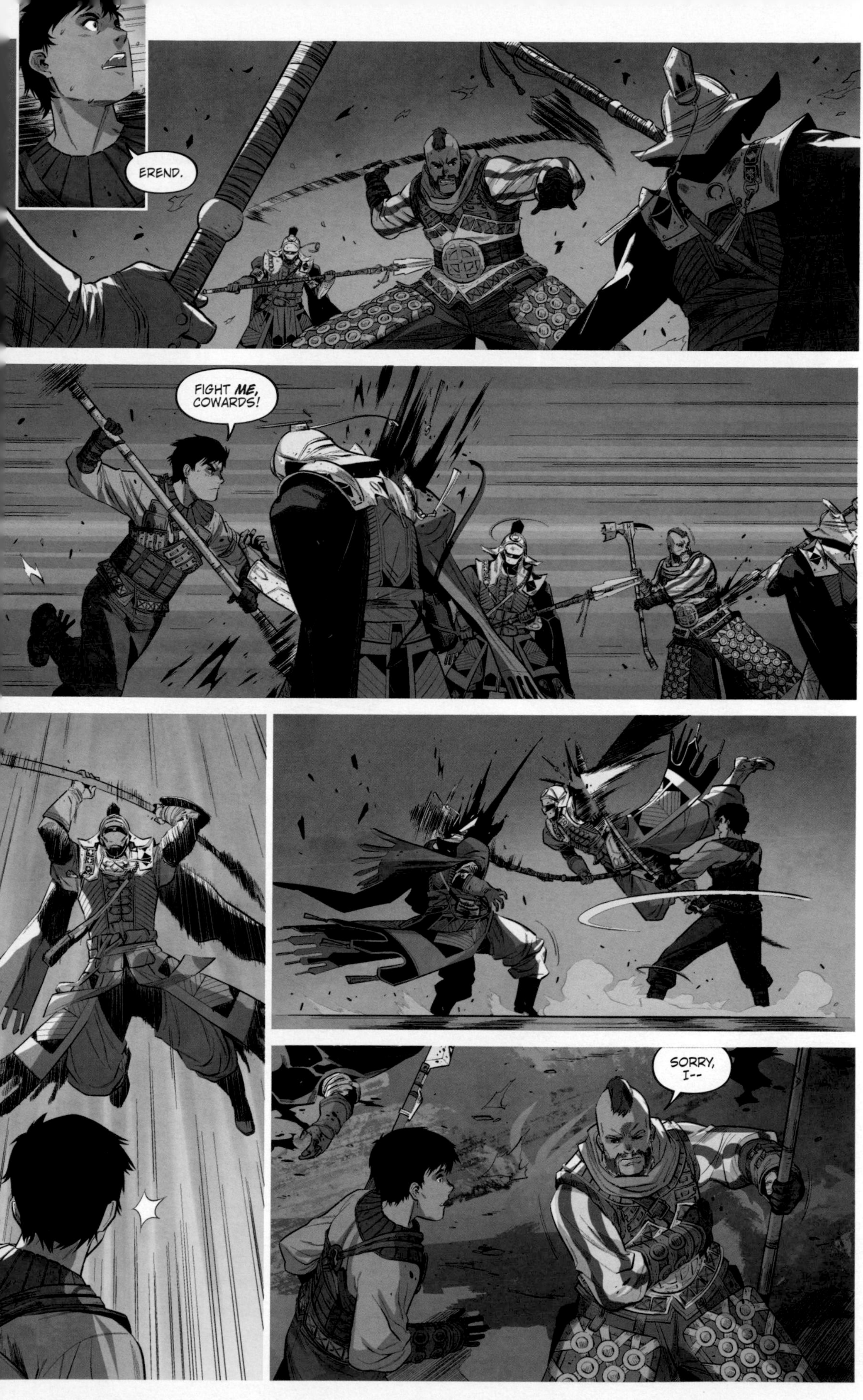
EREND.
FIGHT ME, COWARDS!
SORRY, I--

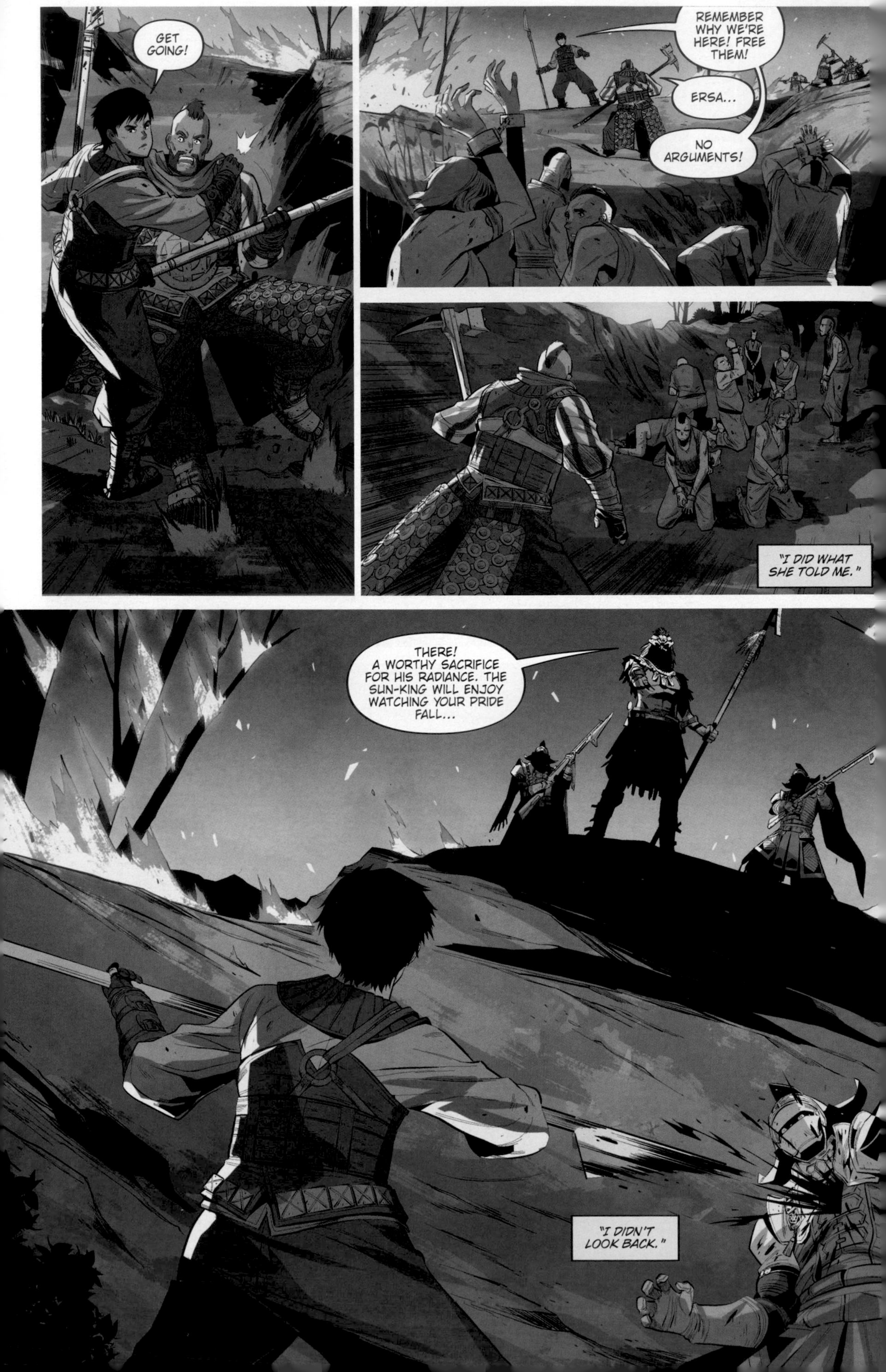
GET GOING!
REMEMBER WHY WE'RE HERE! FREE THEM!
ERSA...
NO ARGUMENTS!
"I DID WHAT SHE TOLD ME."
THERE! A WORTHY SACRIFICE FOR HIS RADIANCE. THE SUN-KING WILL ENJOY WATCHING YOUR PRIDE FALL...
"I DIDN'T LOOK BACK."

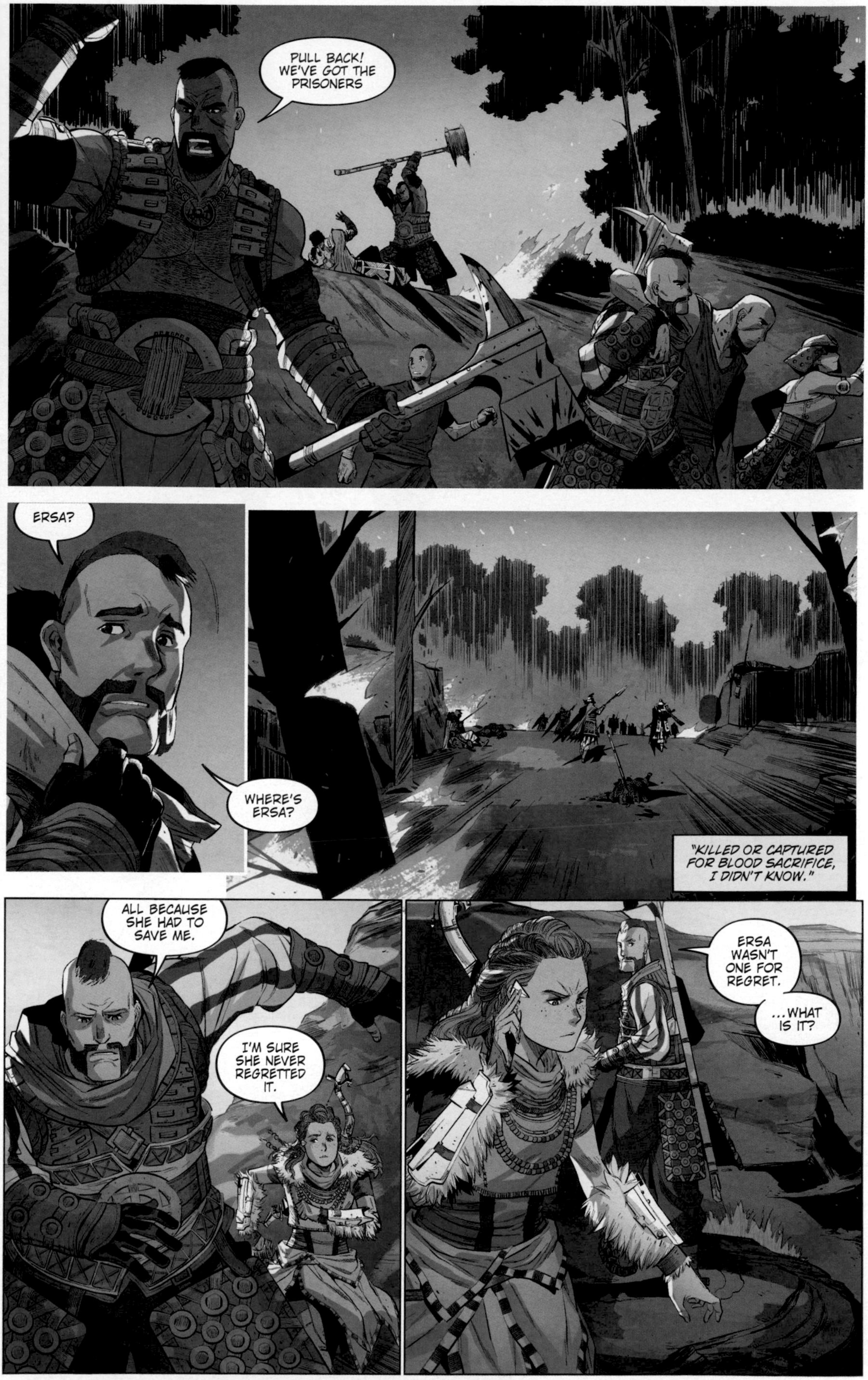
PULL BACK! WE'VE GOT THE PRISONERS
ERSA?
WHERE'S ERSA?
"KILLED OR CAPTURED FOR BLOOD SACRIFICE, I DIDN'T KNOW."
ALL BECAUSE SHE HAD TO SAVE ME.
I'M SURE SHE NEVER REGRETTED IT.
ERSA WASN'T ONE FOR REGRET.
...WHAT IS IT?

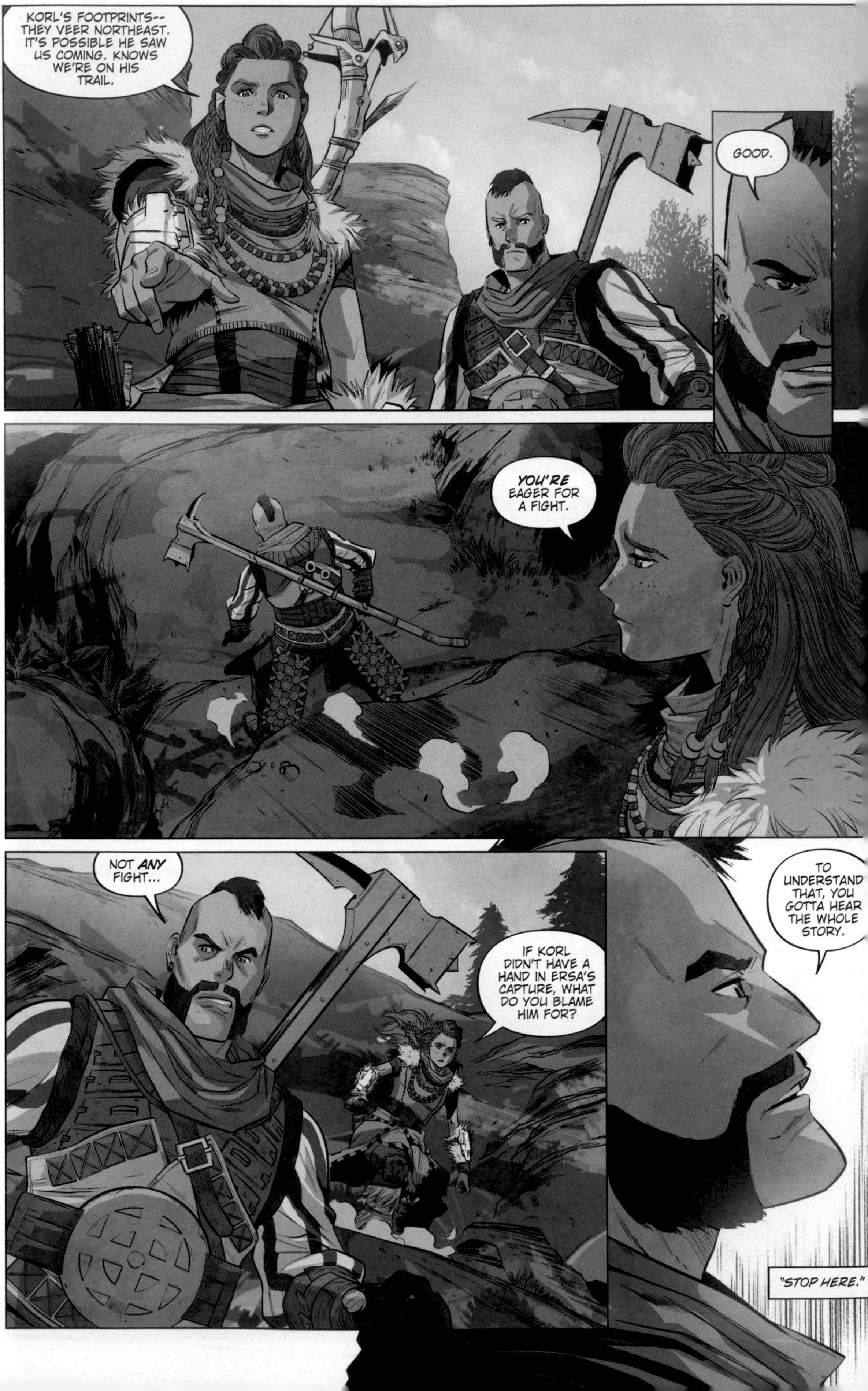

KORL'S FOOTPRINTS-- THEY VEER NORTHEAST. IT'S POSSIBLE HE SAW US COMING. KNOWS WE'RE ON HIS TRAIL.
GOOD.
YOU'RE EAGER FOR A FIGHT.
NOT *ANY* FIGHT...
IF KORL DIDN'T HAVE A HAND IN ERSA'S CAPTURE, WHAT DO YOU BLAME HIM FOR?
TO UNDERSTAND THAT, YOU GOTTA HEAR THE WHOLE STORY.
"STOP HERE."

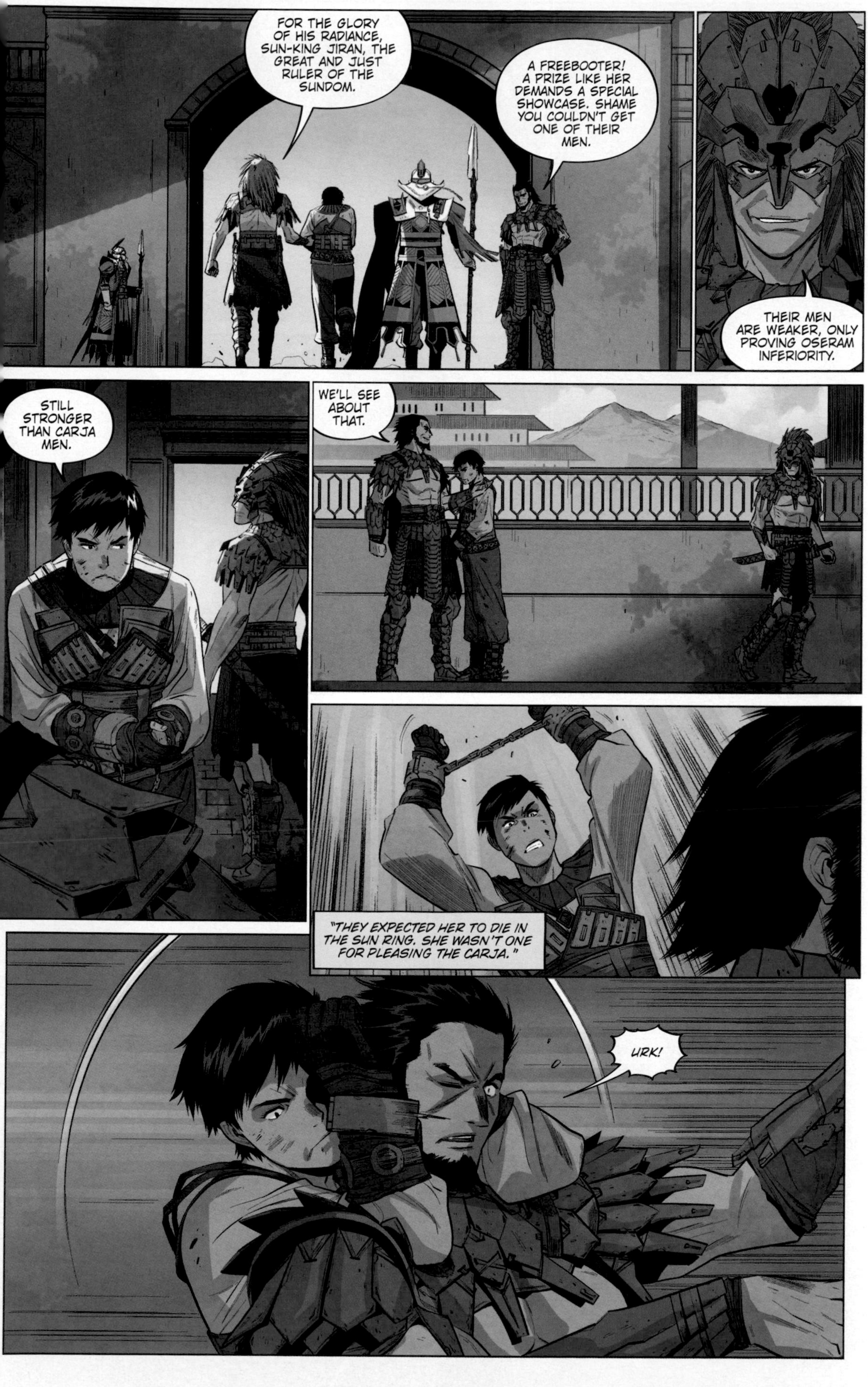
FOR THE GLORY OF HIS RADIANCE, SUN-KING JIRAN, THE GREAT AND JUST RULER OF THE SUNDOM.
A FREEBOOTER! A PRIZE LIKE HER DEMANDS A SPECIAL SHOWCASE. SHAME YOU COULDN'T GET ONE OF THEIR MEN.
THEIR MEN ARE WEAKER, ONLY PROVING OSERAM INFERIORITY.
STILL STRONGER THAN CARJA MEN.
WE'LL SEE ABOUT THAT.
"THEY EXPECTED HER TO DIE IN THE SUN RING. SHE WASN'T ONE FOR PLEASING THE CARJA."
URK!

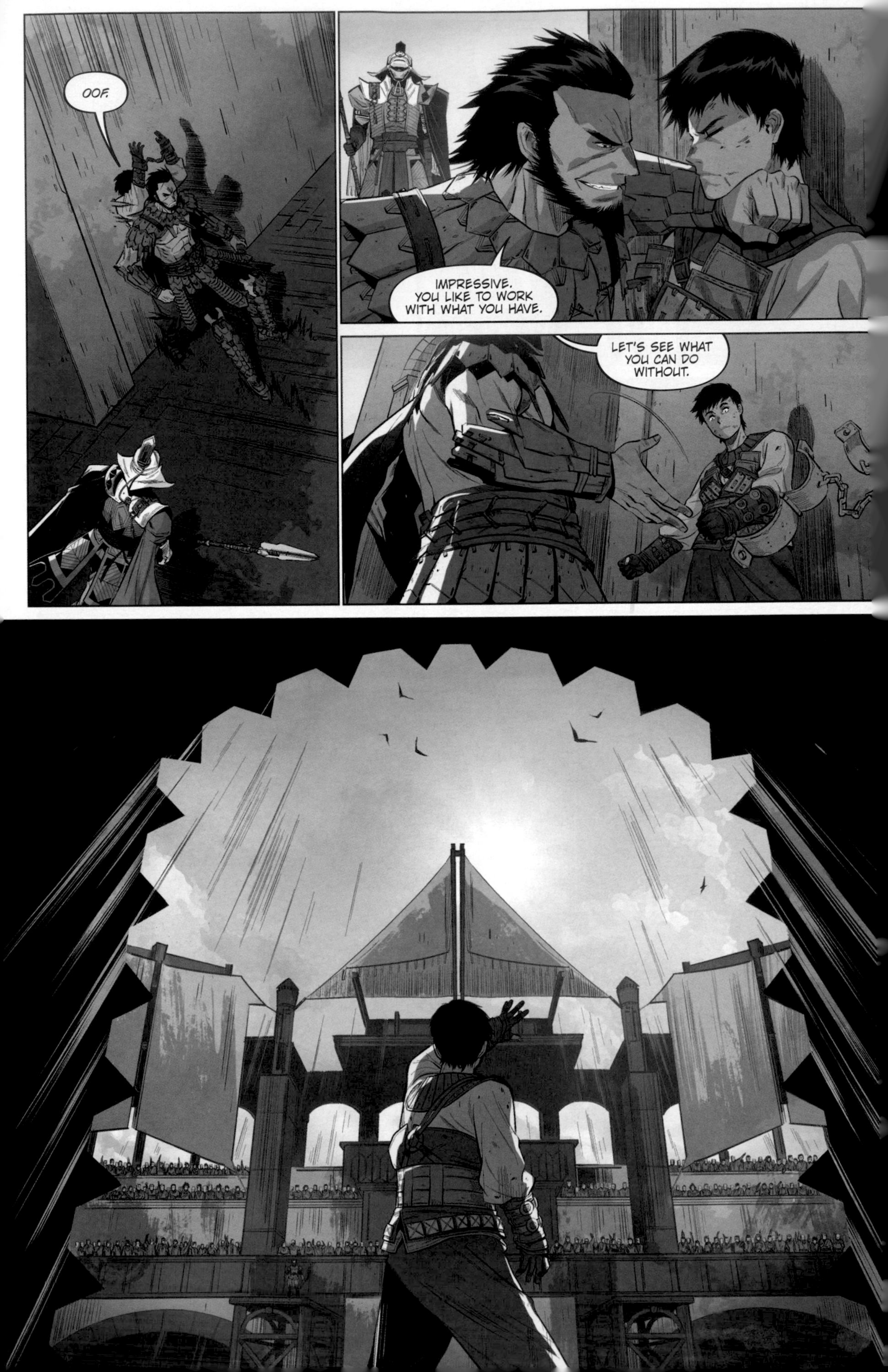
OOF.
IMPRESSIVE. YOU LIKE TO WORK WITH WHAT YOU HAVE.
LET'S SEE WHAT YOU CAN DO WITHOUT.

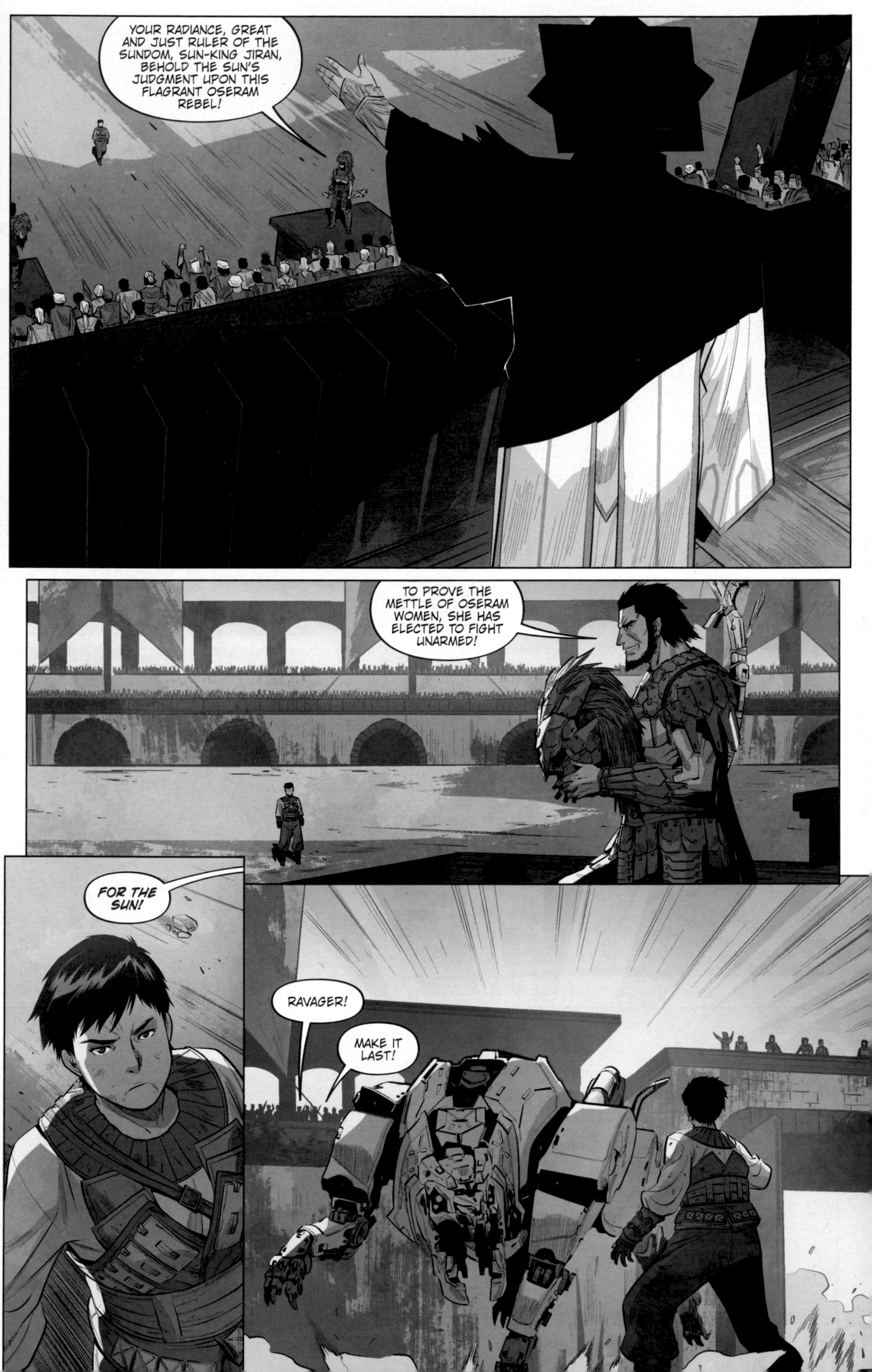
YOUR RADIANCE, GREAT AND JUST RULER OF THE SUNDOM, SUN-KING JIRAN, BEHOLD THE SUN'S JUDGMENT UPON THIS FLAGRANT OSERAM REBEL!
TO PROVE THE METTLE OF OSERAM WOMEN, SHE HAS ELECTED TO FIGHT UNARMED!
FOR THE SUN!
RAVAGER!
MAKE IT LAST!

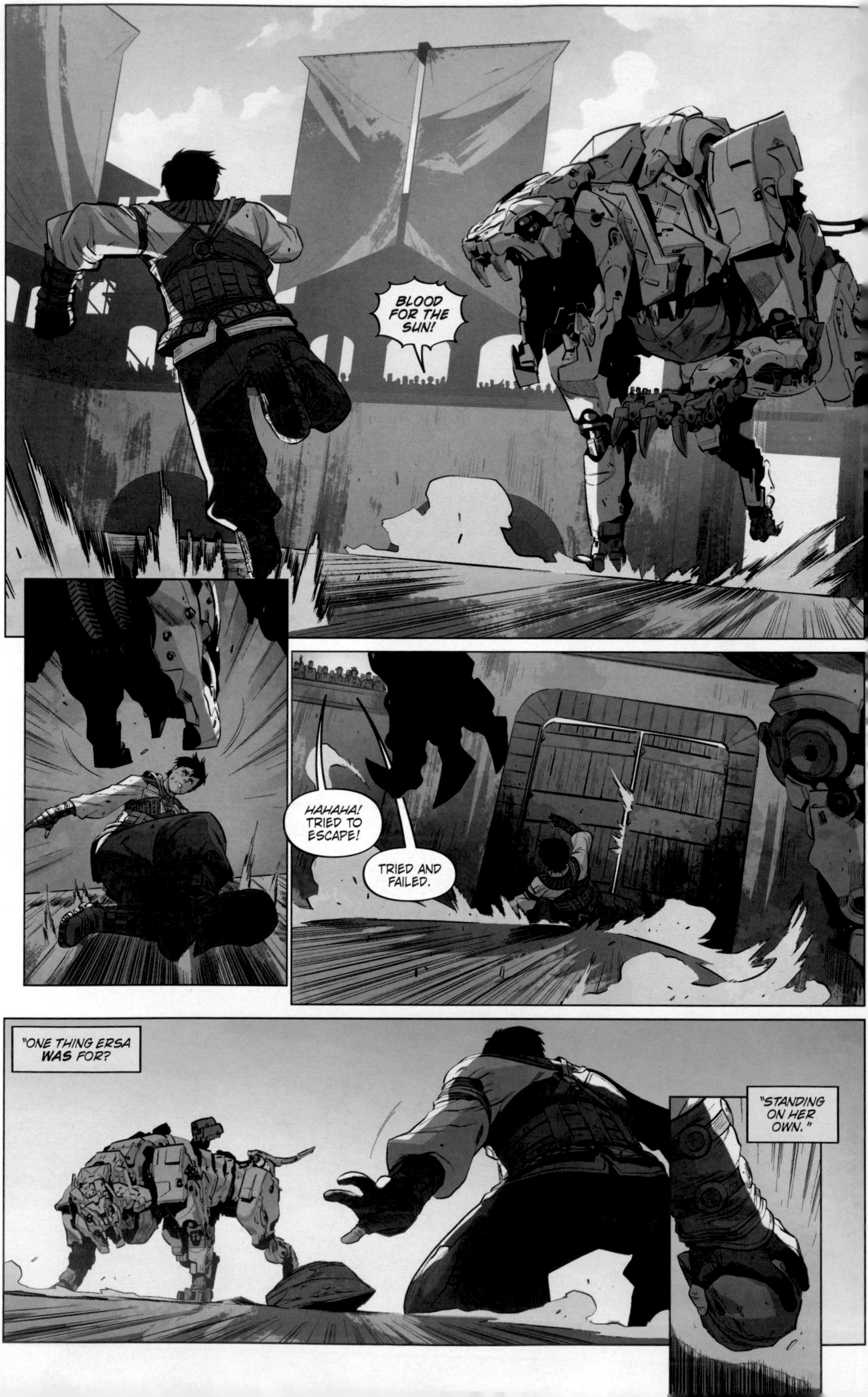
BLOOD FOR THE SUN!
HAHAHA! TRIED TO ESCAPE!
TRIED AND FAILED.
"ONE THING ERSA WAS FOR?
"STANDING ON HER OWN."

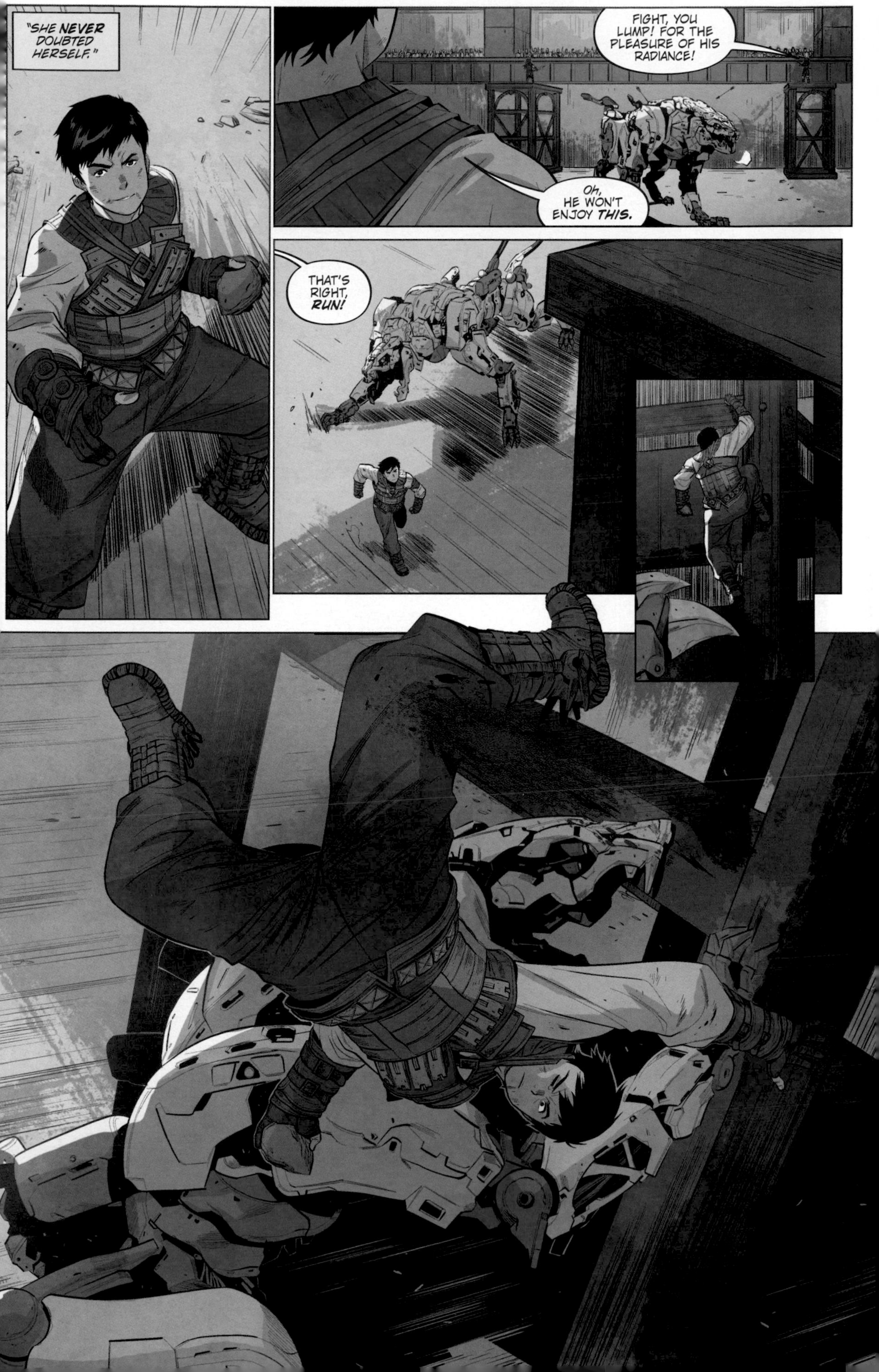
"SHE NEVER DOUBTED HERSELF."
FIGHT, YOU LUMP! FOR THE PLEASURE OF HIS RADIANCE!
Oh, HE WON'T ENJOY THIS.
THAT'S RIGHT, RUN!

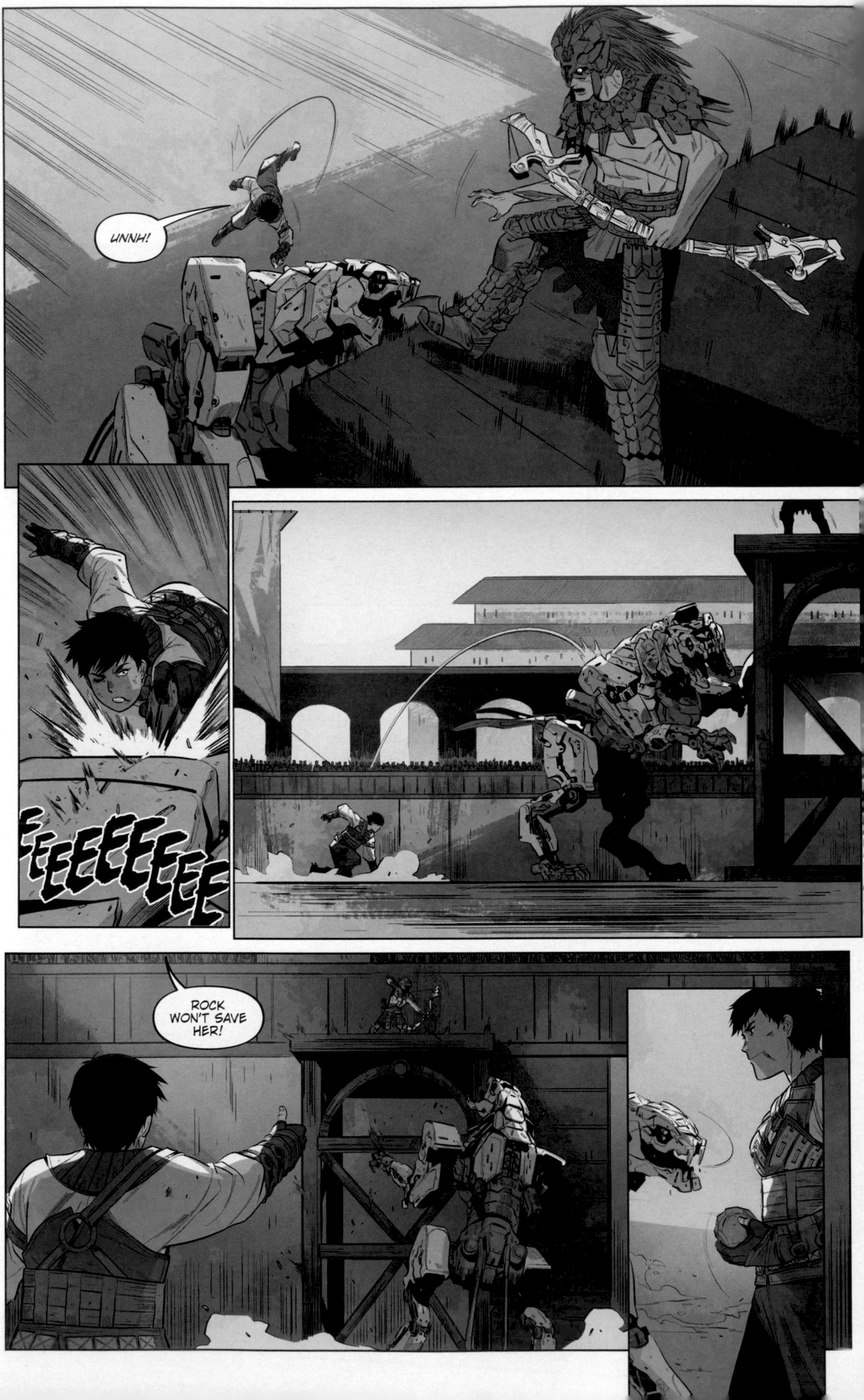
UNNH!
EEEEEEEEEE
ROCK WON'T SAVE HER!

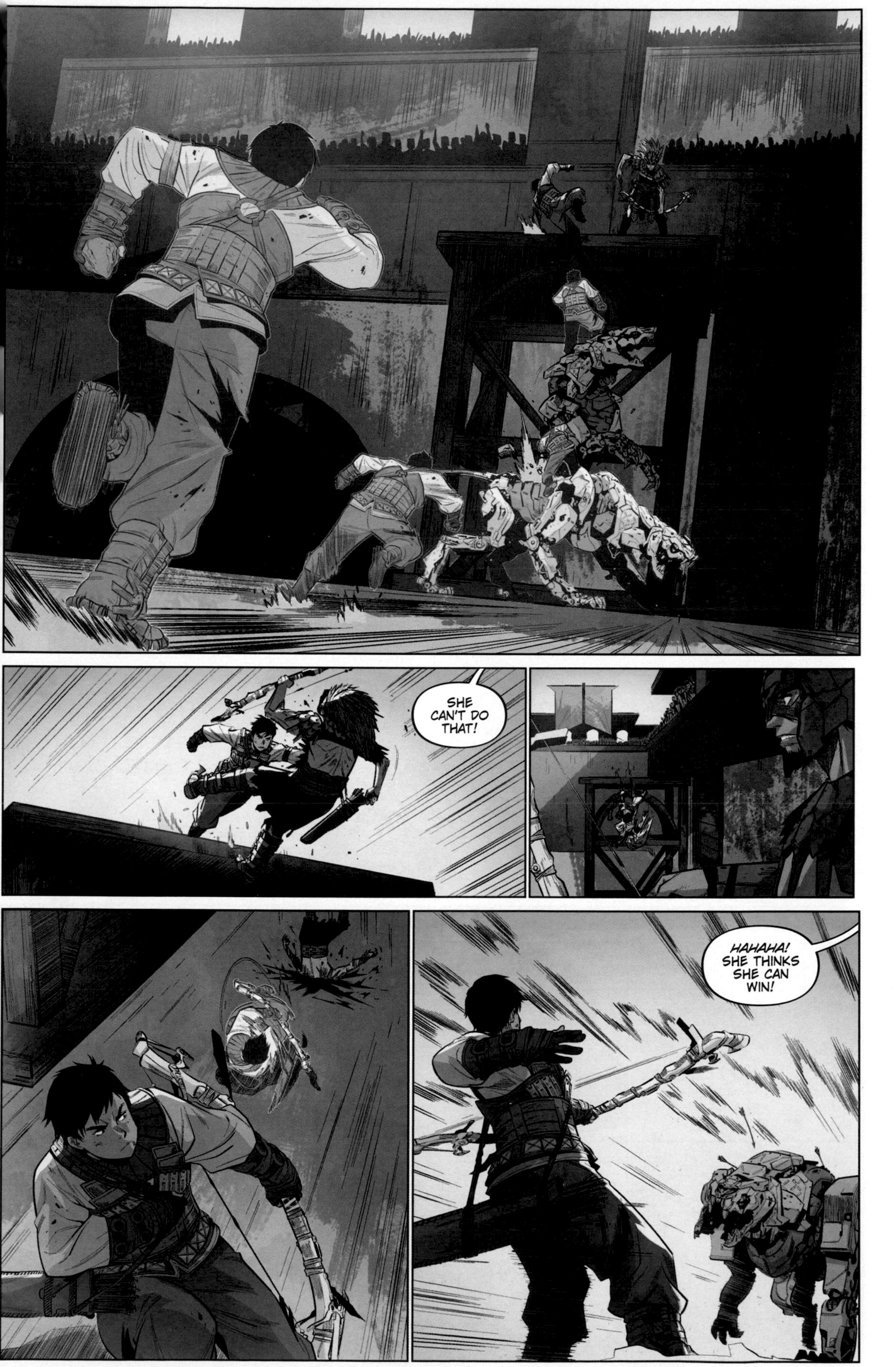
SHE CAN'T DO THAT!
HAHAHA! SHE THINKS SHE CAN WIN!

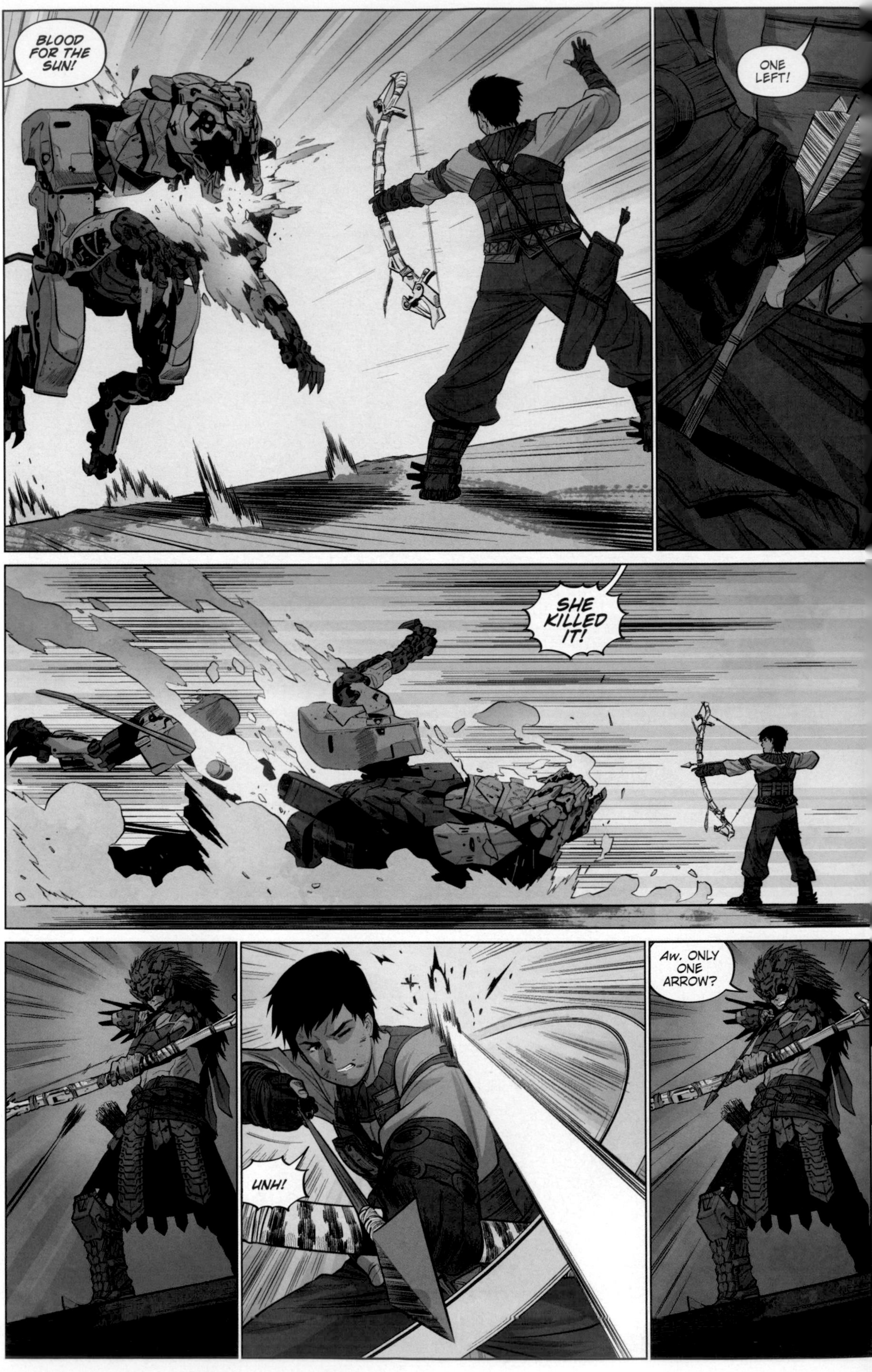
BLOOD FOR THE SUN!
ONE LEFT!
SHE KILLED IT!
UNH!
Aw. ONLY ONE ARROW?

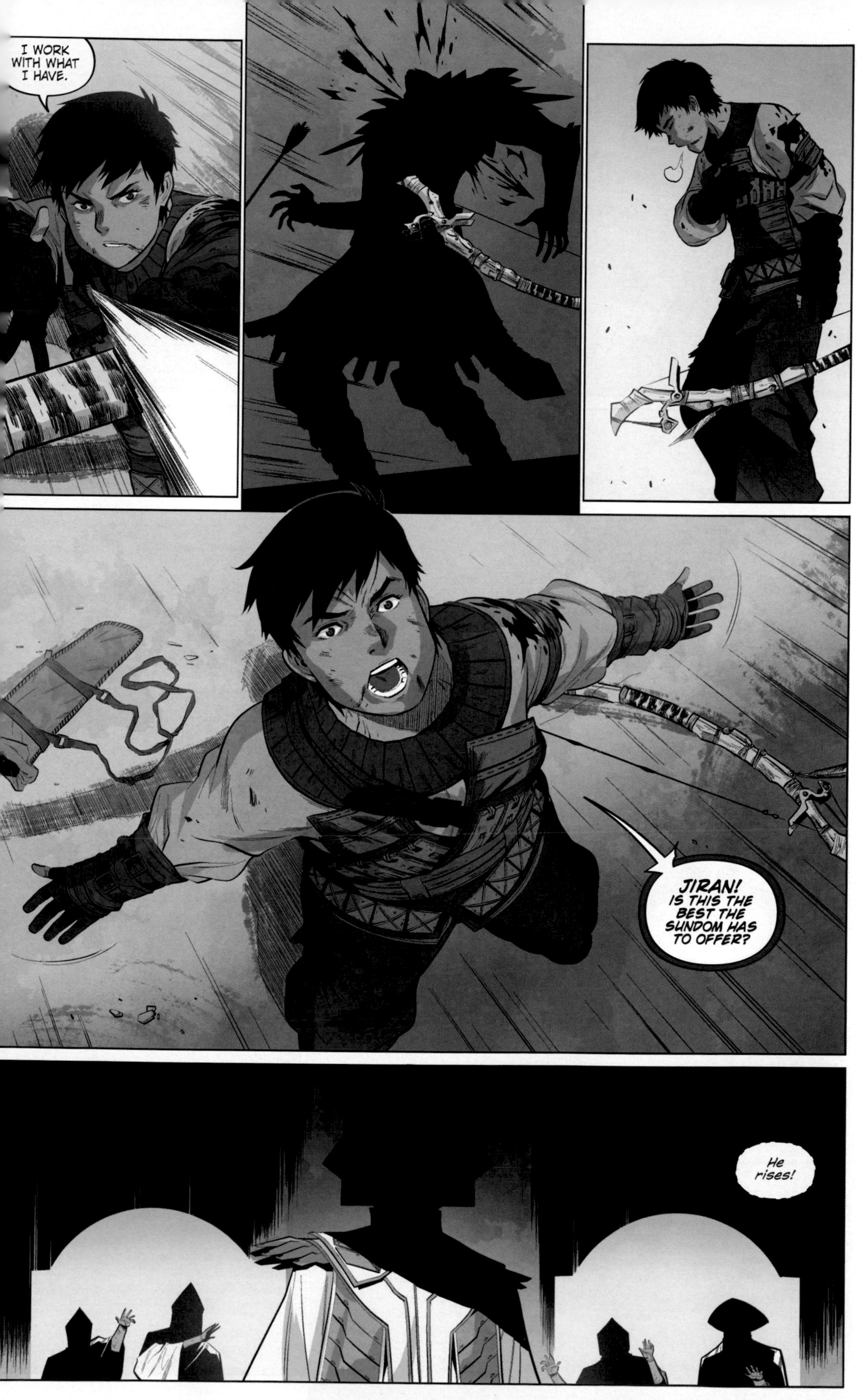
I WORK WITH WHAT I HAVE.
JIRAN! IS THIS THE BEST THE SUNDOM HAS TO OFFER?
He rises!

DELICIOUS. NOW WHAT WILL WE DO WITH YOU?

NO! NOT AGAIN.

KORL CUT THE BRIDGE. SO HE GETS TO RUN FREE?!

EREND...

FORGET IT. CAN WE CLIMB DOWN?

NOT IF WE WANT TO SURVIVE.

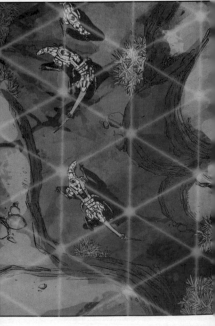

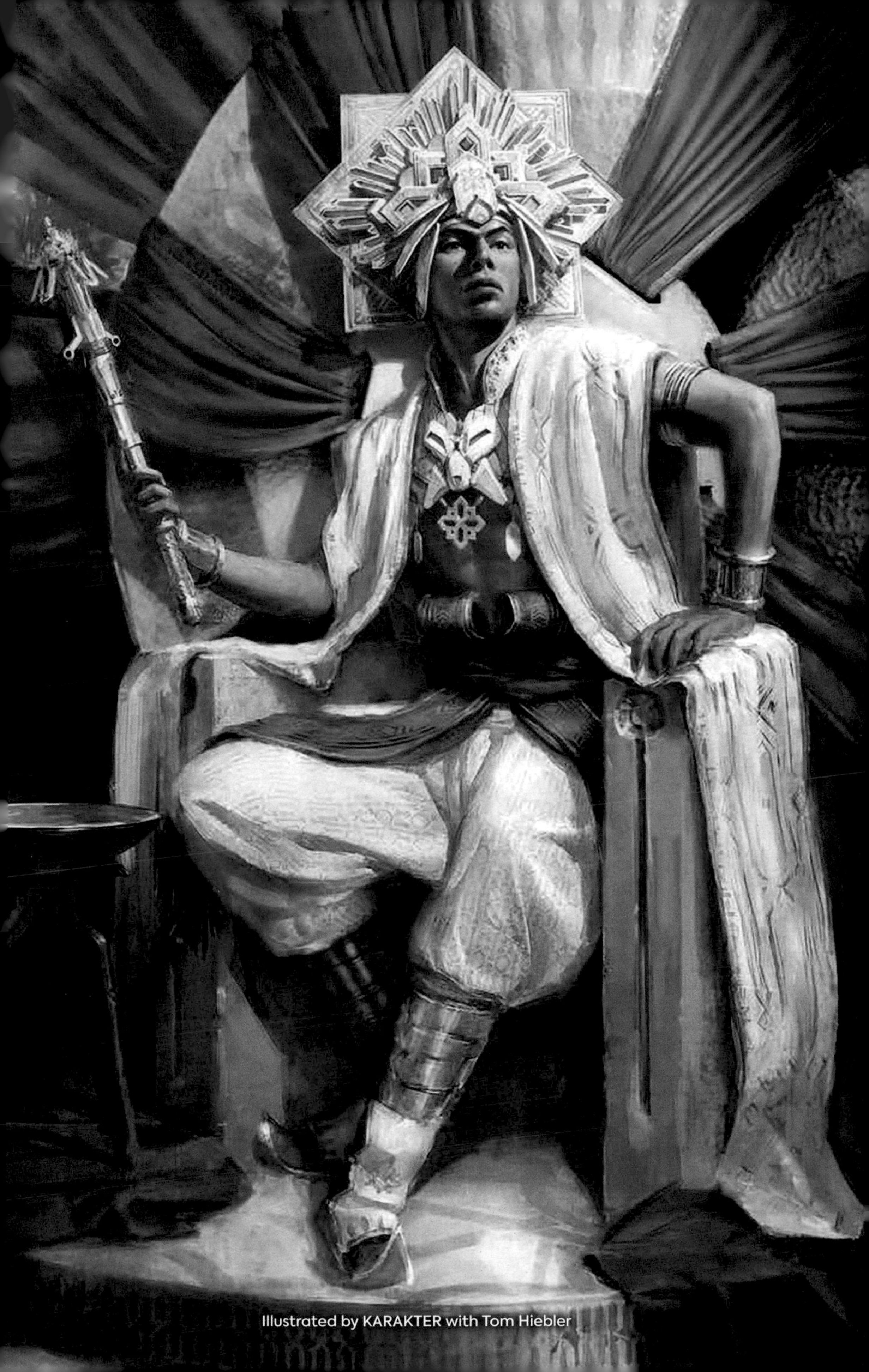

Illustrated by KARAKTER with Tom Hiebler

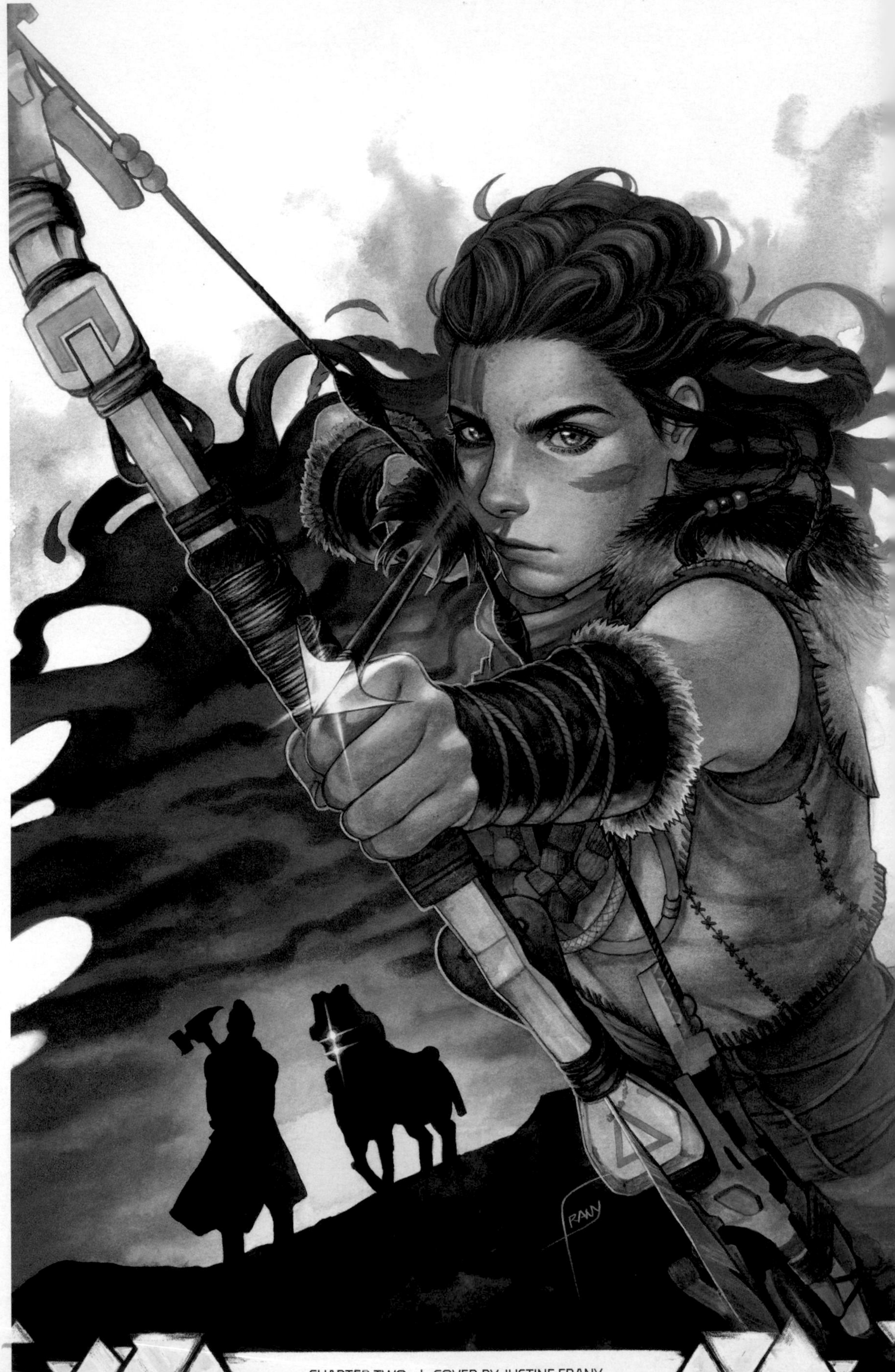
FRANY

CHAPTER TWO | COVER BY JUSTINE FRANY

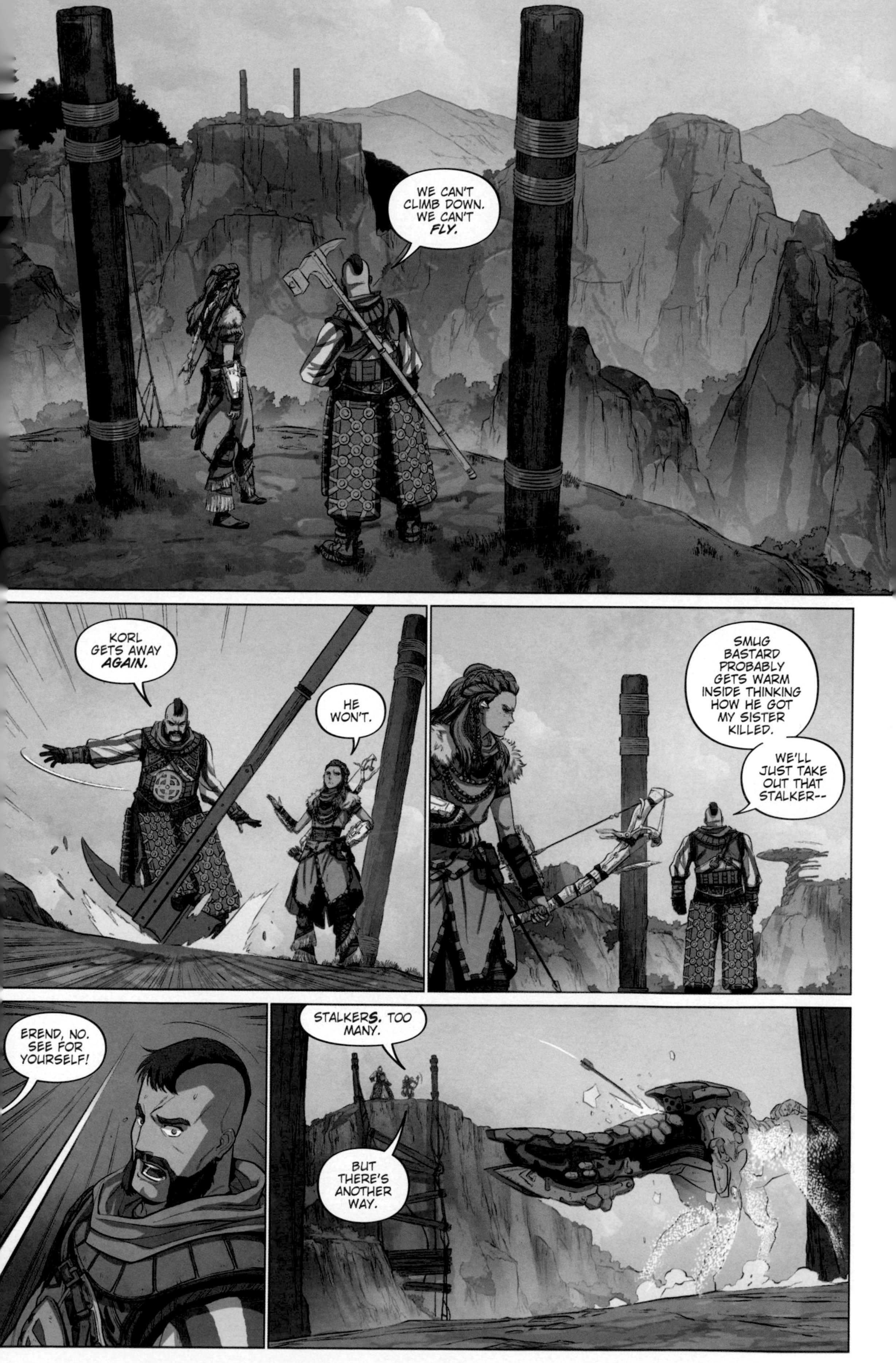
WE CAN'T CLIMB DOWN. WE CAN'T *FLY.*
KORL GETS AWAY *AGAIN.*
HE WON'T.
SMUG BASTARD PROBABLY GETS WARM INSIDE THINKING HOW HE GOT MY SISTER KILLED.
WE'LL JUST TAKE OUT THAT STALKER--
EREND, NO. SEE FOR YOURSELF!
STALKER*S*. TOO MANY.
BUT THERE'S ANOTHER WAY.

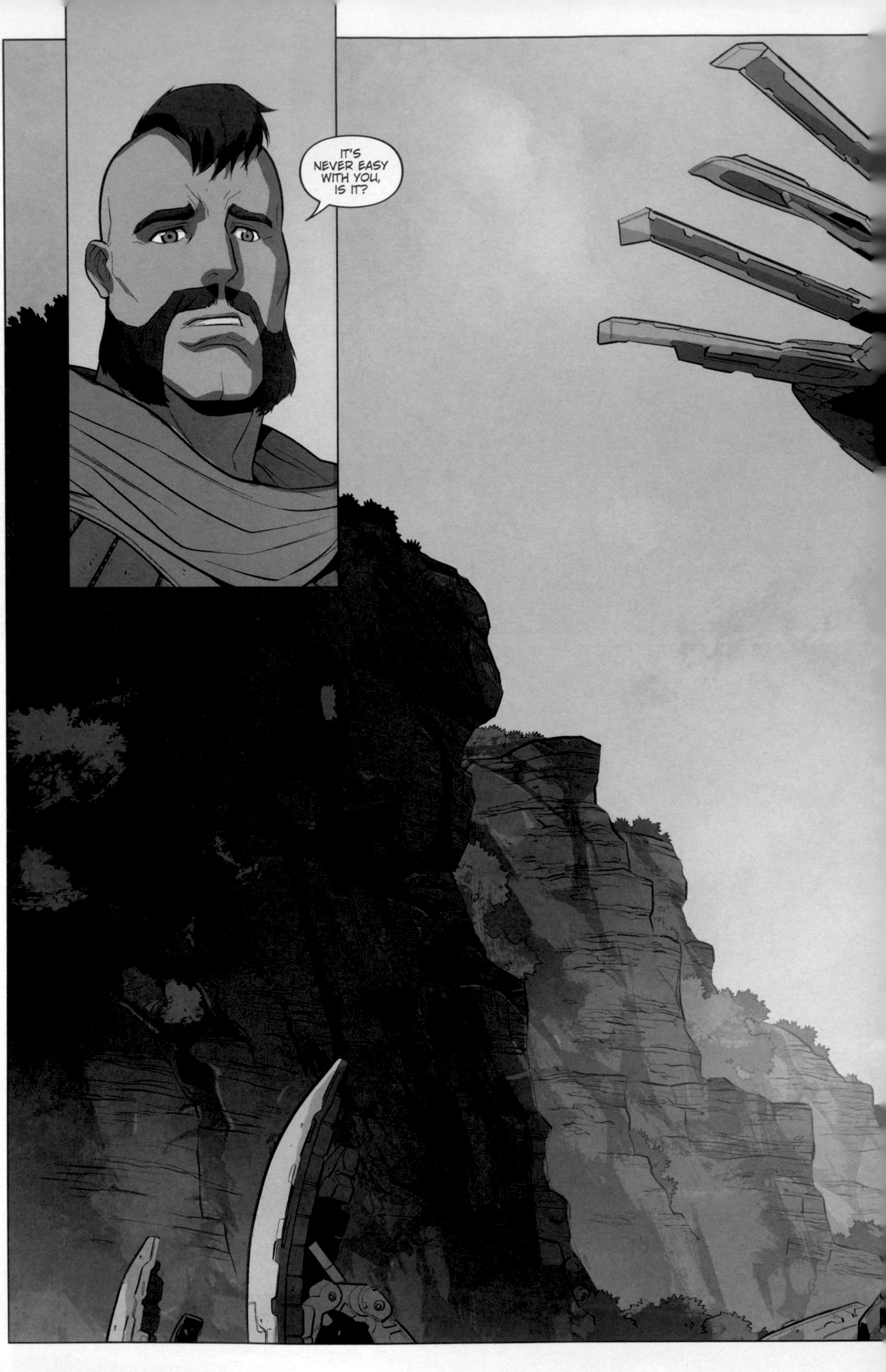
IT'S NEVER EASY WITH YOU, IS IT?

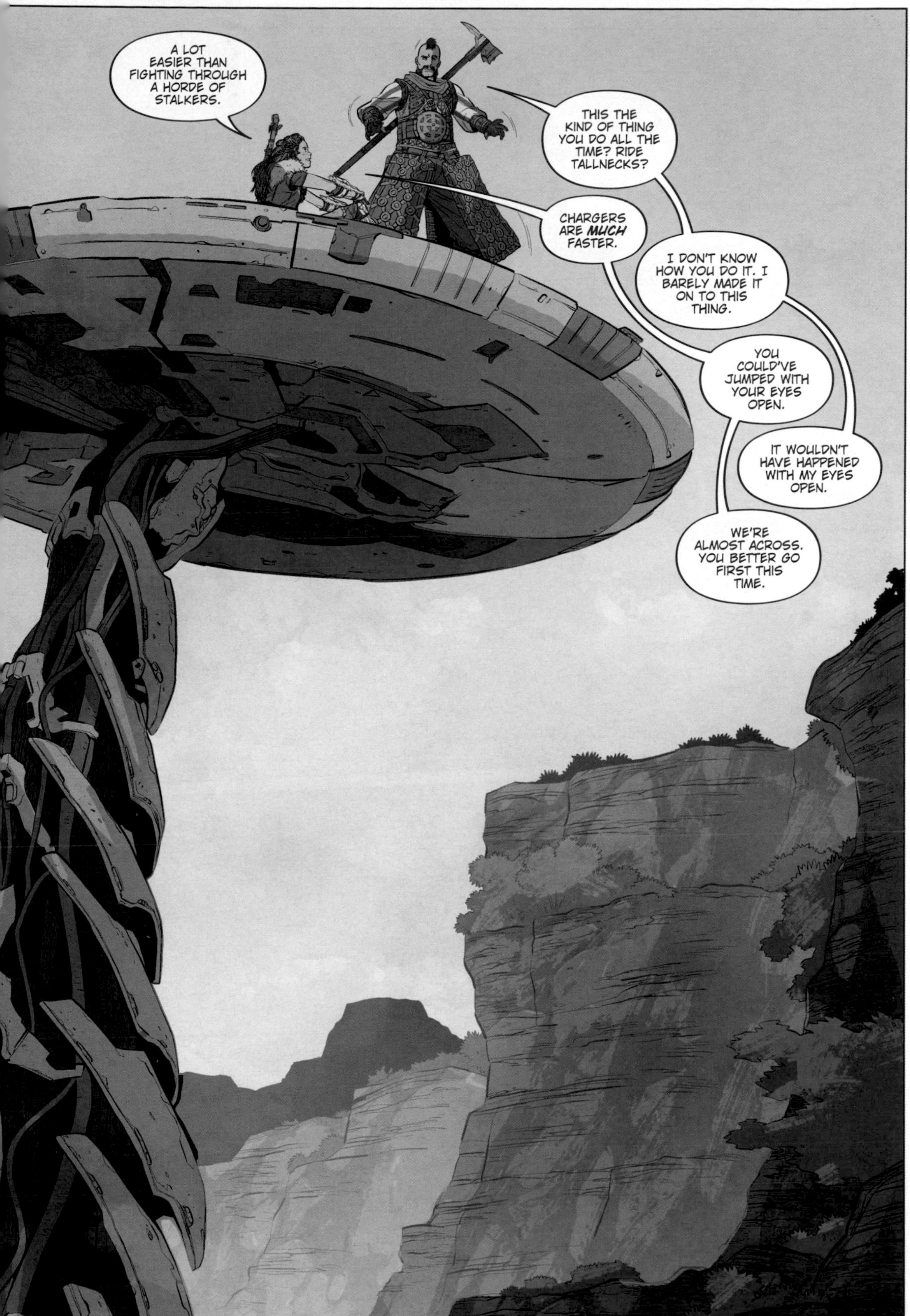
A LOT EASIER THAN FIGHTING THROUGH A HORDE OF STALKERS.
THIS THE KIND OF THING YOU DO ALL THE TIME? RIDE TALLNECKS?
CHARGERS ARE MUCH FASTER.
I DON'T KNOW HOW YOU DO IT. I BARELY MADE IT ON TO THIS THING.
YOU COULD'VE JUMPED WITH YOUR EYES OPEN.
IT WOULDN'T HAVE HAPPENED WITH MY EYES OPEN.
WE'RE ALMOST ACROSS. YOU BETTER GO FIRST THIS TIME.

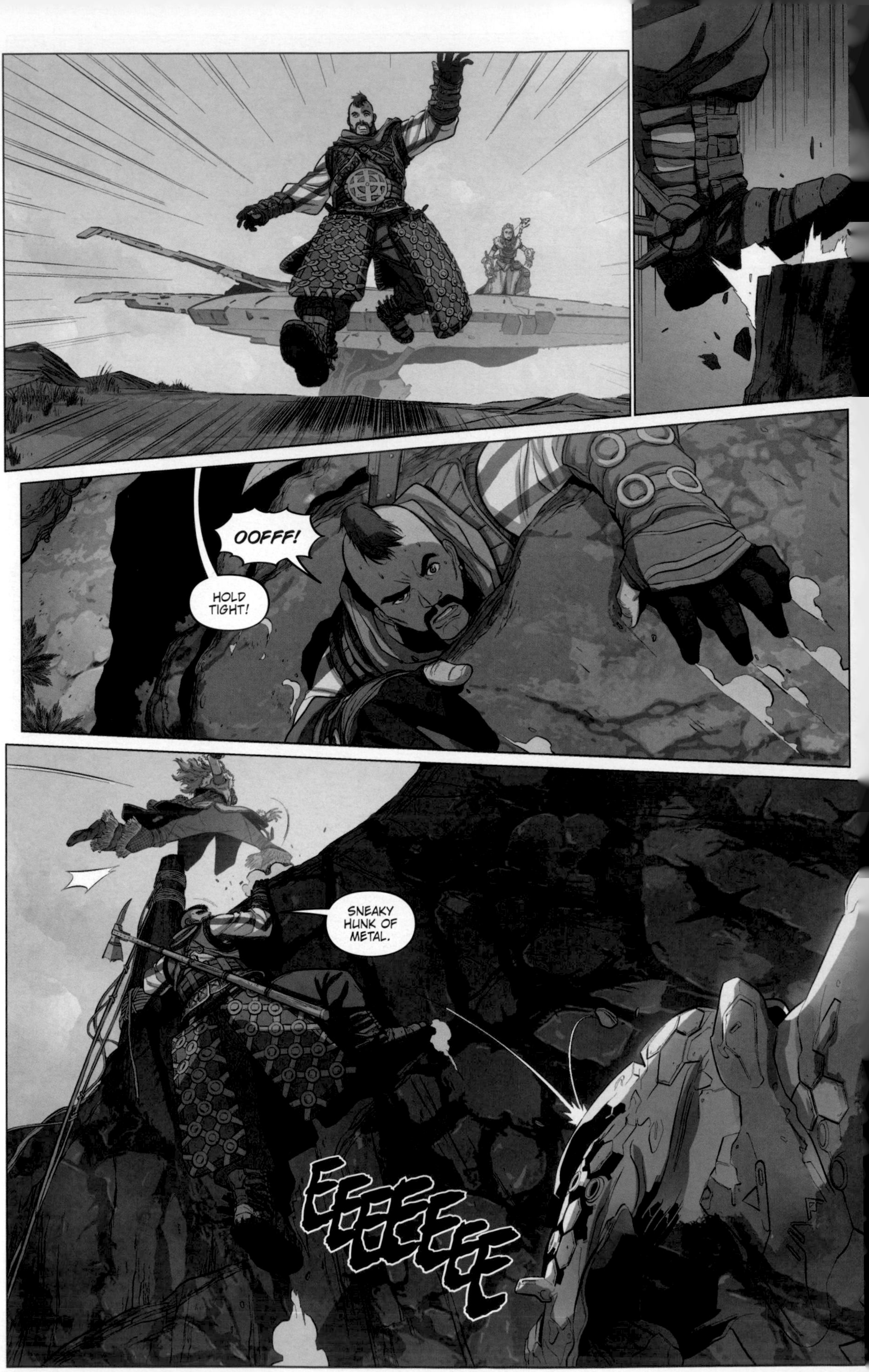
OOFFF!
HOLD TIGHT!
SNEAKY HUNK OF METAL.
EEEEEEEE

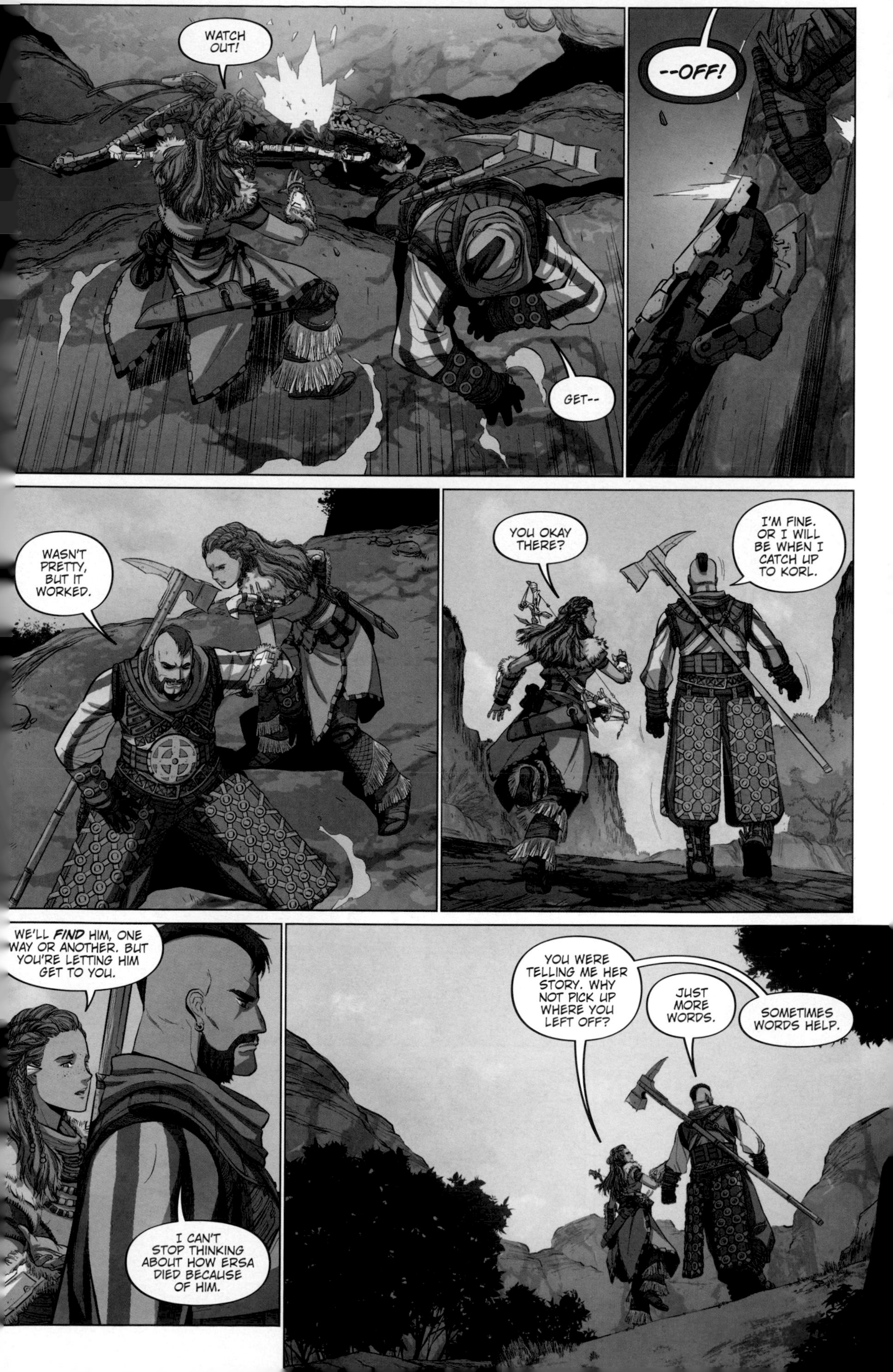
WATCH OUT!
GET--
--OFF!
WASN'T PRETTY, BUT IT WORKED.
YOU OKAY THERE?
I'M FINE. OR I WILL BE WHEN I CATCH UP TO KORL.
WE'LL FIND HIM, ONE WAY OR ANOTHER. BUT YOU'RE LETTING HIM GET TO YOU.
I CAN'T STOP THINKING ABOUT HOW ERSA DIED BECAUSE OF HIM.
YOU WERE TELLING ME HER STORY. WHY NOT PICK UP WHERE YOU LEFT OFF?
JUST MORE WORDS.
SOMETIMES WORDS HELP.

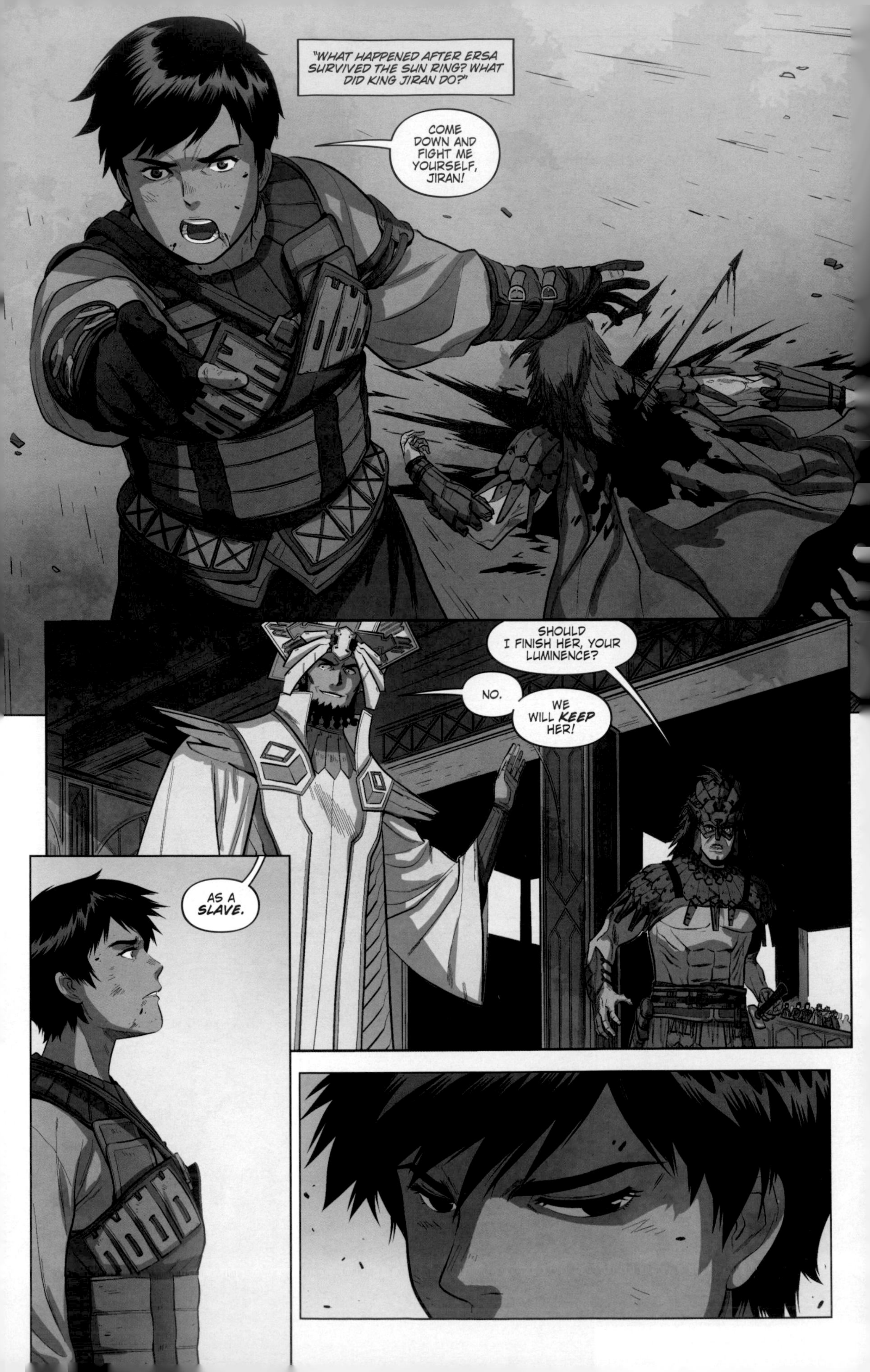
"WHAT HAPPENED AFTER ERSA SURVIVED THE SUN RING? WHAT DID KING JIRAN DO?"
COME DOWN AND FIGHT ME YOURSELF, JIRAN!
SHOULD I FINISH HER, YOUR LUMINENCE?
NO.
WE WILL KEEP HER!
AS A SLAVE.

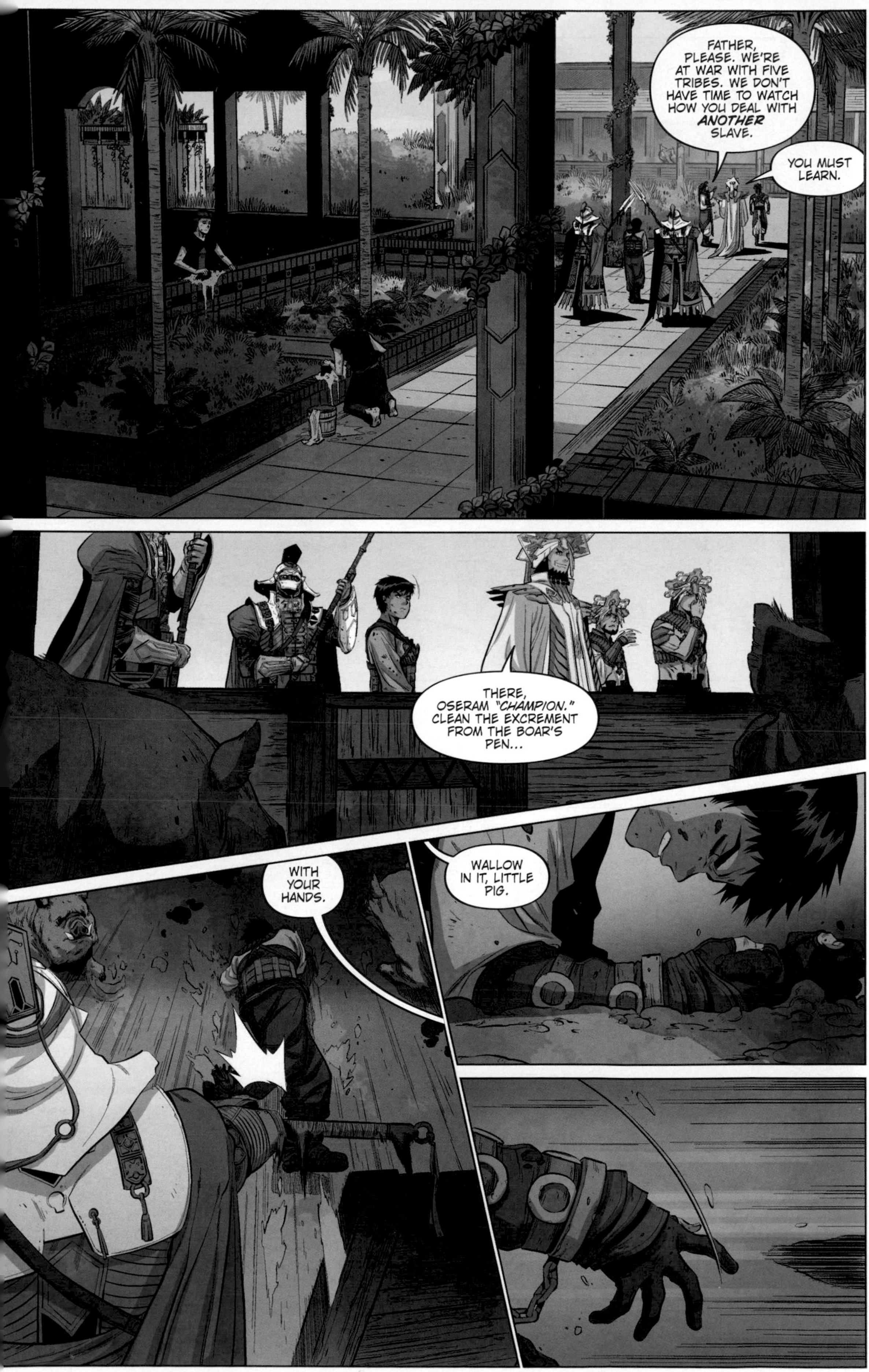
FATHER, PLEASE. WE'RE AT WAR WITH FIVE TRIBES. WE DON'T HAVE TIME TO WATCH HOW YOU DEAL WITH ANOTHER SLAVE.
YOU MUST LEARN.
THERE, OSERAM "CHAMPION." CLEAN THE EXCREMENT FROM THE BOAR'S PEN...
WITH YOUR HANDS.
WALLOW IN IT, LITTLE PIG.

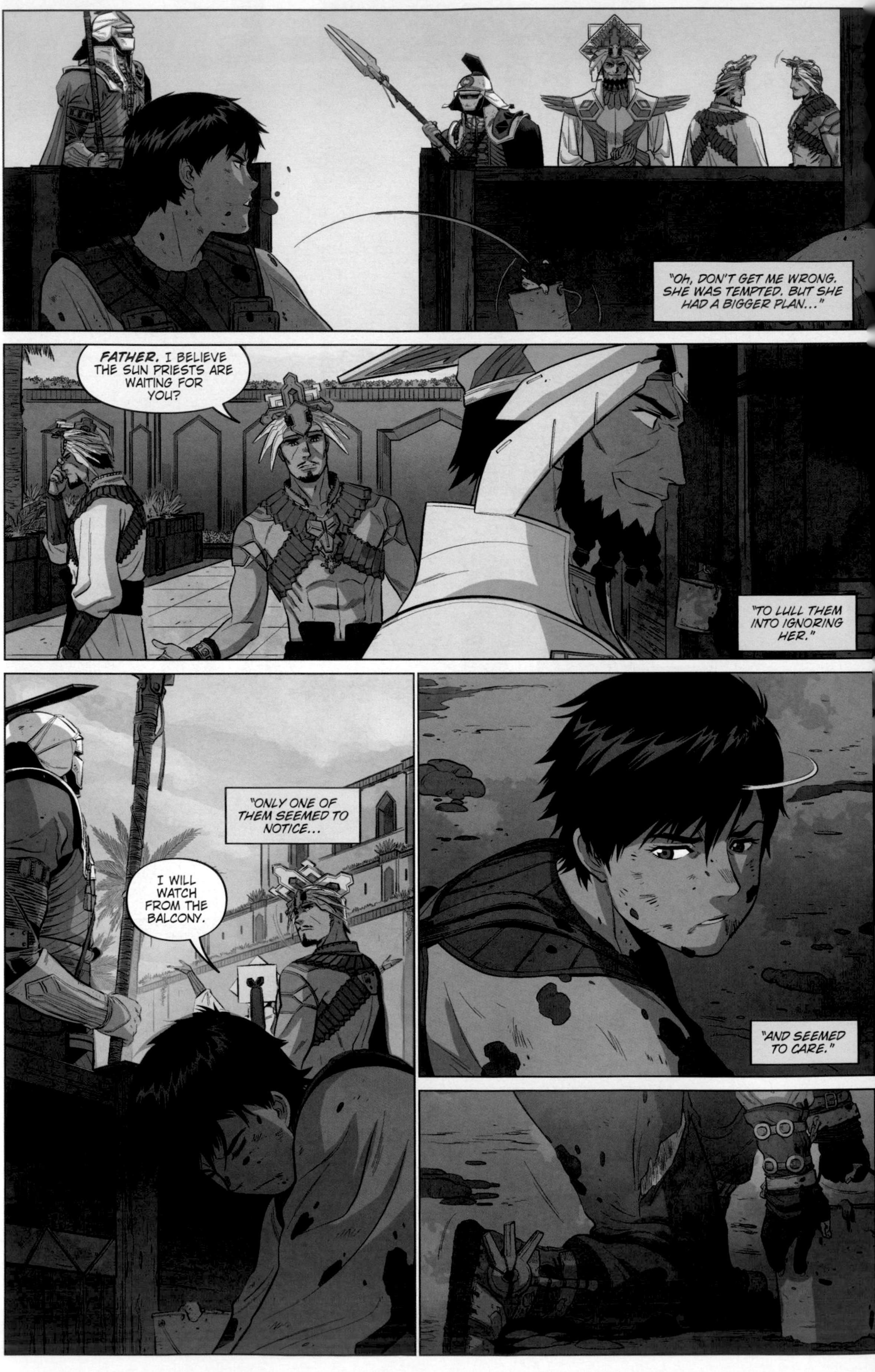
"Oh, DON'T GET ME WRONG. SHE WAS TEMPTED. BUT SHE HAD A BIGGER PLAN..."
FATHER. I BELIEVE THE SUN PRIESTS ARE WAITING FOR YOU?
"TO LULL THEM INTO IGNORING HER."
"ONLY ONE OF THEM SEEMED TO NOTICE...
I WILL WATCH FROM THE BALCONY.
"AND SEEMED TO CARE."

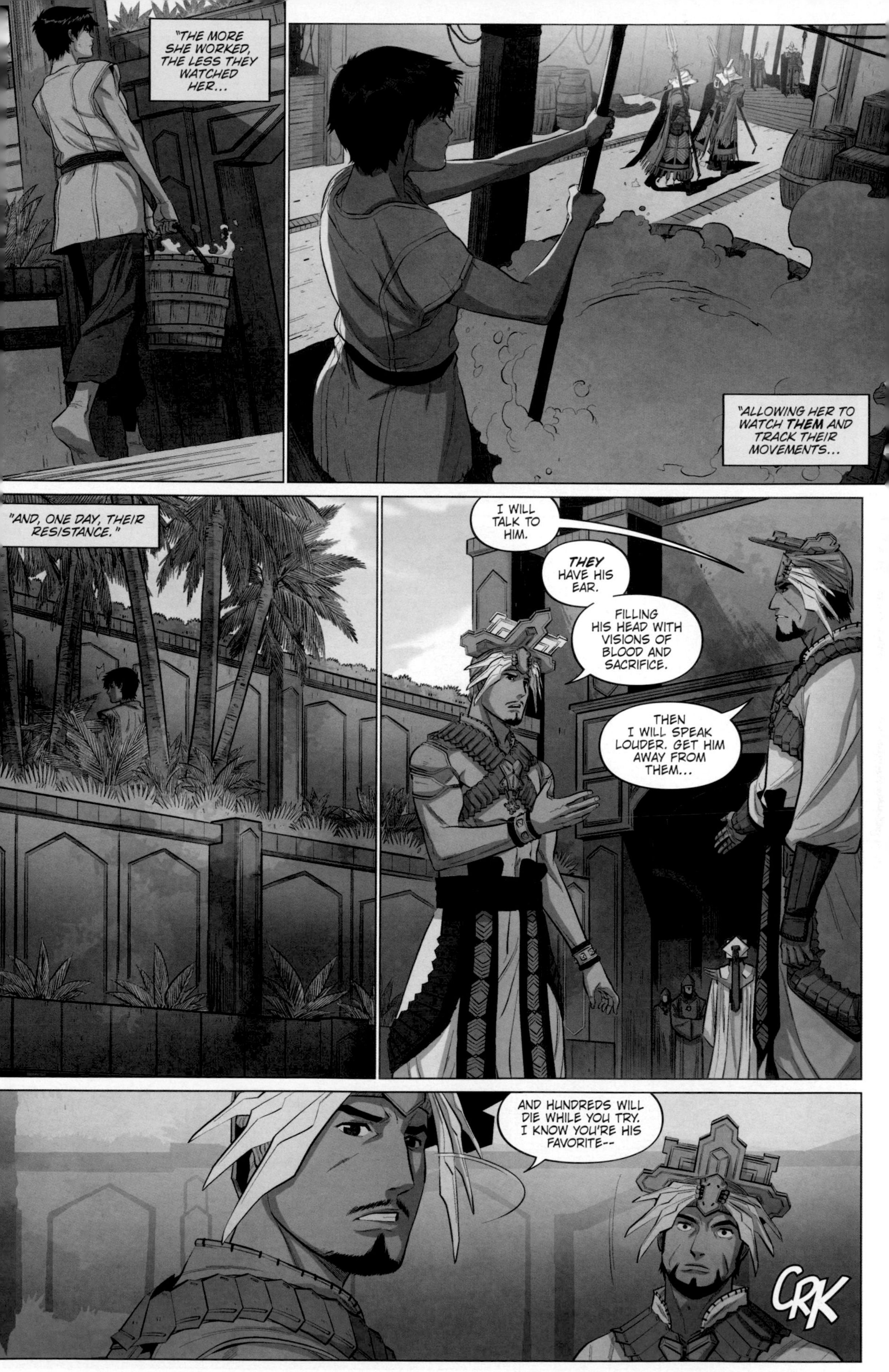
"THE MORE SHE WORKED, THE LESS THEY WATCHED HER...
"ALLOWING HER TO WATCH THEM AND TRACK THEIR MOVEMENTS...
"AND, ONE DAY, THEIR RESISTANCE."
I WILL TALK TO HIM.
THEY HAVE HIS EAR.
FILLING HIS HEAD WITH VISIONS OF BLOOD AND SACRIFICE.
THEN I WILL SPEAK LOUDER. GET HIM AWAY FROM THEM...
AND HUNDREDS WILL DIE WHILE YOU TRY. I KNOW YOU'RE HIS FAVORITE--
CRK

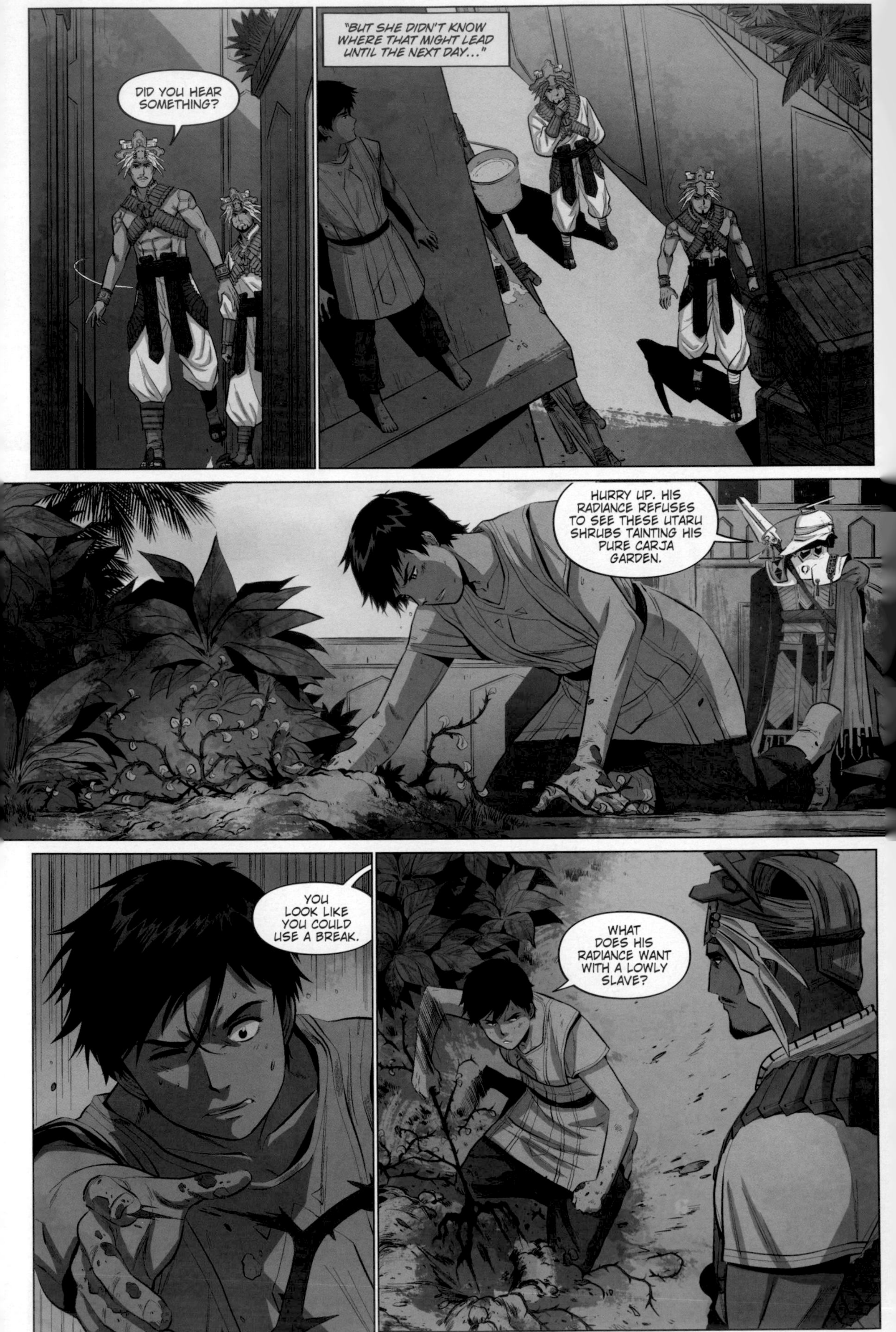
DID YOU HEAR SOMETHING?
"BUT SHE DIDN'T KNOW WHERE THAT MIGHT LEAD UNTIL THE NEXT DAY..."
HURRY UP. HIS RADIANCE REFUSES TO SEE THESE UTARU SHRUBS TAINTING HIS PURE CARJA GARDEN.
YOU LOOK LIKE YOU COULD USE A BREAK.
WHAT DOES HIS RADIANCE WANT WITH A LOWLY SLAVE?

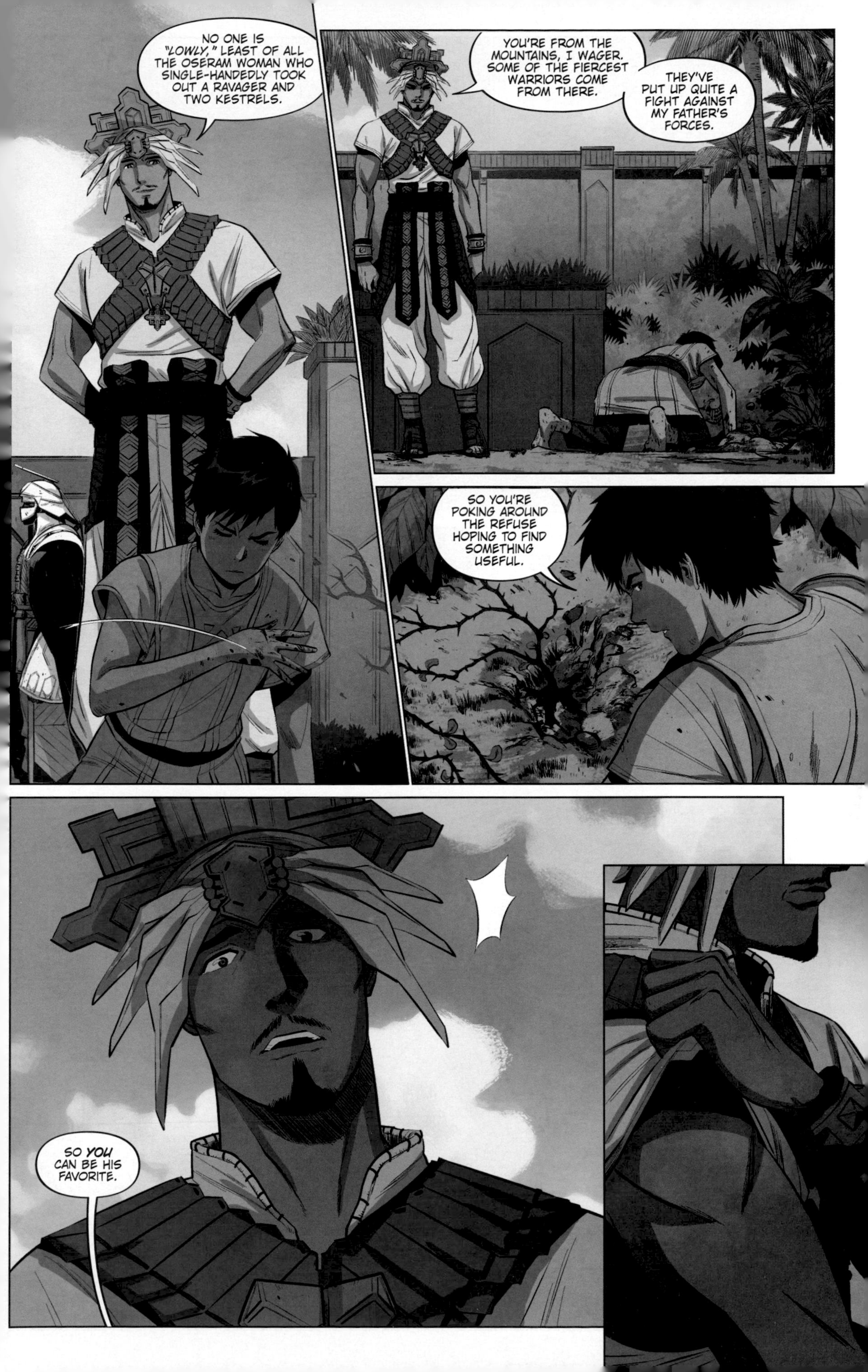
NO ONE IS "LOWLY," LEAST OF ALL THE OSERAM WOMAN WHO SINGLE-HANDEDLY TOOK OUT A RAVAGER AND TWO KESTRELS.
YOU'RE FROM THE MOUNTAINS, I WAGER. SOME OF THE FIERCEST WARRIORS COME FROM THERE.
THEY'VE PUT UP QUITE A FIGHT AGAINST MY FATHER'S FORCES.
SO YOU'RE POKING AROUND THE REFUSE HOPING TO FIND SOMETHING USEFUL.
SO YOU CAN BE HIS FAVORITE.

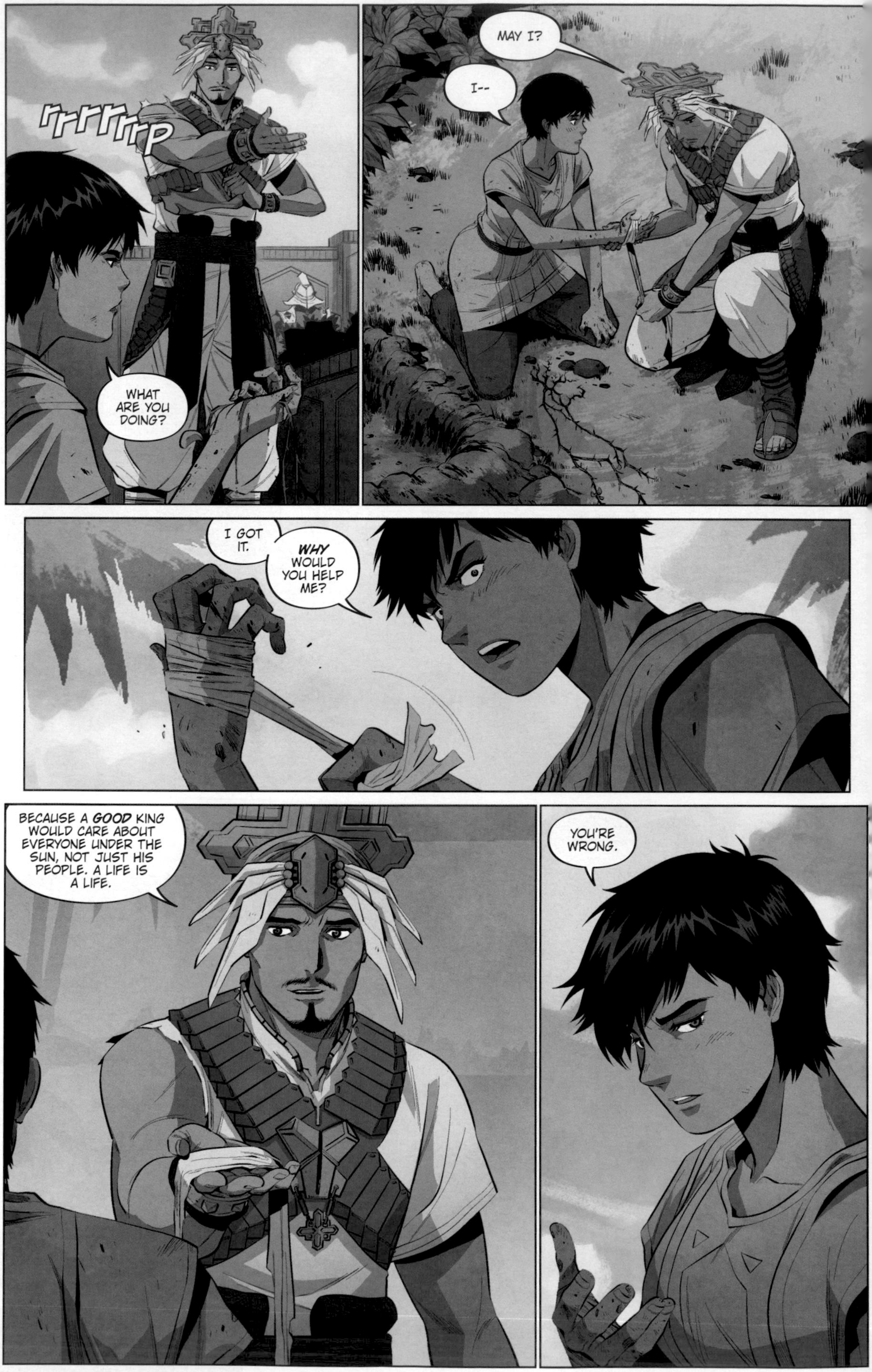
rrrrrrp
WHAT ARE YOU DOING?
MAY I?
I--
I GOT IT.
WHY WOULD YOU HELP ME?
BECAUSE A GOOD KING WOULD CARE ABOUT EVERYONE UNDER THE SUN, NOT JUST HIS PEOPLE. A LIFE IS A LIFE.
YOU'RE WRONG.

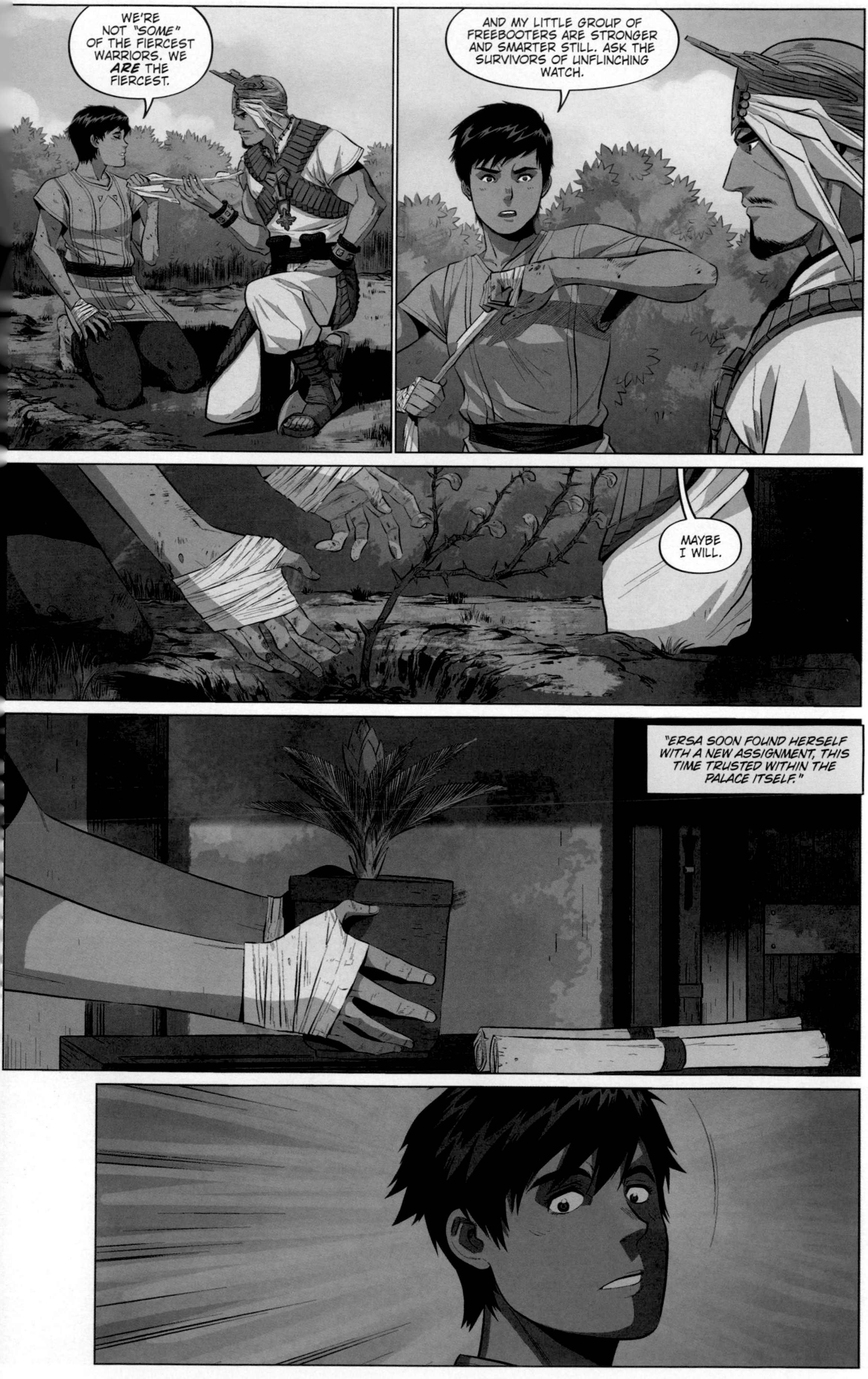
WE'RE NOT "SOME" OF THE FIERCEST WARRIORS. WE ARE THE FIERCEST.
AND MY LITTLE GROUP OF FREEBOOTERS ARE STRONGER AND SMARTER STILL. ASK THE SURVIVORS OF UNFLINCHING WATCH.
MAYBE I WILL.
"ERSA SOON FOUND HERSELF WITH A NEW ASSIGNMENT, THIS TIME TRUSTED WITHIN THE PALACE ITSELF."

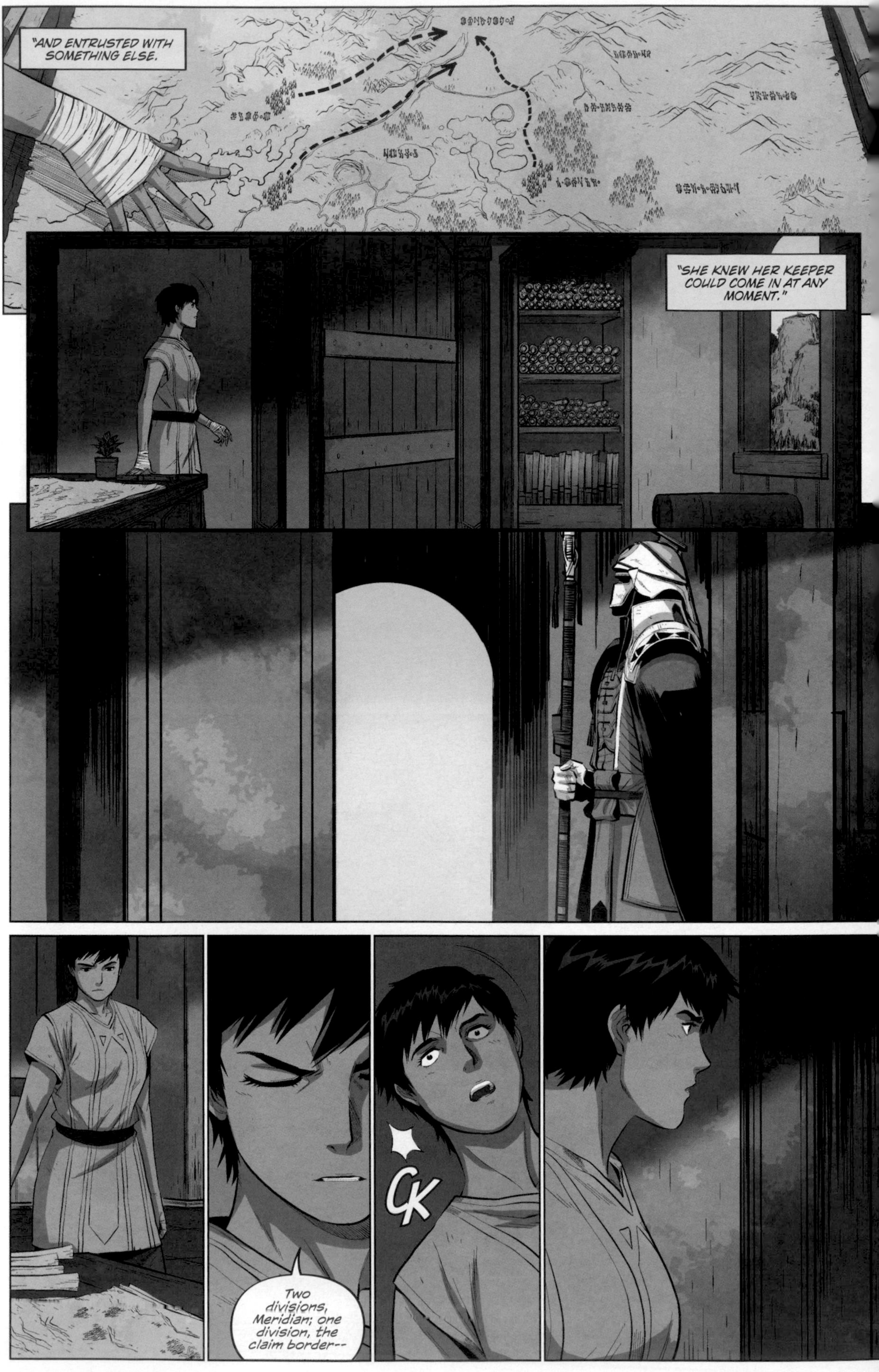
"AND ENTRUSTED WITH SOMETHING ELSE.
"SHE KNEW HER KEEPER COULD COME IN AT ANY MOMENT."
CK
Two divisions, Meridian; one division, the claim border--

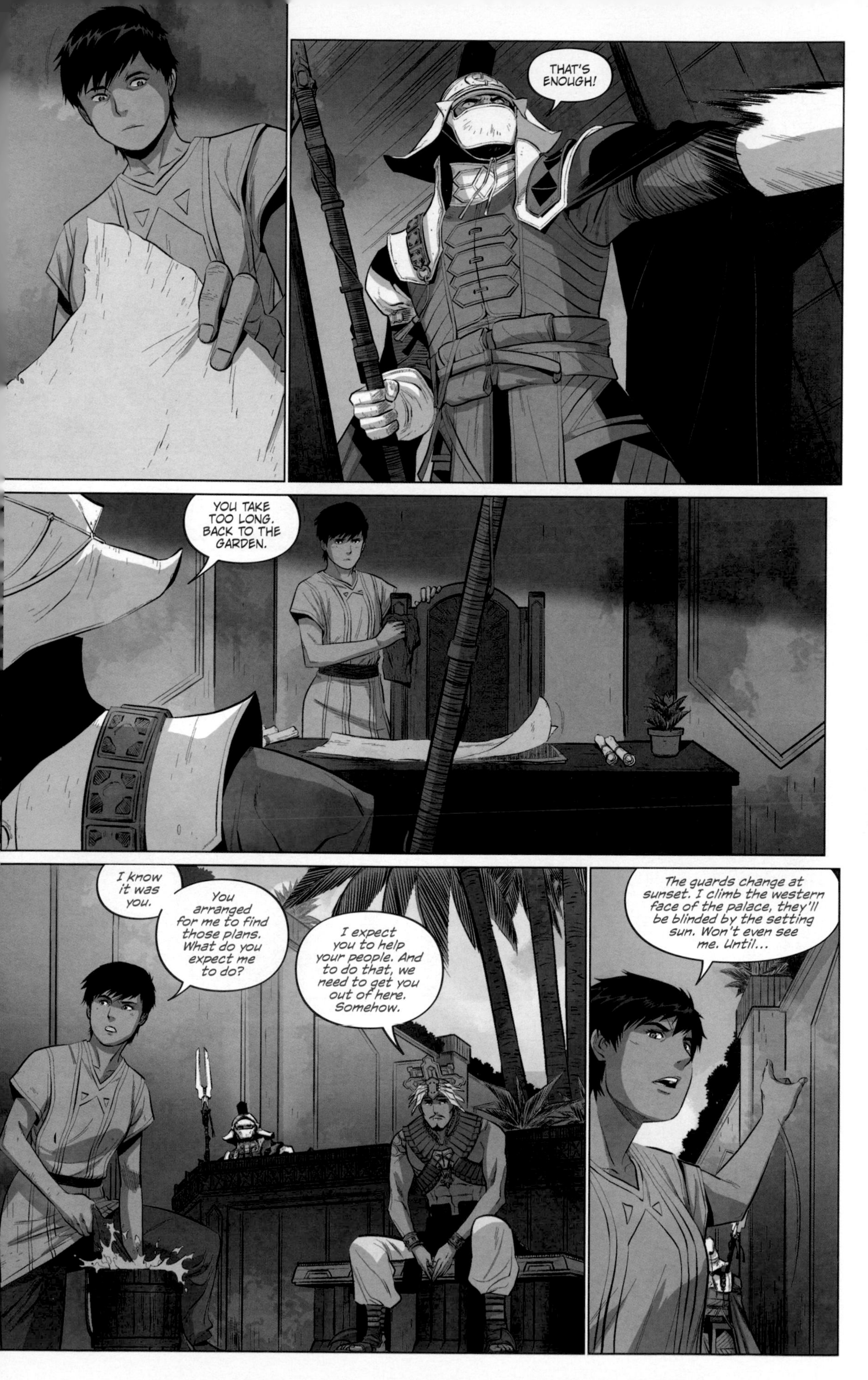
THAT'S ENOUGH!
YOU TAKE TOO LONG. BACK TO THE GARDEN.
I know it was you.
You arranged for me to find those plans. What do you expect me to do?
I expect you to help your people. And to do that, we need to get you out of here. Somehow.
The guards change at sunset. I climb the western face of the palace, they'll be blinded by the setting sun. Won't even see me. Until...

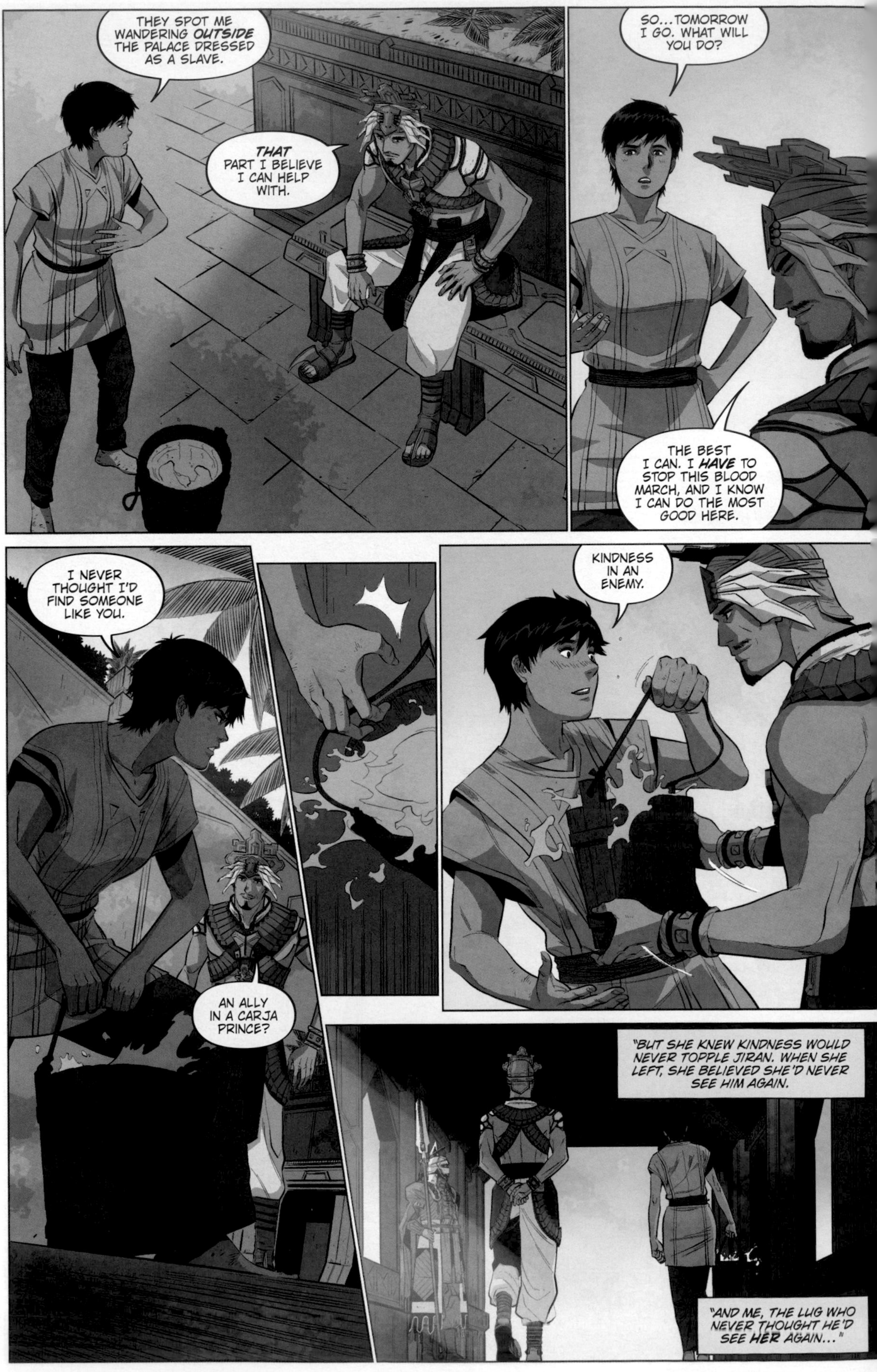
THEY SPOT ME WANDERING OUTSIDE THE PALACE DRESSED AS A SLAVE.
THAT PART I BELIEVE I CAN HELP WITH.
SO...TOMORROW I GO. WHAT WILL YOU DO?
THE BEST I CAN. I HAVE TO STOP THIS BLOOD MARCH, AND I KNOW I CAN DO THE MOST GOOD HERE.
I NEVER THOUGHT I'D FIND SOMEONE LIKE YOU.
AN ALLY IN A CARJA PRINCE?
KINDNESS IN AN ENEMY.
"BUT SHE KNEW KINDNESS WOULD NEVER TOPPLE JIRAN. WHEN SHE LEFT, SHE BELIEVED SHE'D NEVER SEE HIM AGAIN.
"AND ME, THE LUG WHO NEVER THOUGHT HE'D SEE HER AGAIN..."

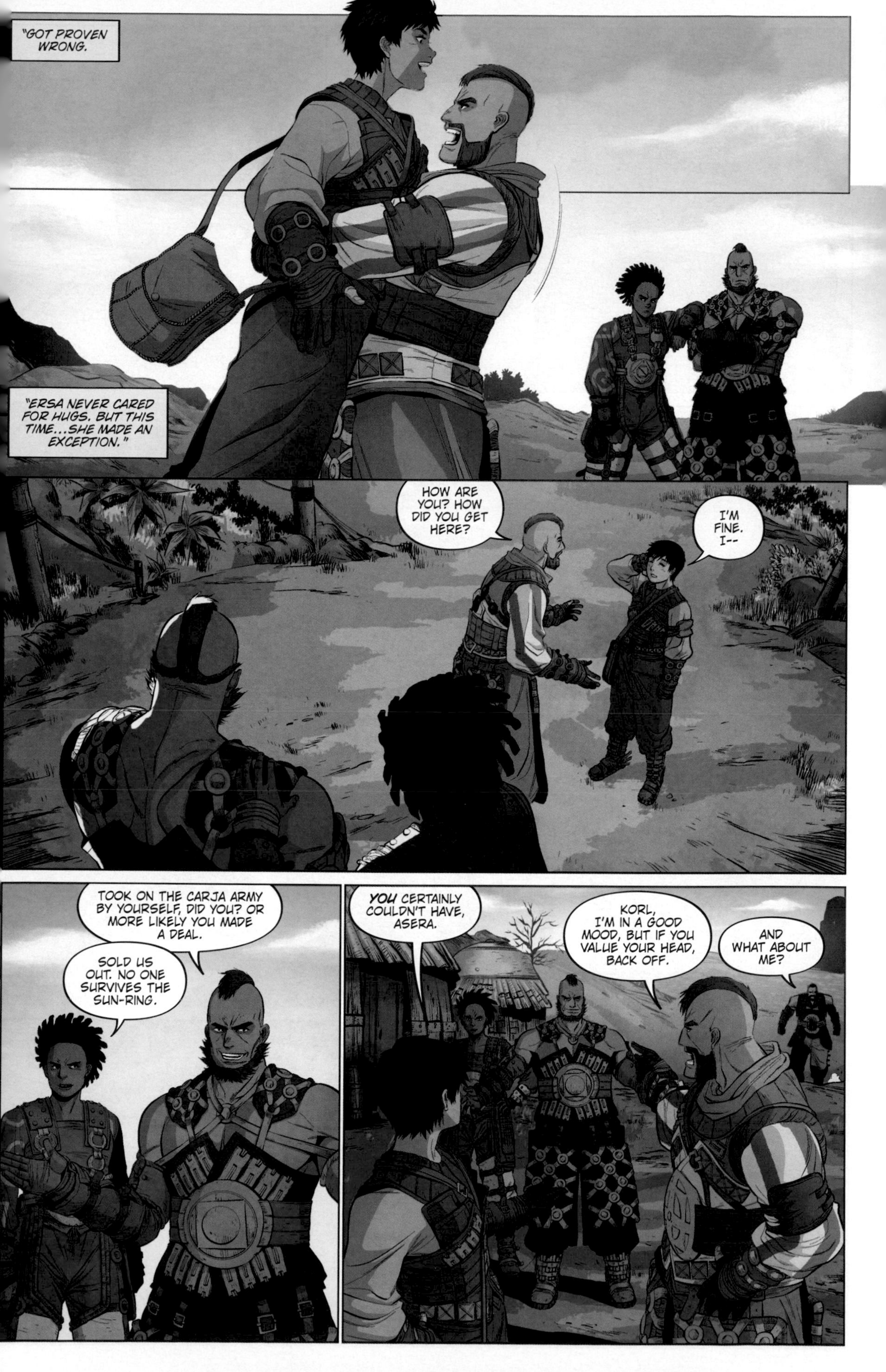
"GOT PROVEN WRONG.
"ERSA NEVER CARED FOR HUGS. BUT THIS TIME...SHE MADE AN EXCEPTION."
HOW ARE YOU? HOW DID YOU GET HERE?
I'M FINE. I--
TOOK ON THE CARJA ARMY BY YOURSELF, DID YOU? OR MORE LIKELY YOU MADE A DEAL.
SOLD US OUT. NO ONE SURVIVES THE SUN-RING.
YOU CERTAINLY COULDN'T HAVE, ASERA.
KORL, I'M IN A GOOD MOOD, BUT IF YOU VALUE YOUR HEAD, BACK OFF.
AND WHAT ABOUT ME?

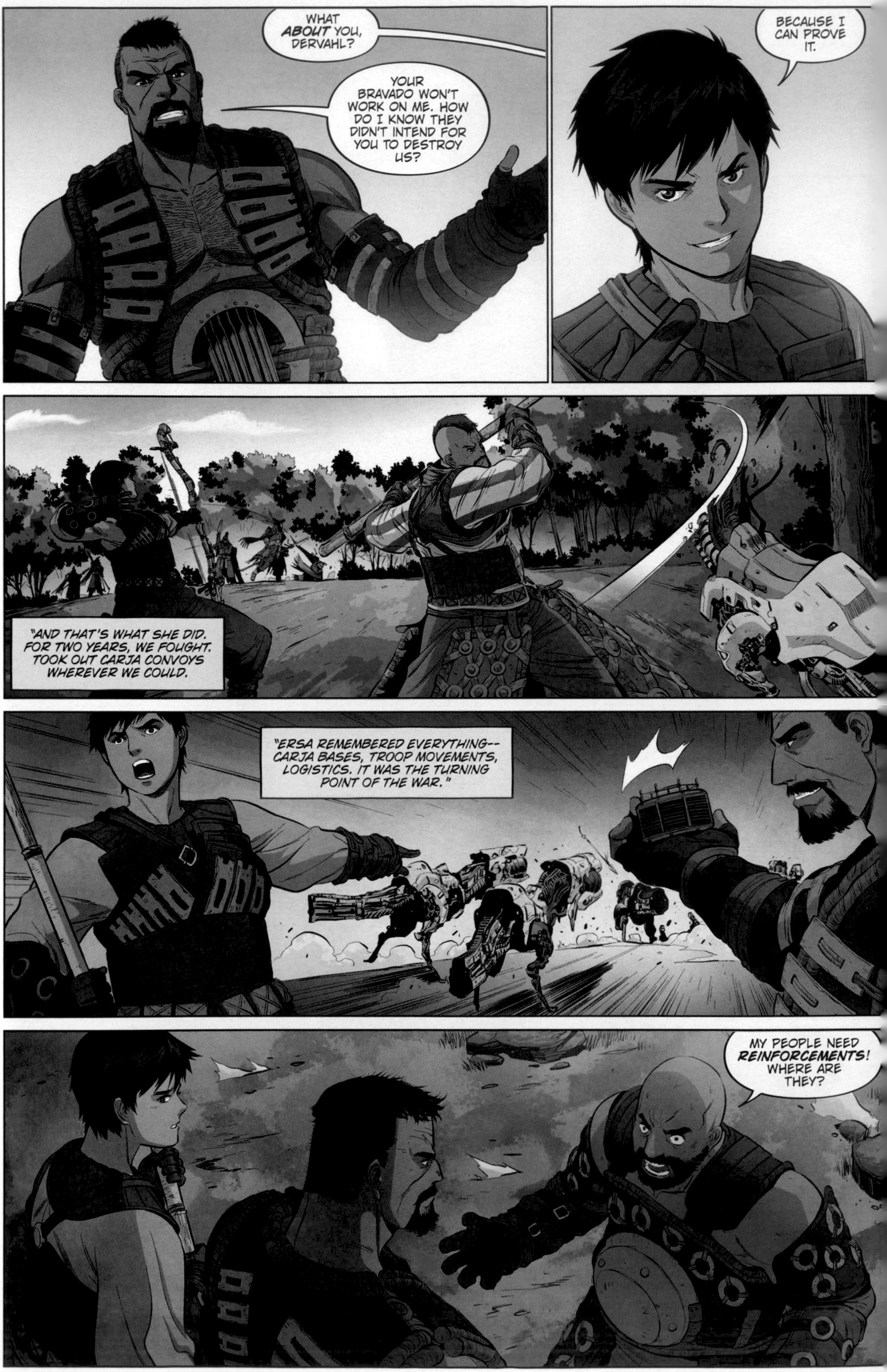
WHAT ABOUT YOU, DERVAHL?
YOUR BRAVADO WON'T WORK ON ME. HOW DO I KNOW THEY DIDN'T INTEND FOR YOU TO DESTROY US?
BECAUSE I CAN PROVE IT.
"AND THAT'S WHAT SHE DID. FOR TWO YEARS, WE FOUGHT. TOOK OUT CARJA CONVOYS WHEREVER WE COULD.
"ERSA REMEMBERED EVERYTHING-- CARJA BASES, TROOP MOVEMENTS, LOGISTICS. IT WAS THE TURNING POINT OF THE WAR."
MY PEOPLE NEED REINFORCEMENTS! WHERE ARE THEY?

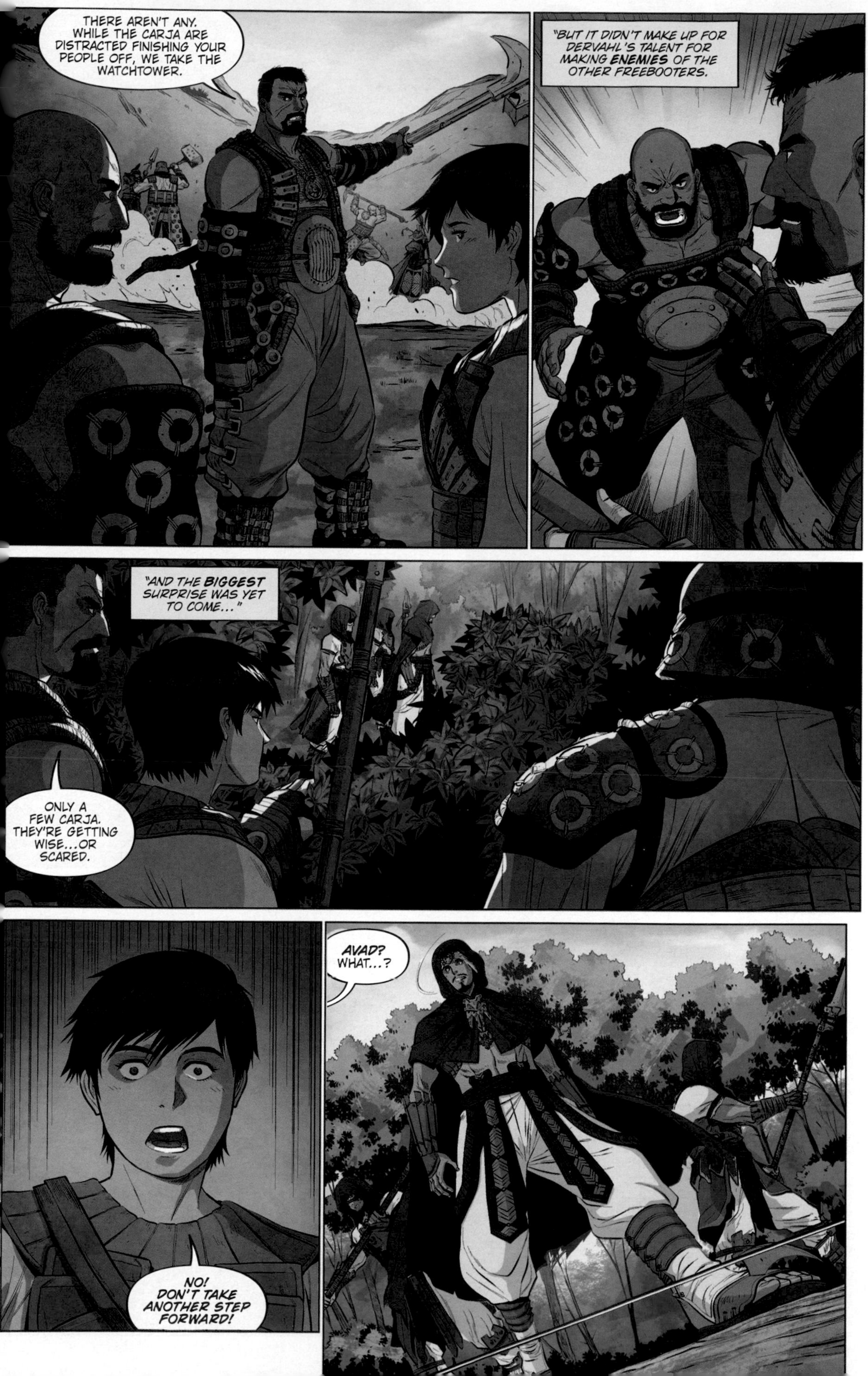

THERE AREN'T ANY. WHILE THE CARJA ARE DISTRACTED FINISHING YOUR PEOPLE OFF, WE TAKE THE WATCHTOWER.
"BUT IT DIDN'T MAKE UP FOR DERVAHL'S TALENT FOR MAKING ENEMIES OF THE OTHER FREEBOOTERS.
"AND THE BIGGEST SURPRISE WAS YET TO COME..."
ONLY A FEW CARJA. THEY'RE GETTING WISE...OR SCARED.
NO! DON'T TAKE ANOTHER STEP FORWARD!
AVAD? WHAT...?

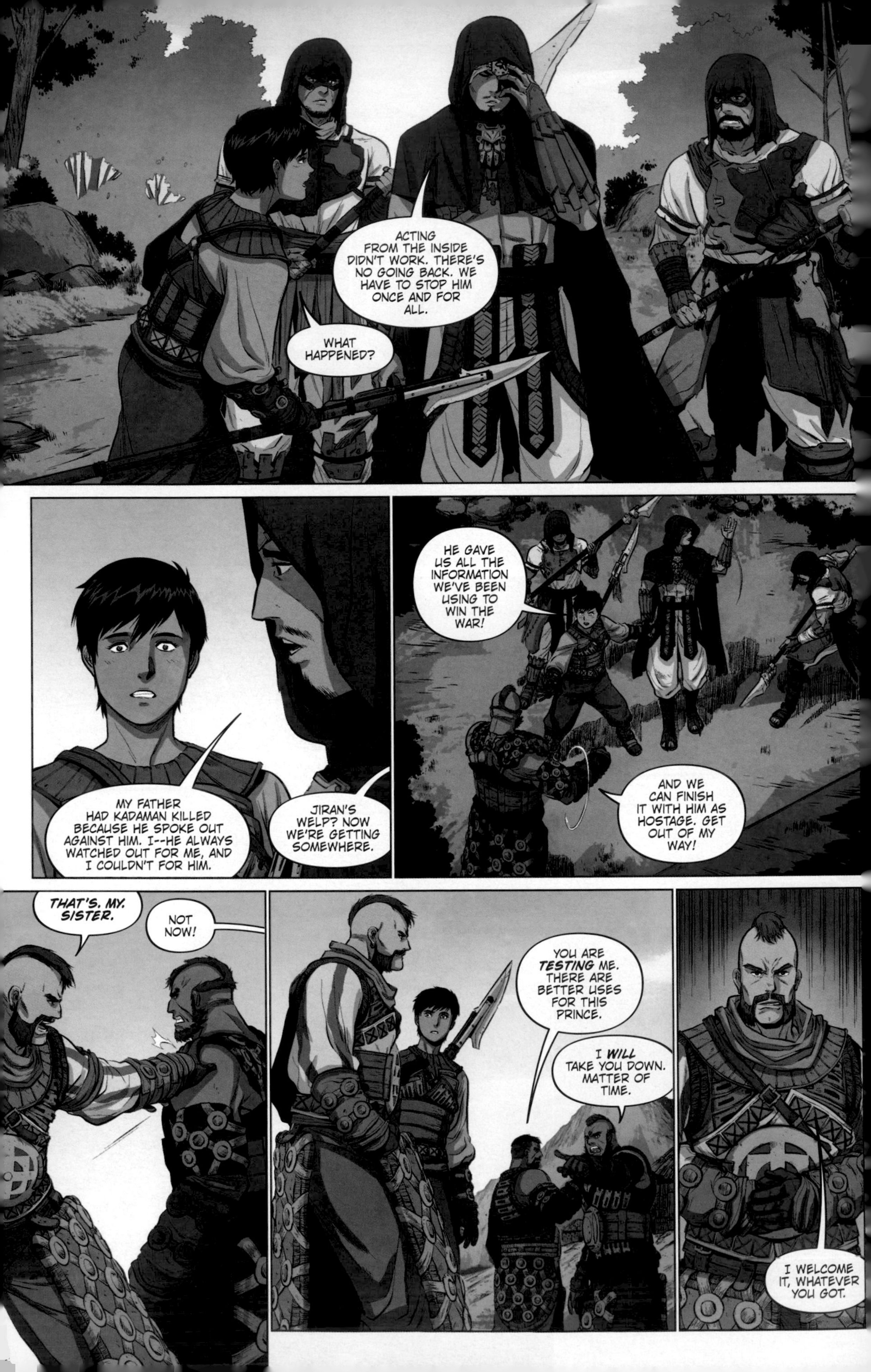
ACTING FROM THE INSIDE DIDN'T WORK. THERE'S NO GOING BACK. WE HAVE TO STOP HIM ONCE AND FOR ALL.
WHAT HAPPENED?
MY FATHER HAD KADAMAN KILLED BECAUSE HE SPOKE OUT AGAINST HIM. I--HE ALWAYS WATCHED OUT FOR ME, AND I COULDN'T FOR HIM.
JIRAN'S WELP? NOW WE'RE GETTING SOMEWHERE.
HE GAVE US ALL THE INFORMATION WE'VE BEEN USING TO WIN THE WAR!
AND WE CAN FINISH IT WITH HIM AS HOSTAGE. GET OUT OF MY WAY!
THAT'S. MY. SISTER.
NOT NOW!
YOU ARE TESTING ME. THERE ARE BETTER USES FOR THIS PRINCE.
I WILL TAKE YOU DOWN. MATTER OF TIME.
I WELCOME IT, WHATEVER YOU GOT.

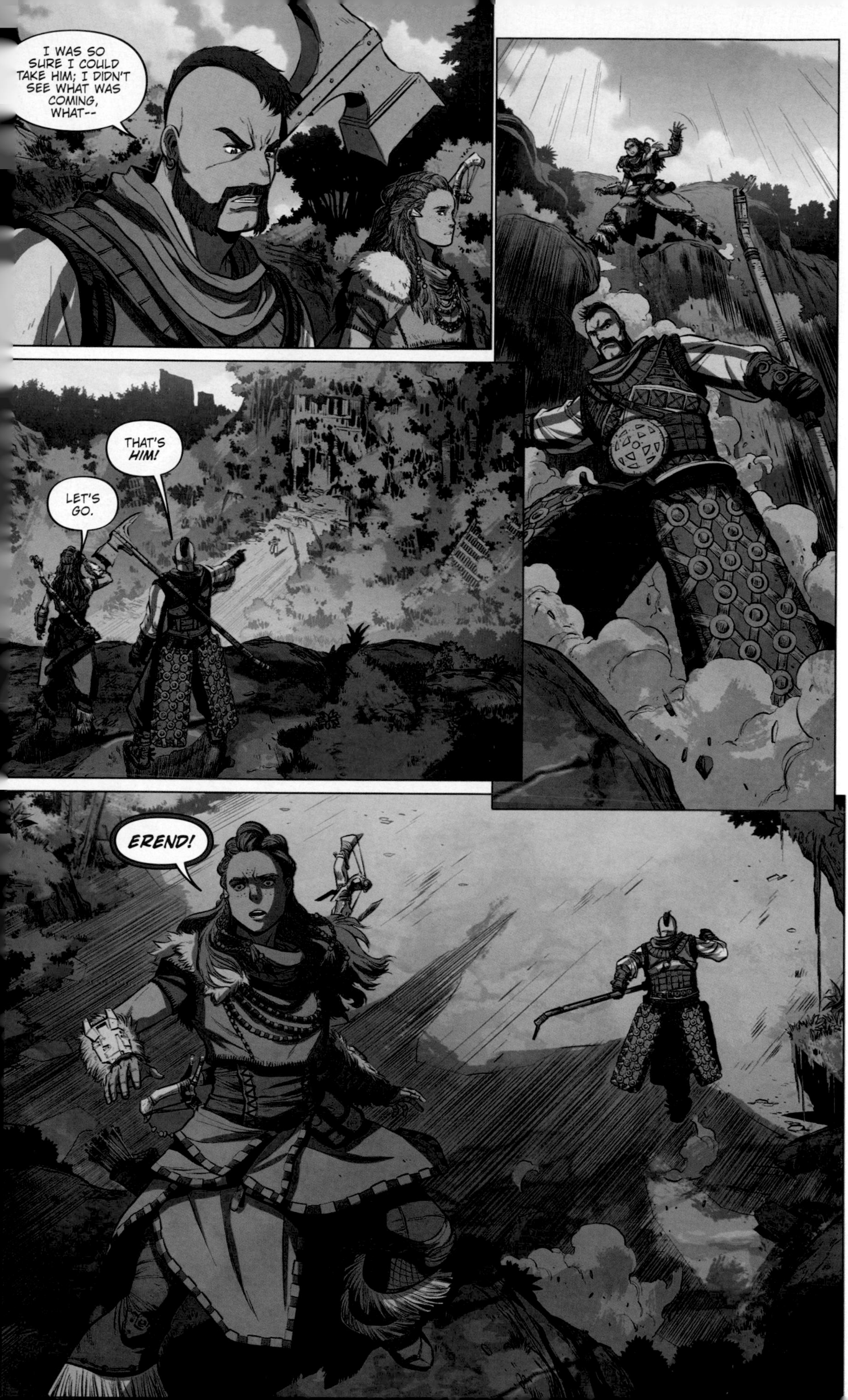
I WAS SO SURE I COULD TAKE HIM; I DIDN'T SEE WHAT WAS COMING, WHAT--
THAT'S HIM!
LET'S GO.
EREND!

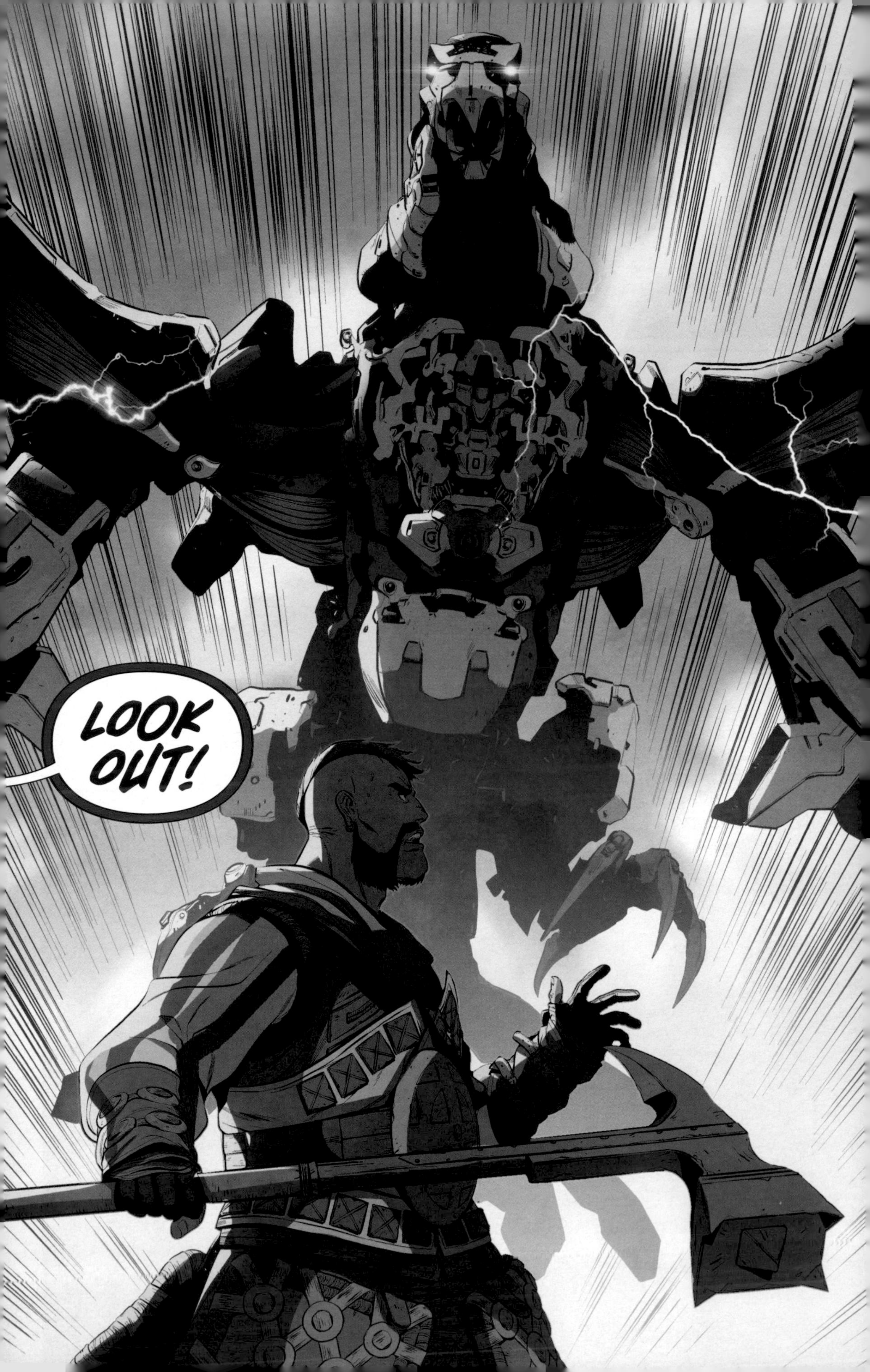
LOOK OUT!

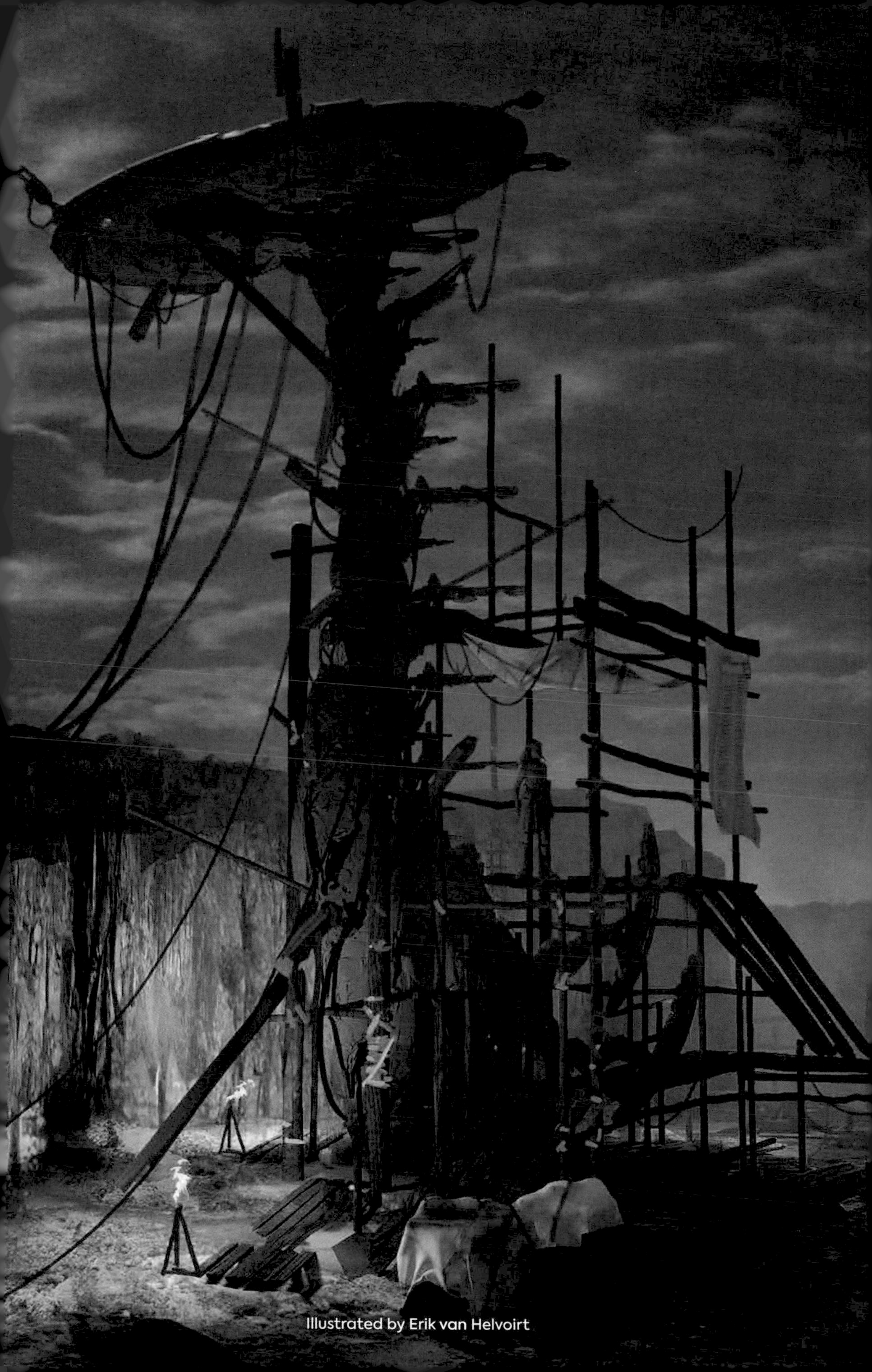

Illustrated by Erik van Helvoirt

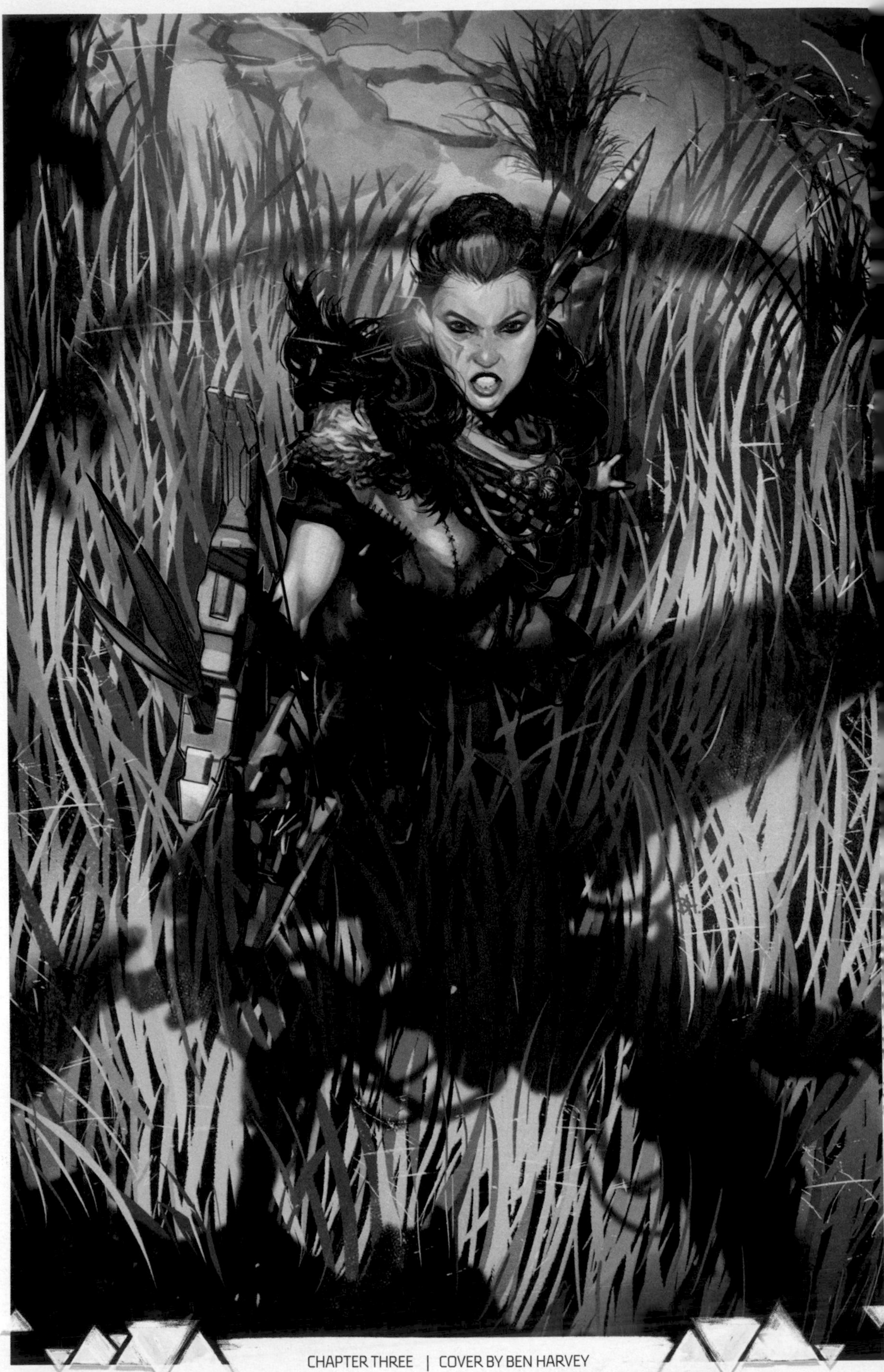

CHAPTER THREE | COVER BY BEN HARVEY

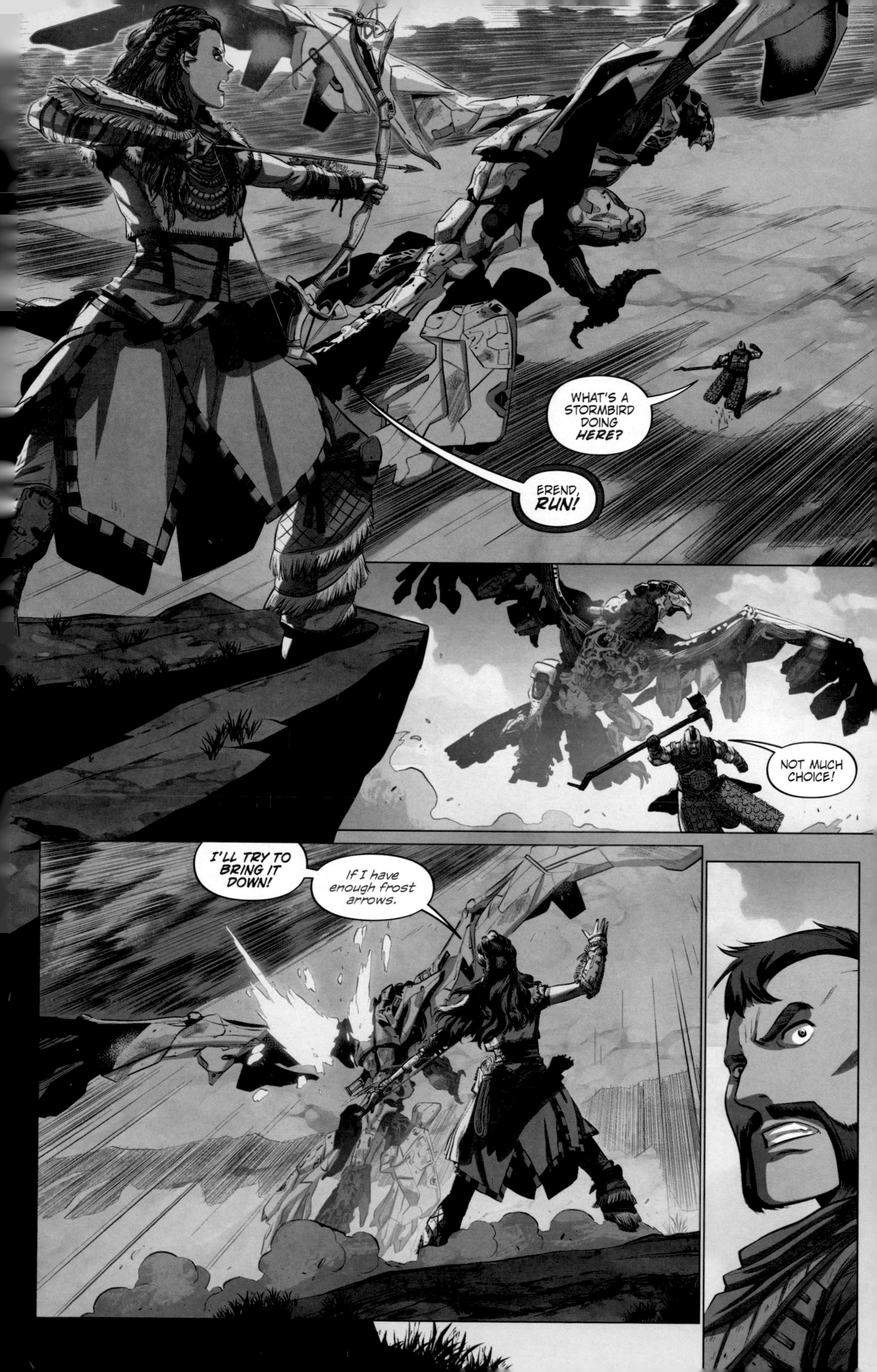
WHAT'S A STORMBIRD DOING HERE?
EREND, RUN!
NOT MUCH CHOICE!
I'LL TRY TO BRING IT DOWN!
If I have enough frost arrows.

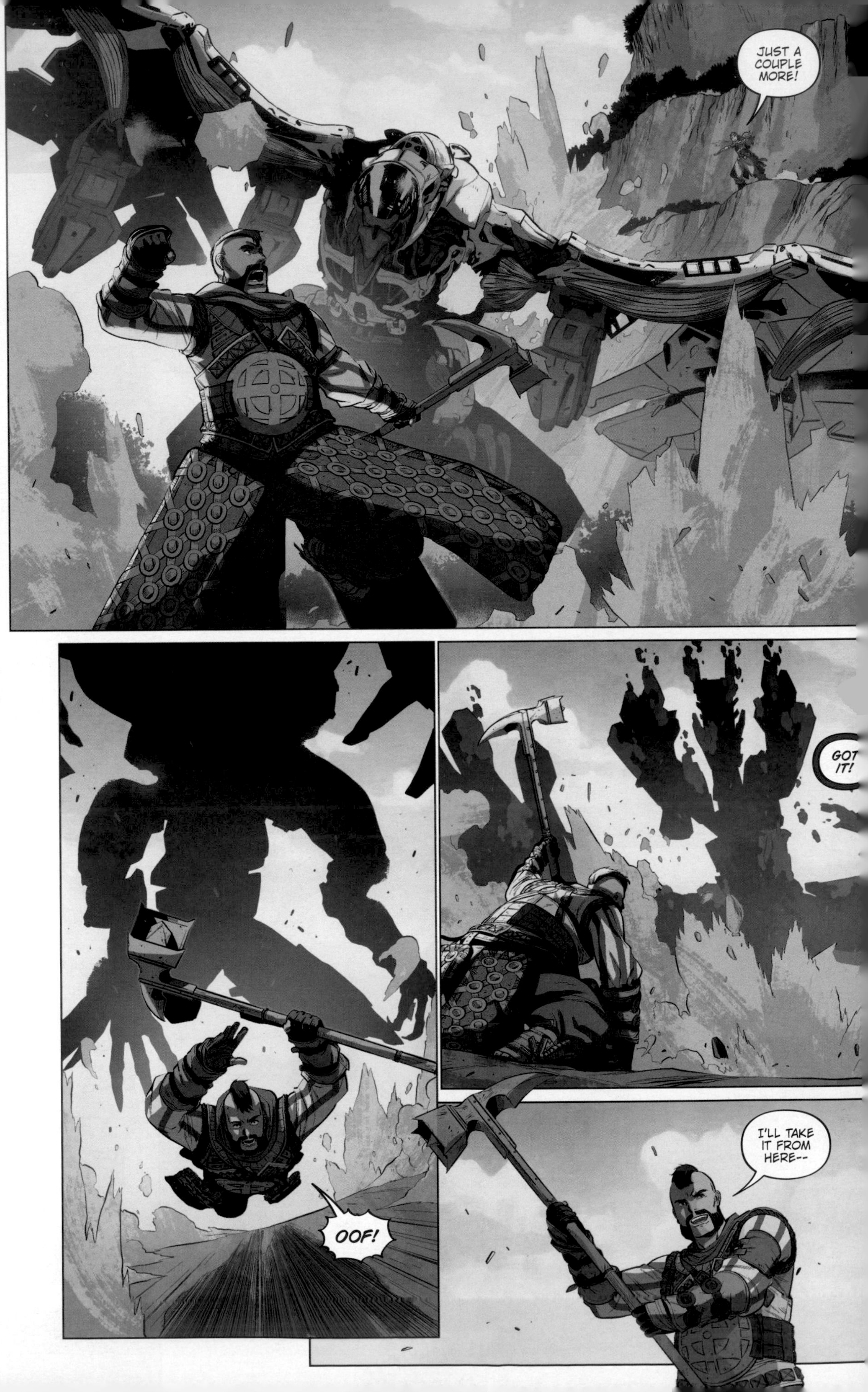
JUST A COUPLE MORE!
OOF!
GOT IT!
I'LL TAKE IT FROM HERE--

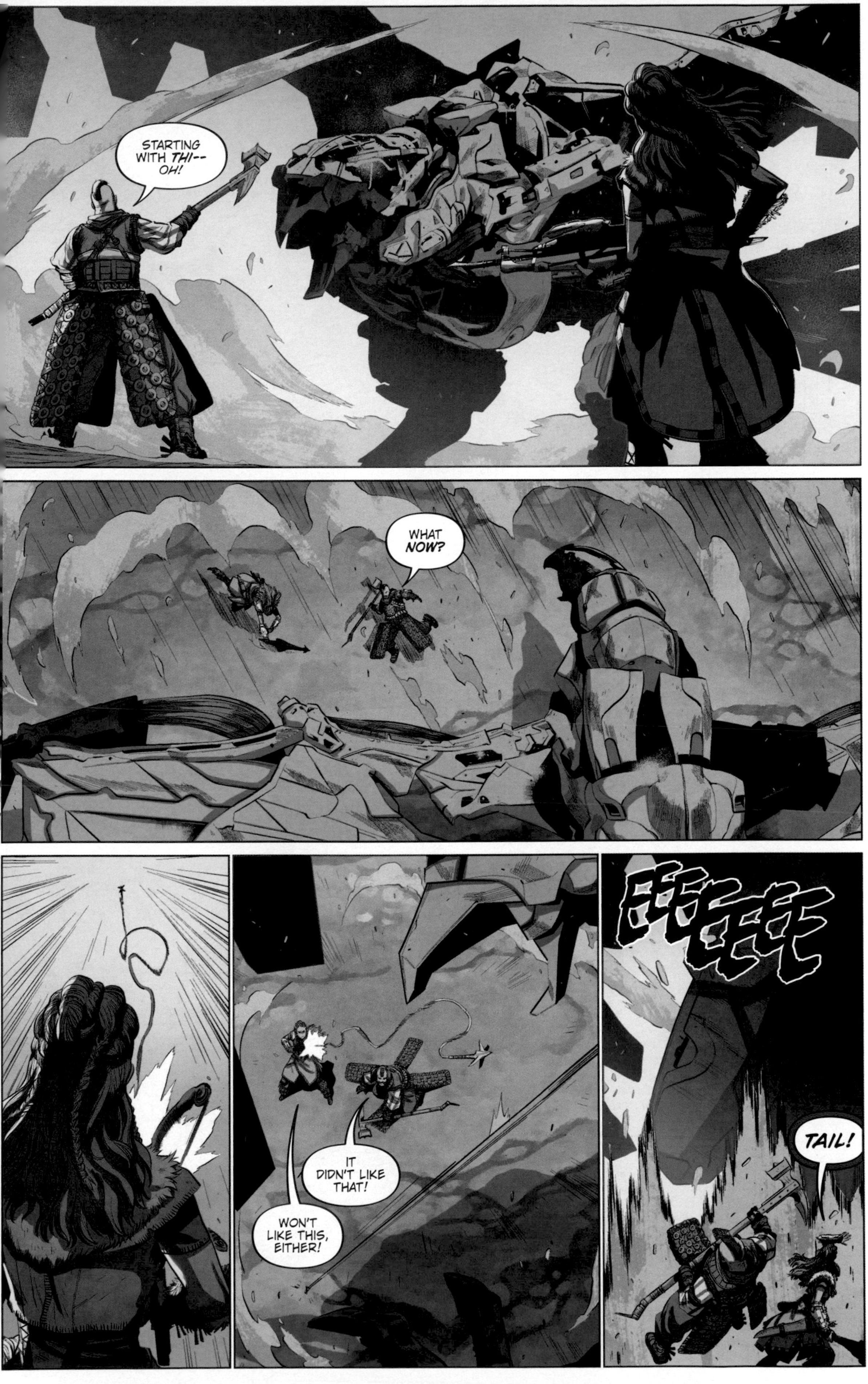

STARTING WITH *THI*-- OH!
WHAT *NOW?*
IT DIDN'T LIKE THAT!
WON'T LIKE THIS, EITHER!
EEEEEEEE
TAIL!

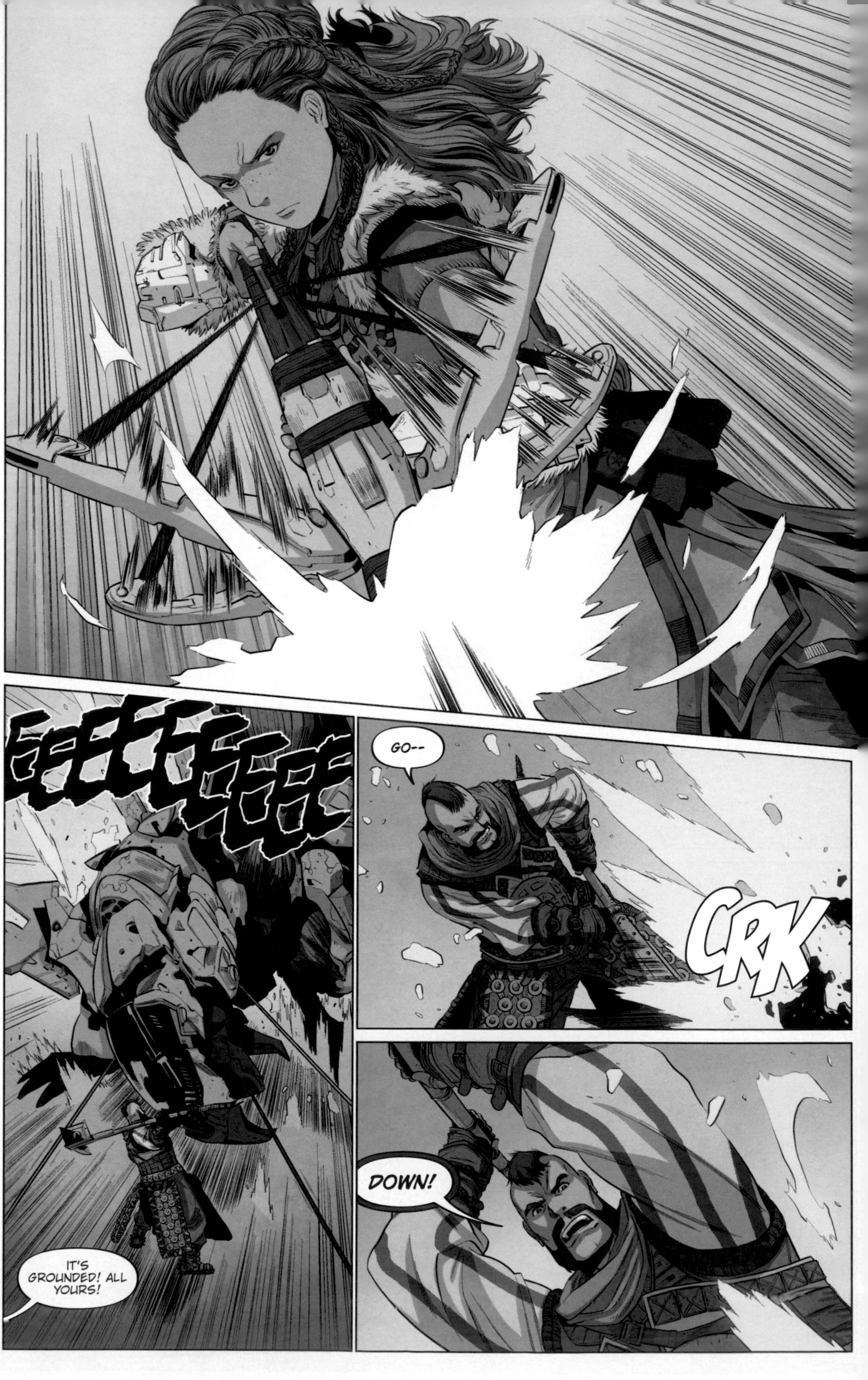
EEEEEEEEEEE
IT'S GROUNDED! ALL YOURS!
GO--
CRK
DOWN!

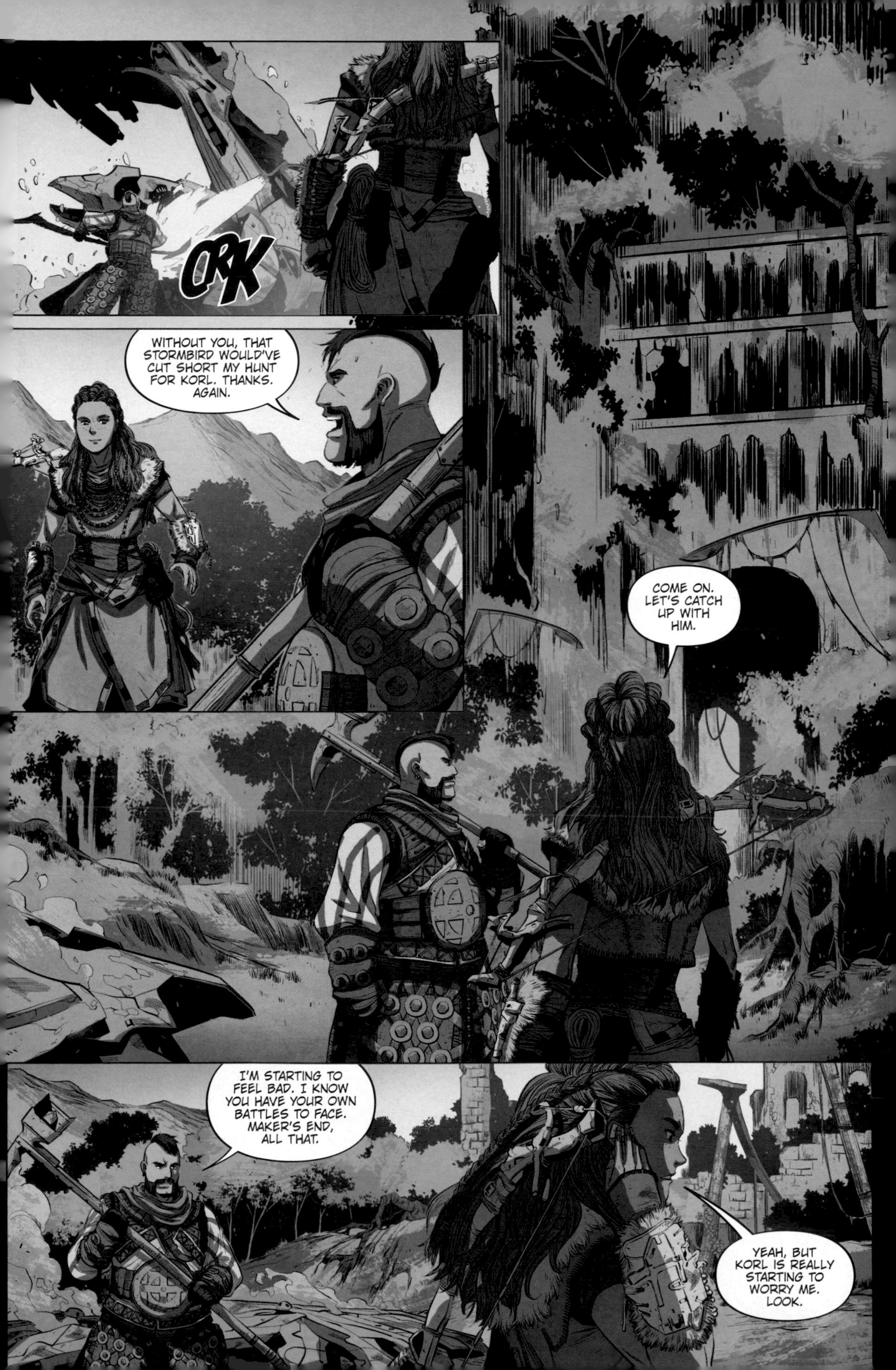
CRK
WITHOUT YOU, THAT STORMBIRD WOULD'VE CUT SHORT MY HUNT FOR KORL. THANKS. AGAIN.
COME ON. LET'S CATCH UP WITH HIM.
I'M STARTING TO FEEL BAD. I KNOW YOU HAVE YOUR OWN BATTLES TO FACE. MAKER'S END, ALL THAT.
YEAH, BUT KORL IS REALLY STARTING TO WORRY ME. LOOK.

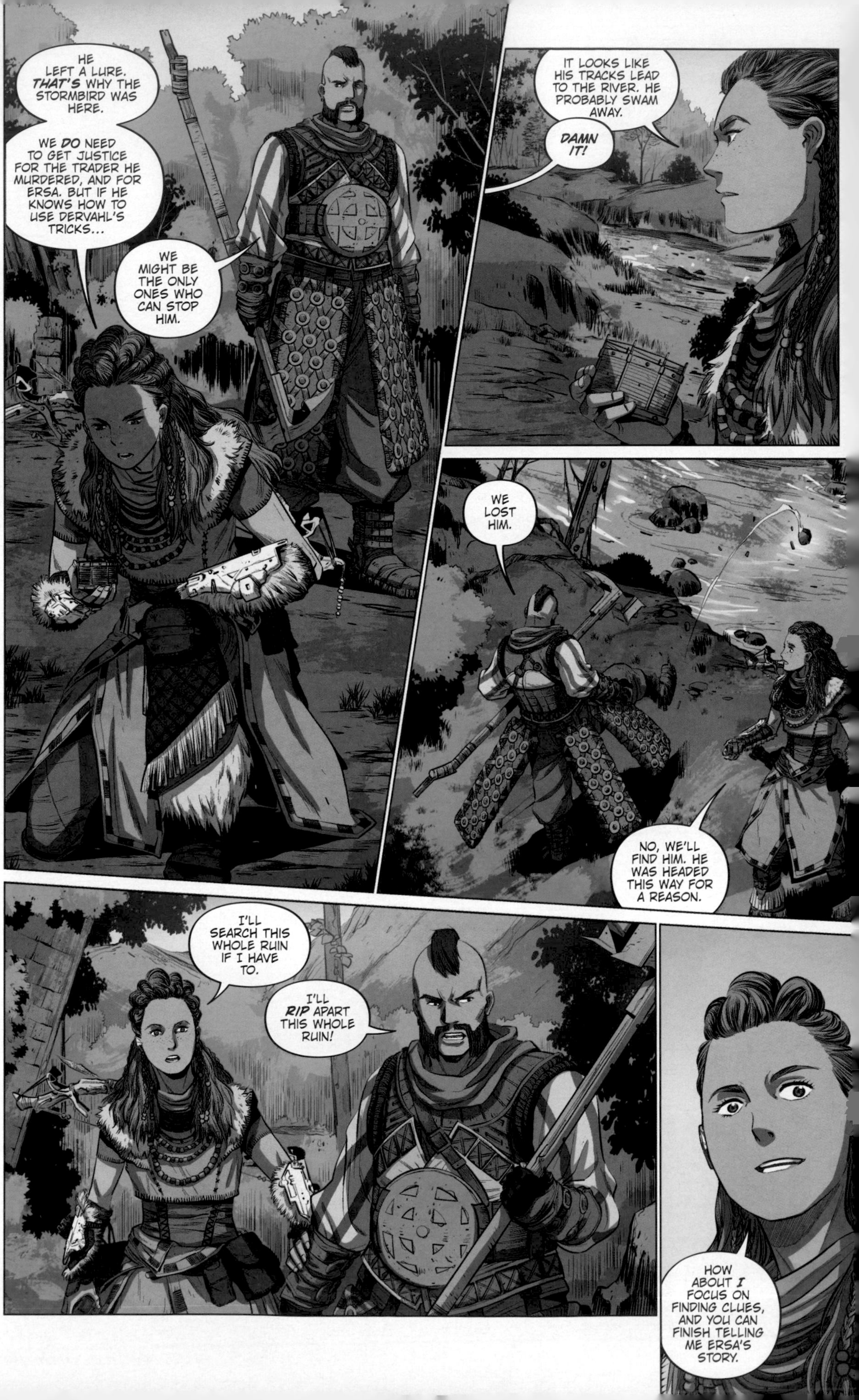
HE LEFT A LURE. THAT'S WHY THE STORMBIRD WAS HERE.
WE DO NEED TO GET JUSTICE FOR THE TRADER HE MURDERED, AND FOR ERSA. BUT IF HE KNOWS HOW TO USE DERVAHL'S TRICKS...
WE MIGHT BE THE ONLY ONES WHO CAN STOP HIM.
IT LOOKS LIKE HIS TRACKS LEAD TO THE RIVER. HE PROBABLY SWAM AWAY.
DAMN IT!
WE LOST HIM.
NO, WE'LL FIND HIM. HE WAS HEADED THIS WAY FOR A REASON.
I'LL SEARCH THIS WHOLE RUIN IF I HAVE TO.
I'LL RIP APART THIS WHOLE RUIN!
HOW ABOUT I FOCUS ON FINDING CLUES, AND YOU CAN FINISH TELLING ME ERSA'S STORY.

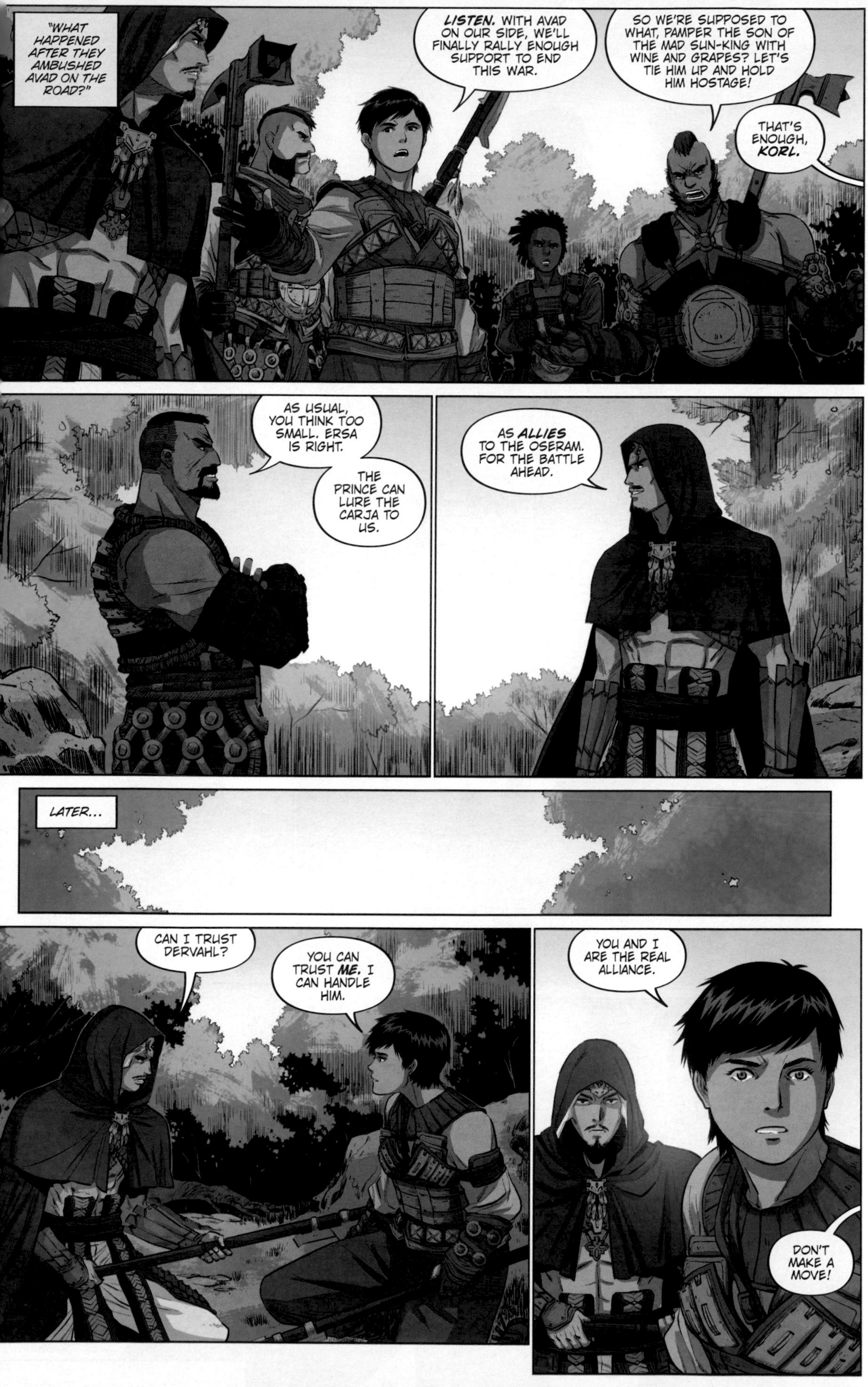
"WHAT HAPPENED AFTER THEY AMBUSHED AVAD ON THE ROAD?"
LISTEN. WITH AVAD ON OUR SIDE, WE'LL FINALLY RALLY ENOUGH SUPPORT TO END THIS WAR.
SO WE'RE SUPPOSED TO WHAT, PAMPER THE SON OF THE MAD SUN-KING WITH WINE AND GRAPES? LET'S TIE HIM UP AND HOLD HIM HOSTAGE!
THAT'S ENOUGH, KORL.
AS USUAL, YOU THINK TOO SMALL. ERSA IS RIGHT.
THE PRINCE CAN LURE THE CARJA TO US.
AS ALLIES TO THE OSERAM. FOR THE BATTLE AHEAD.
LATER...
CAN I TRUST DERVAHL?
YOU CAN TRUST ME. I CAN HANDLE HIM.
YOU AND I ARE THE REAL ALLIANCE.
DON'T MAKE A MOVE!

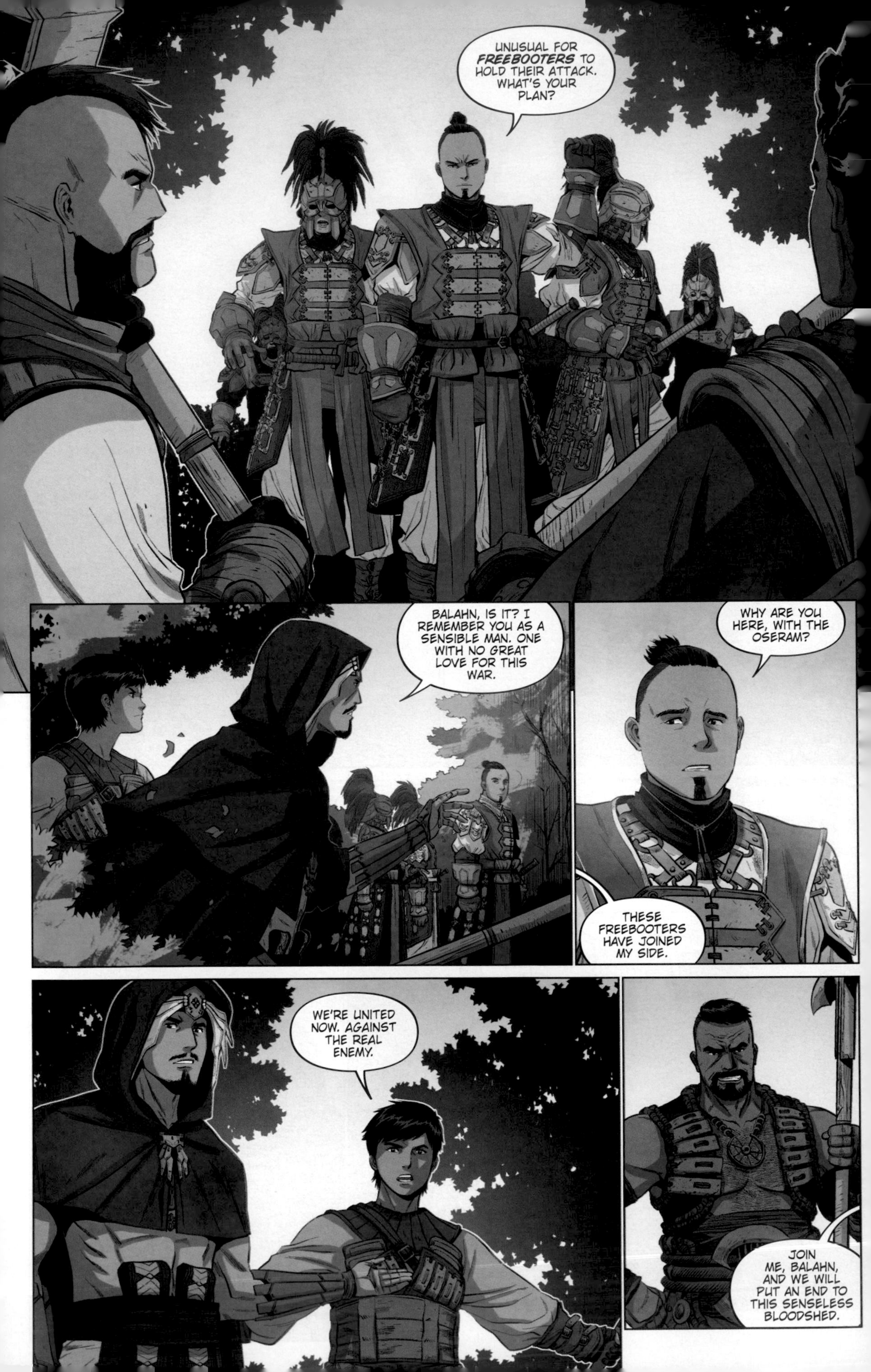
UNUSUAL FOR **FREEBOOTERS** TO HOLD THEIR ATTACK. WHAT'S YOUR PLAN?
BALAHN, IS IT? I REMEMBER YOU AS A SENSIBLE MAN. ONE WITH NO GREAT LOVE FOR THIS WAR.
WHY ARE YOU HERE, WITH THE OSERAM?
THESE FREEBOOTERS HAVE JOINED MY SIDE.
WE'RE UNITED NOW. AGAINST THE REAL ENEMY.
JOIN ME, BALAHN, AND WE WILL PUT AN END TO THIS SENSELESS BLOODSHED.

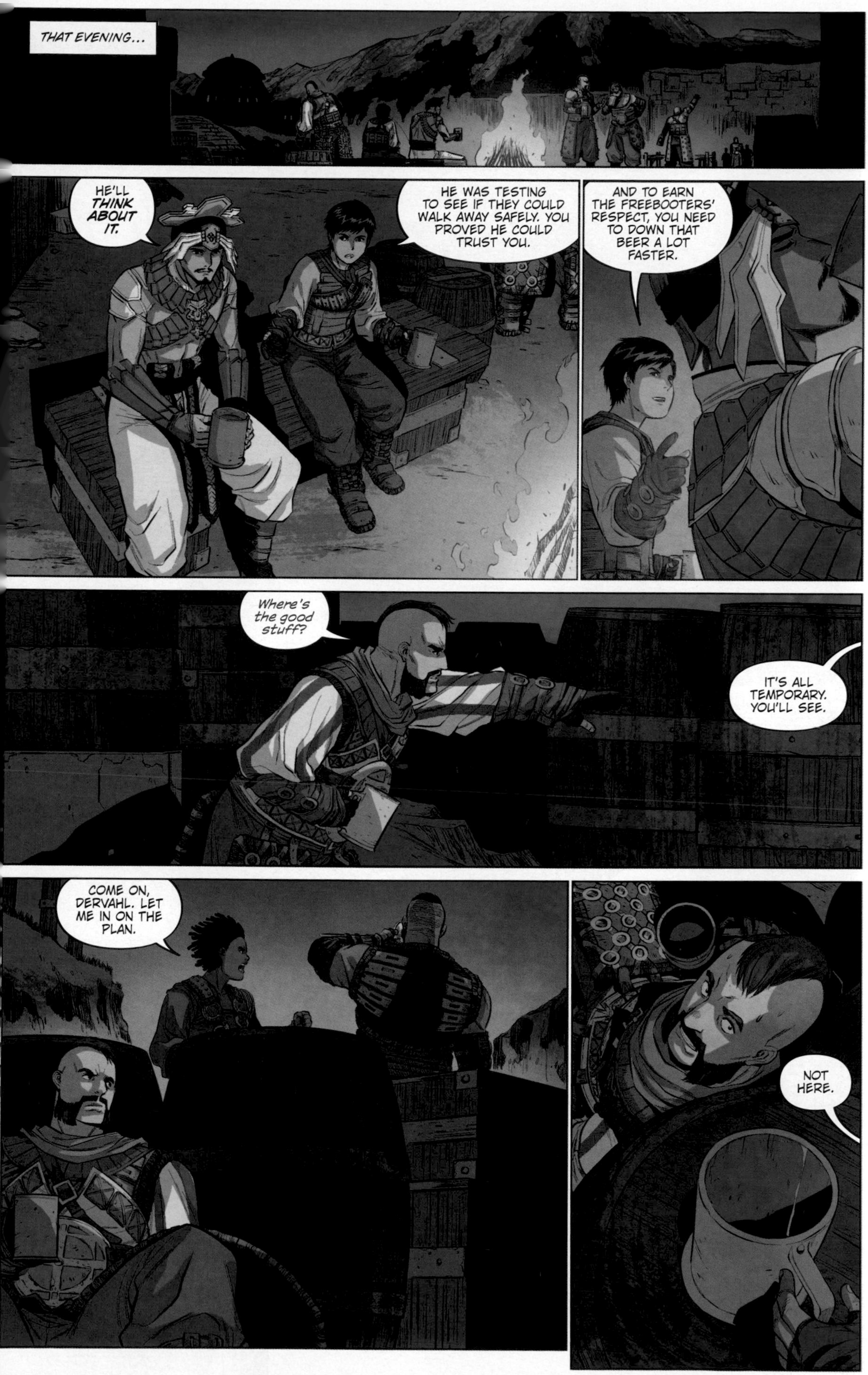
THAT EVENING...
HE'LL THINK ABOUT IT.
HE WAS TESTING TO SEE IF THEY COULD WALK AWAY SAFELY. YOU PROVED HE COULD TRUST YOU.
AND TO EARN THE FREEBOOTERS' RESPECT, YOU NEED TO DOWN THAT BEER A LOT FASTER.
Where's the good stuff?
IT'S ALL TEMPORARY. YOU'LL SEE.
COME ON, DERVAHL. LET ME IN ON THE PLAN.
NOT HERE.

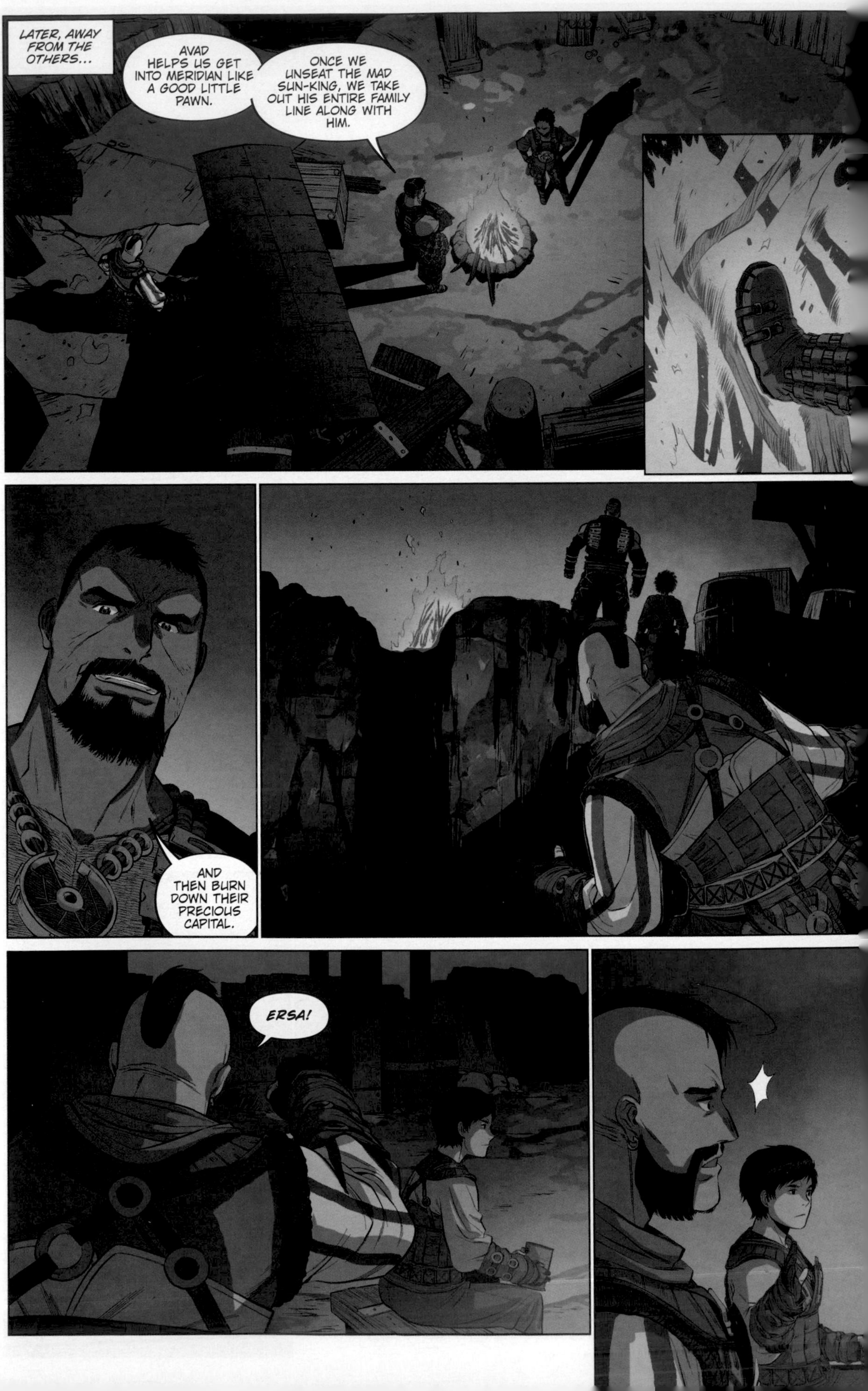
LATER, AWAY FROM THE OTHERS...
AVAD HELPS US GET INTO MERIDIAN LIKE A GOOD LITTLE PAWN.
ONCE WE UNSEAT THE MAD SUN-KING, WE TAKE OUT HIS ENTIRE FAMILY LINE ALONG WITH HIM.
AND THEN BURN DOWN THEIR PRECIOUS CAPITAL.
ERSA!

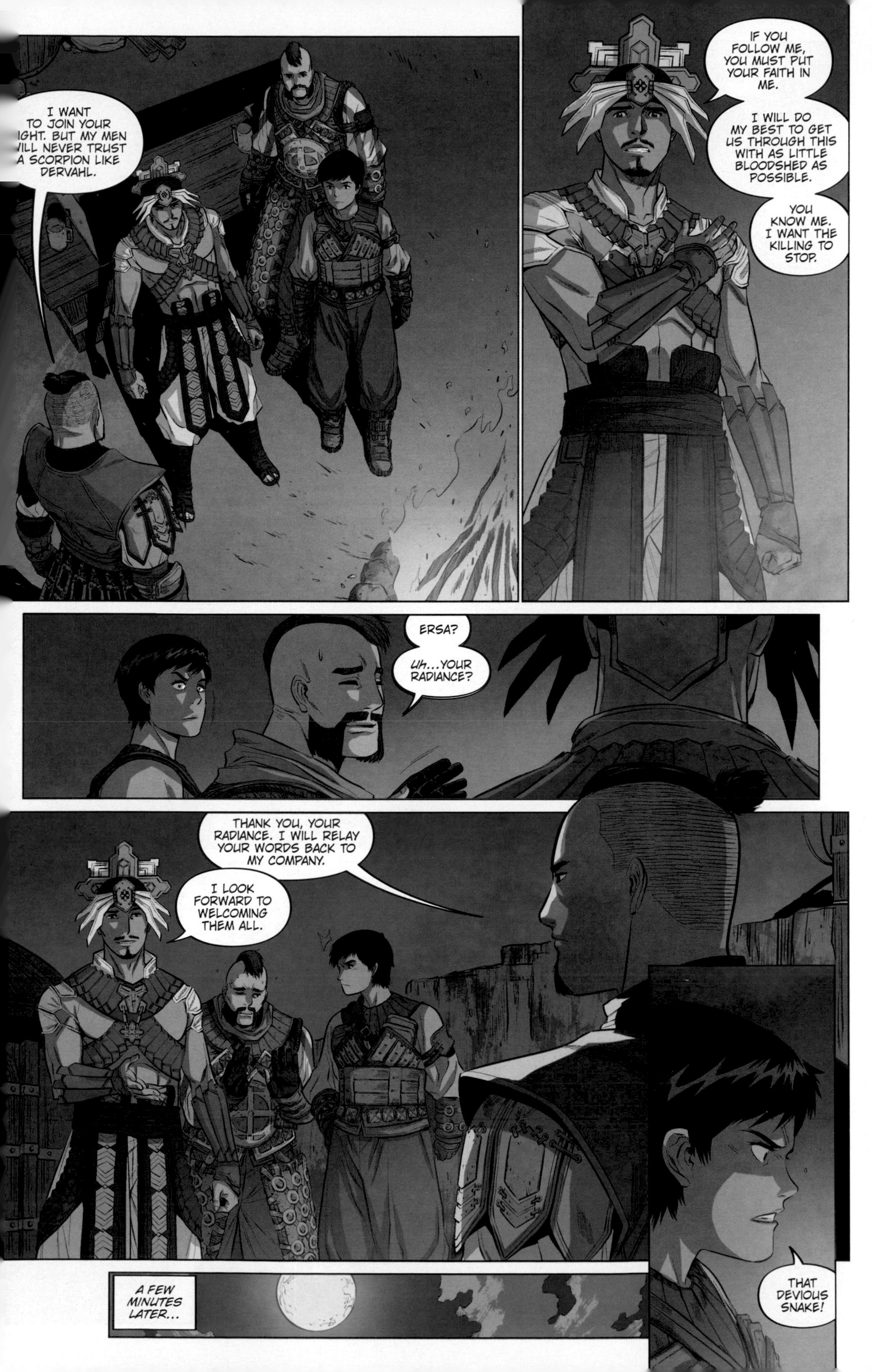
I WANT TO JOIN YOUR FIGHT. BUT MY MEN WILL NEVER TRUST A SCORPION LIKE DERVAHL.
IF YOU FOLLOW ME, YOU MUST PUT YOUR FAITH IN ME.
I WILL DO MY BEST TO GET US THROUGH THIS WITH AS LITTLE BLOODSHED AS POSSIBLE.
YOU KNOW ME. I WANT THE KILLING TO STOP.
ERSA?
Uh...YOUR RADIANCE?
THANK YOU, YOUR RADIANCE. I WILL RELAY YOUR WORDS BACK TO MY COMPANY.
I LOOK FORWARD TO WELCOMING THEM ALL.
A FEW MINUTES LATER...
THAT DEVIOUS SNAKE!

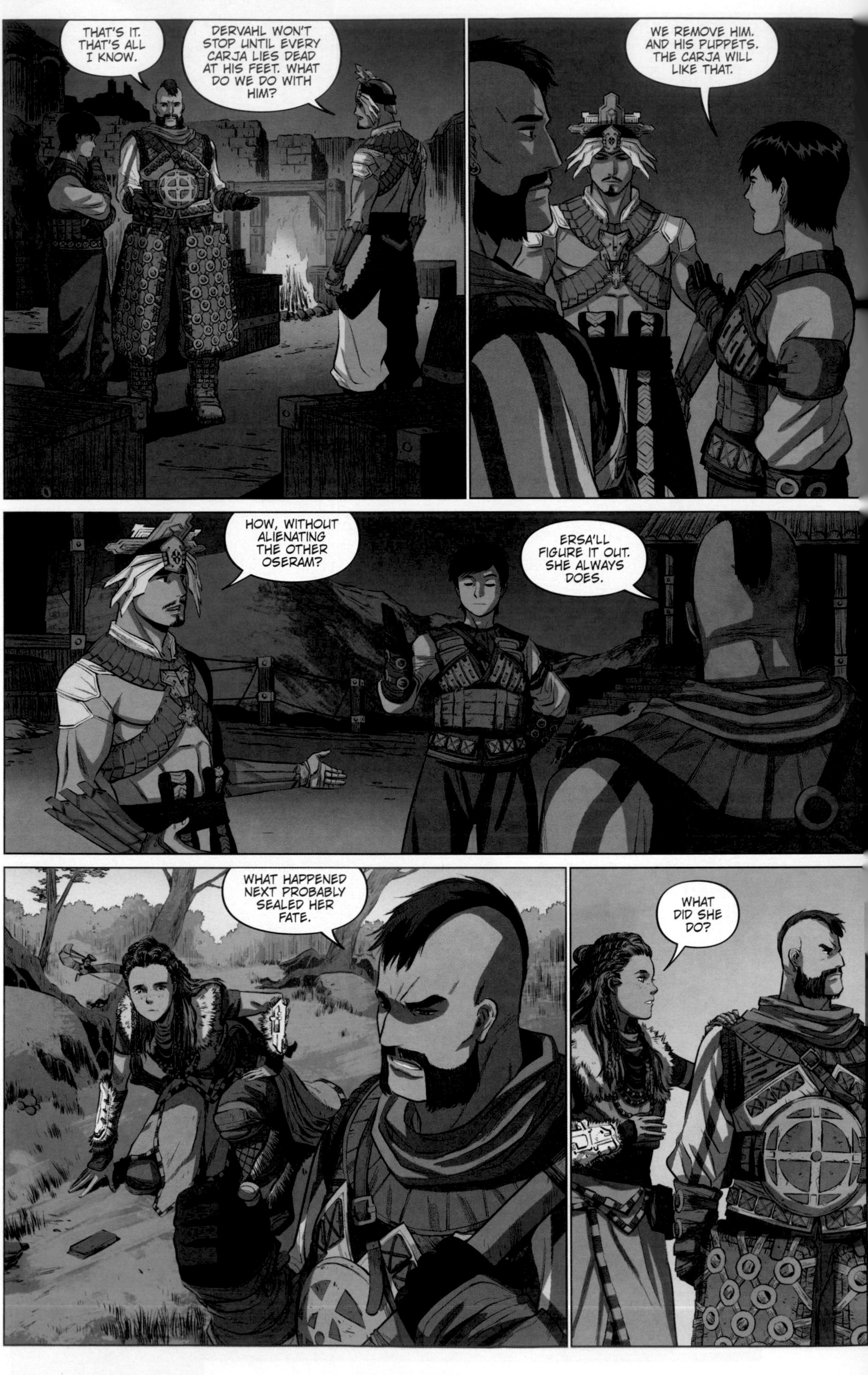
THAT'S IT. THAT'S ALL I KNOW.
DERVAHL WON'T STOP UNTIL EVERY CARJA LIES DEAD AT HIS FEET. WHAT DO WE DO WITH HIM?
WE REMOVE HIM. AND HIS PUPPETS. THE CARJA WILL LIKE THAT.
HOW, WITHOUT ALIENATING THE OTHER OSERAM?
ERSA'LL FIGURE IT OUT. SHE ALWAYS DOES.
WHAT HAPPENED NEXT PROBABLY SEALED HER FATE.
WHAT DID SHE DO?

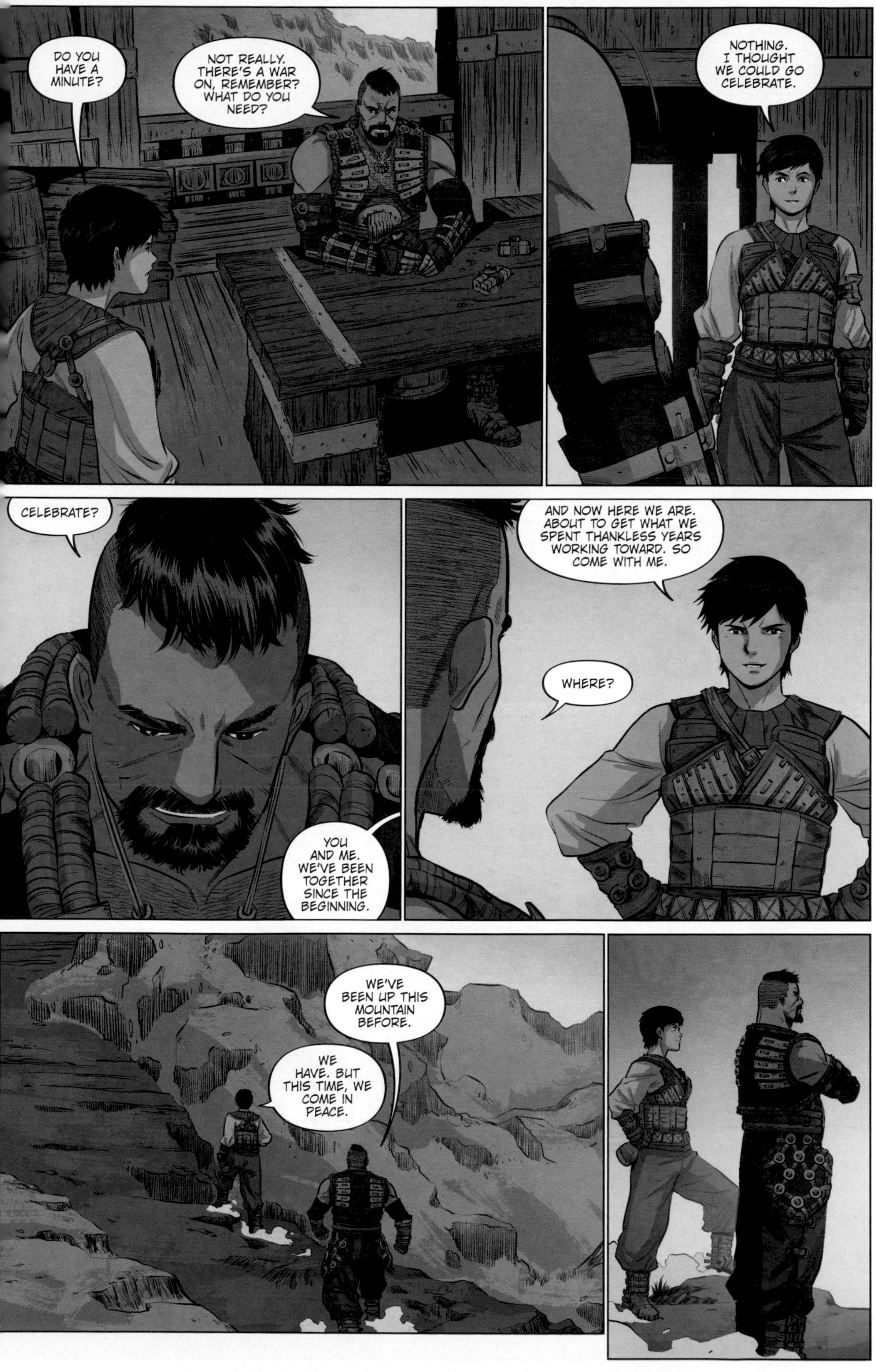
DO YOU HAVE A MINUTE?
NOT REALLY. THERE'S A WAR ON, REMEMBER? WHAT DO YOU NEED?
NOTHING. I THOUGHT WE COULD GO CELEBRATE.
CELEBRATE?
YOU AND ME. WE'VE BEEN TOGETHER SINCE THE BEGINNING.
AND NOW HERE WE ARE. ABOUT TO GET WHAT WE SPENT THANKLESS YEARS WORKING TOWARD. SO COME WITH ME.
WHERE?
WE'VE BEEN UP THIS MOUNTAIN BEFORE.
WE HAVE. BUT THIS TIME, WE COME IN PEACE.

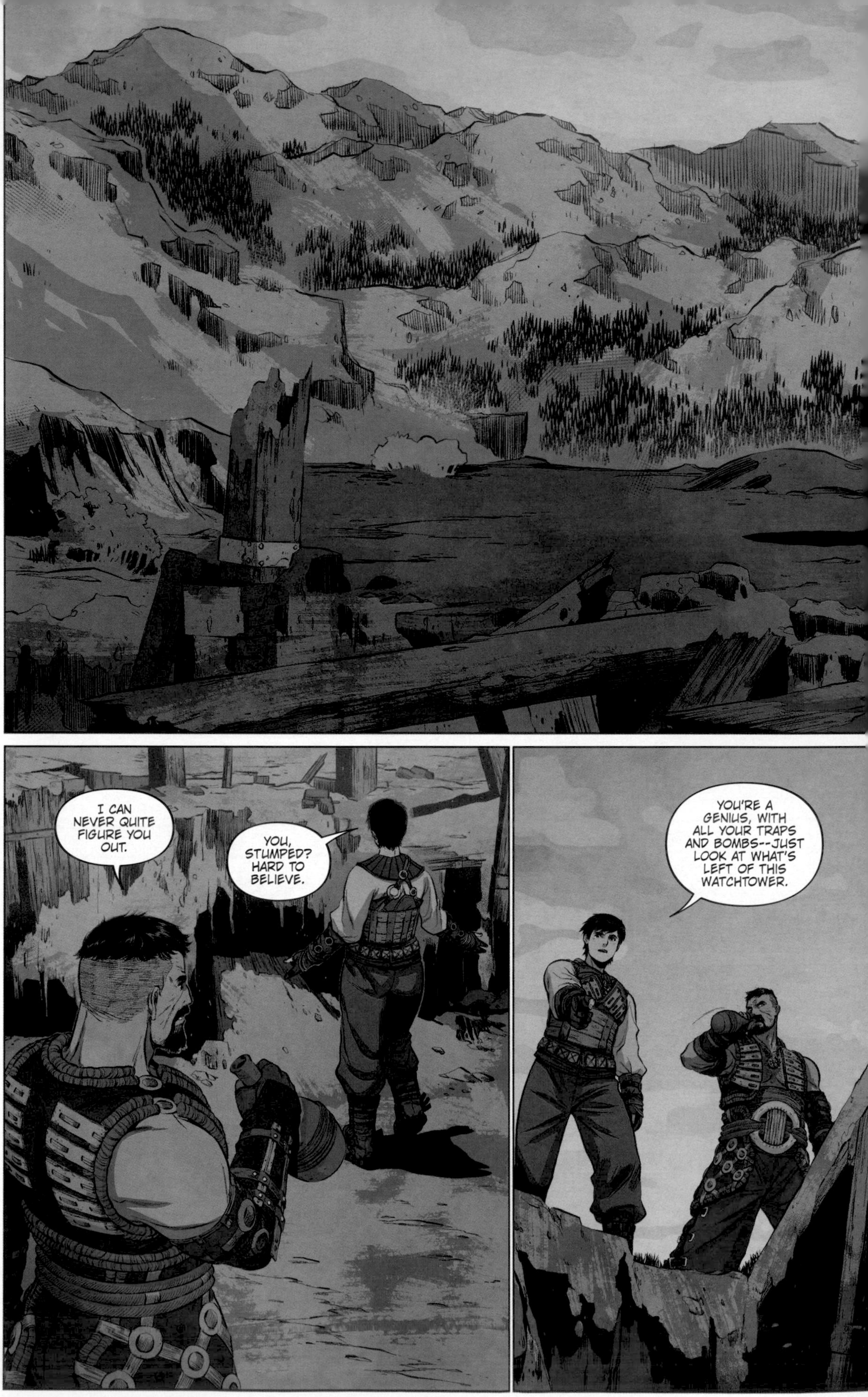
I CAN NEVER QUITE FIGURE YOU OUT.
YOU, STUMPED? HARD TO BELIEVE.
YOU'RE A GENIUS, WITH ALL YOUR TRAPS AND BOMBS--JUST LOOK AT WHAT'S LEFT OF THIS WATCHTOWER.

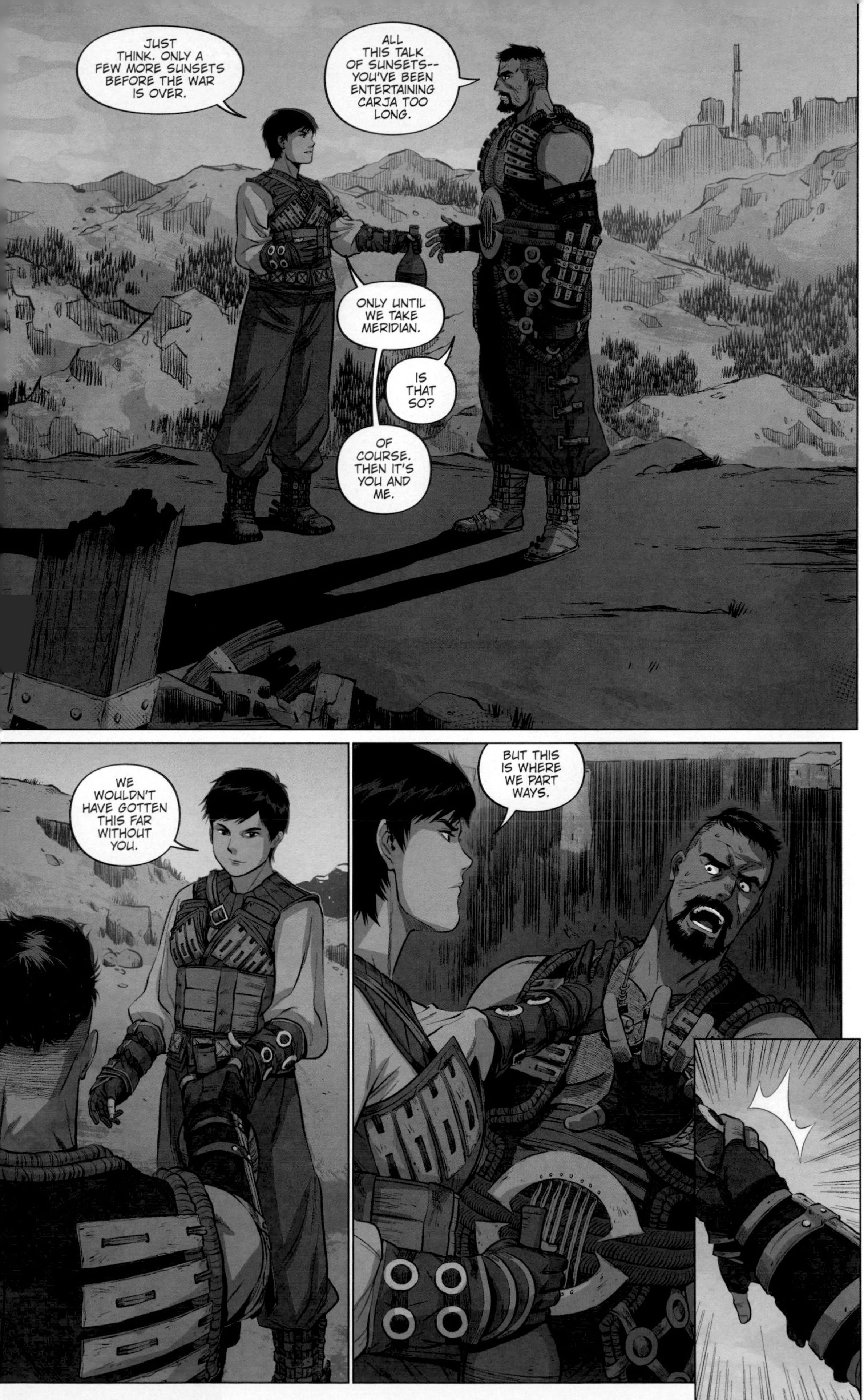
JUST THINK. ONLY A FEW MORE SUNSETS BEFORE THE WAR IS OVER.
ALL THIS TALK OF SUNSETS-- YOU'VE BEEN ENTERTAINING CARJA TOO LONG.
ONLY UNTIL WE TAKE MERIDIAN.
IS THAT SO?
OF COURSE. THEN IT'S YOU AND ME.
WE WOULDN'T HAVE GOTTEN THIS FAR WITHOUT YOU.
BUT THIS IS WHERE WE PART WAYS.

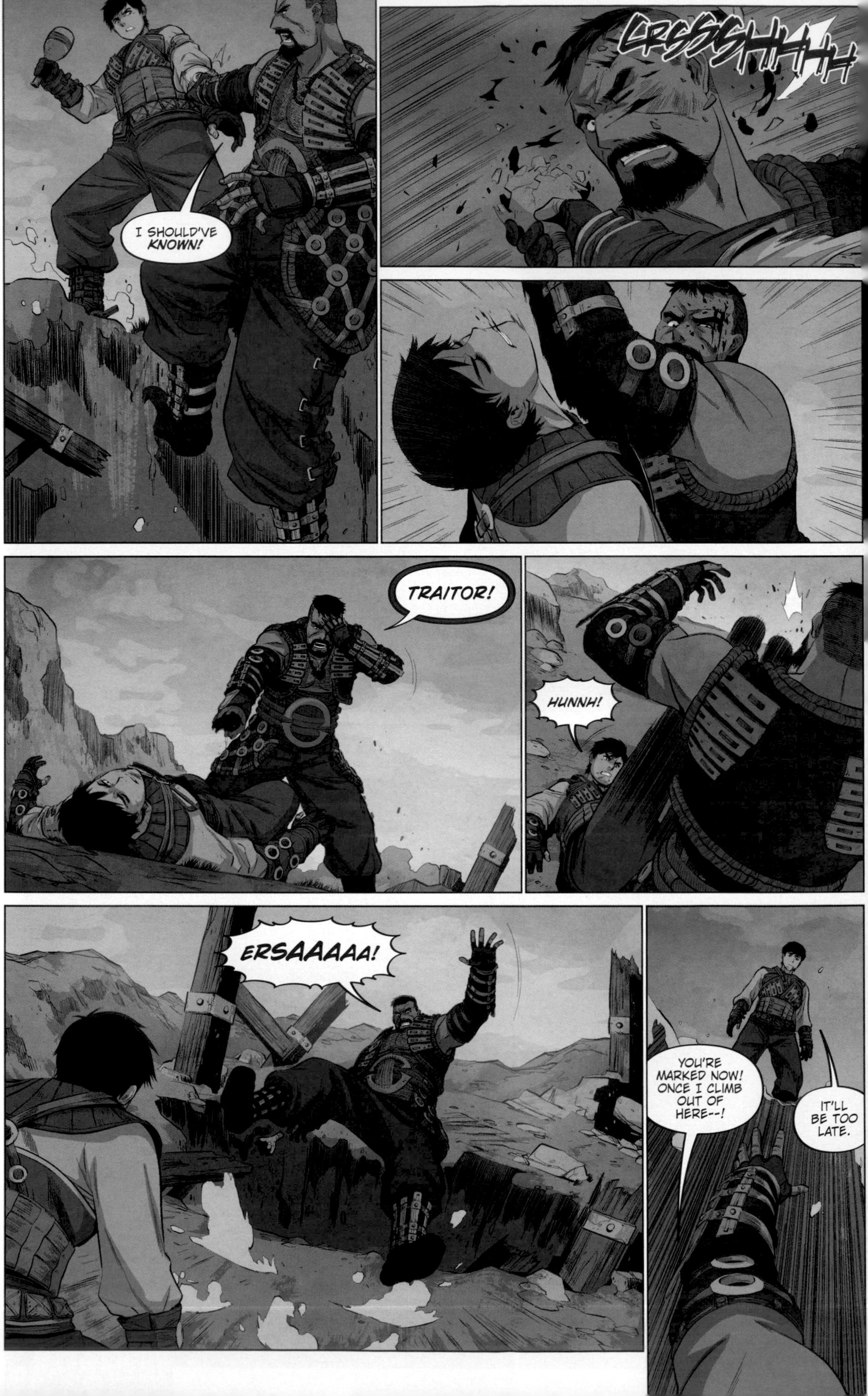
I SHOULD'VE KNOWN!
CRSSSHHHH
TRAITOR!
HUNNH!
ERSAAAAA!
YOU'RE MARKED NOW! ONCE I CLIMB OUT OF HERE--!
IT'LL BE TOO LATE.

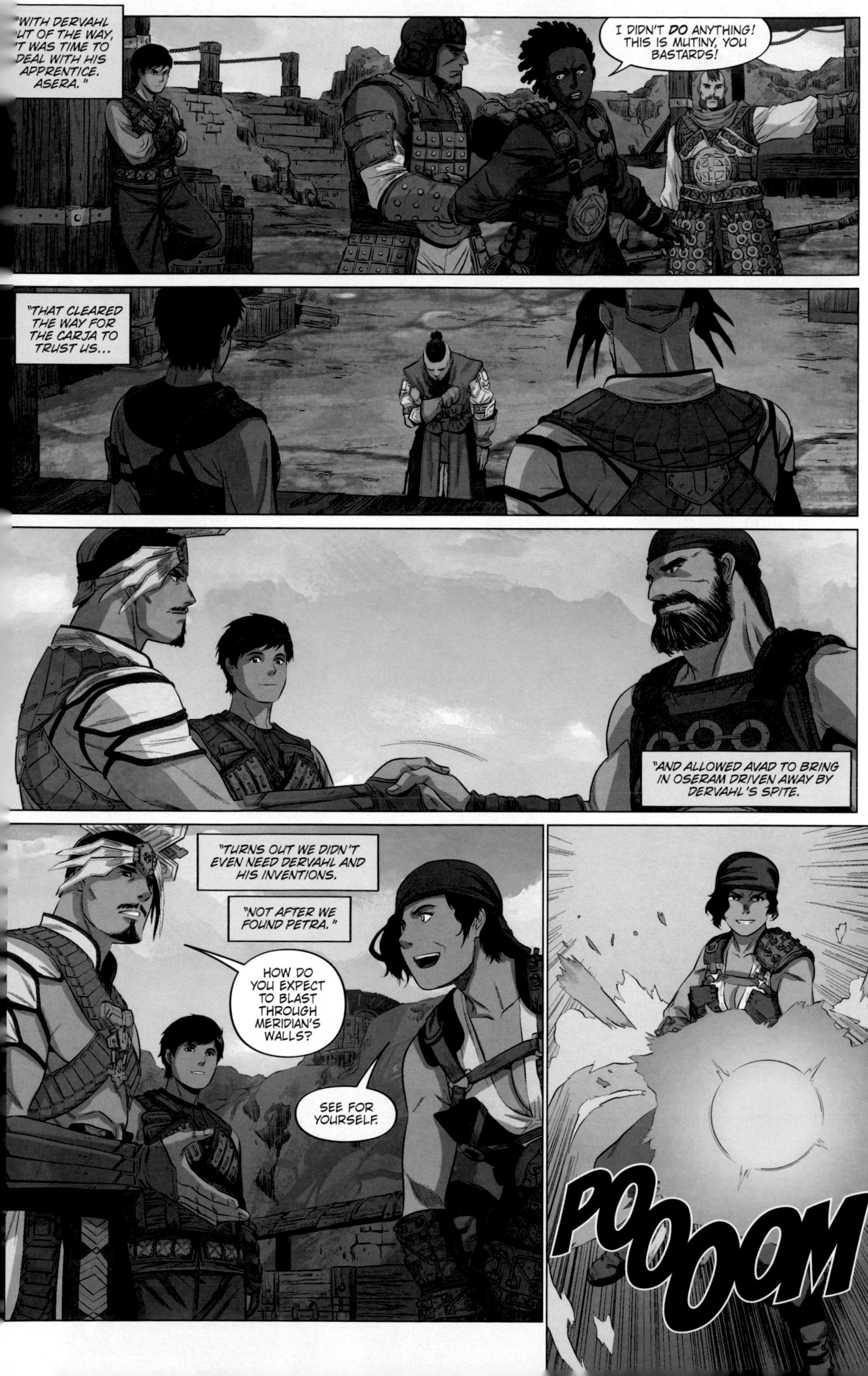
"WITH DERVAHL UT OF THE WAY, T WAS TIME TO DEAL WITH HIS APPRENTICE. ASERA."
I DIDN'T DO ANYTHING! THIS IS MUTINY, YOU BASTARDS!
"THAT CLEARED THE WAY FOR THE CARJA TO TRUST US...
"AND ALLOWED AVAD TO BRING IN OSERAM DRIVEN AWAY BY DERVAHL'S SPITE.
"TURNS OUT WE DIDN'T EVEN NEED DERVAHL AND HIS INVENTIONS.
"NOT AFTER WE FOUND PETRA."
HOW DO YOU EXPECT TO BLAST THROUGH MERIDIAN'S WALLS?
SEE FOR YOURSELF.
POOOOOM

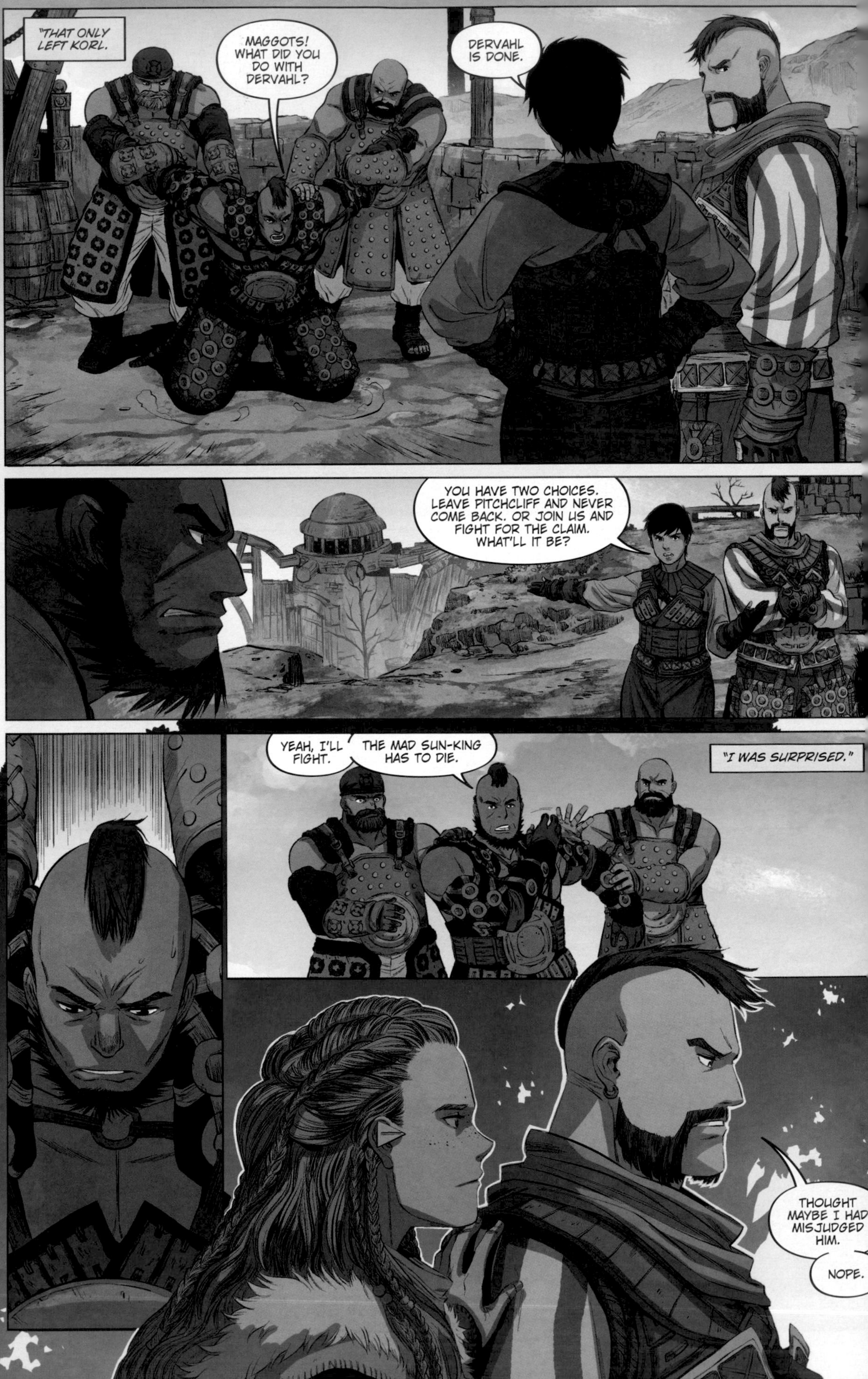
"THAT ONLY LEFT KORL.
MAGGOTS! WHAT DID YOU DO WITH DERVAHL?
DERVAHL IS DONE.
YOU HAVE TWO CHOICES. LEAVE PITCHCLIFF AND NEVER COME BACK. OR JOIN US AND FIGHT FOR THE CLAIM. WHAT'LL IT BE?
YEAH, I'LL FIGHT.
THE MAD SUN-KING HAS TO DIE.
"I WAS SURPRISED."
THOUGHT MAYBE I HAD MISJUDGED HIM.
NOPE.

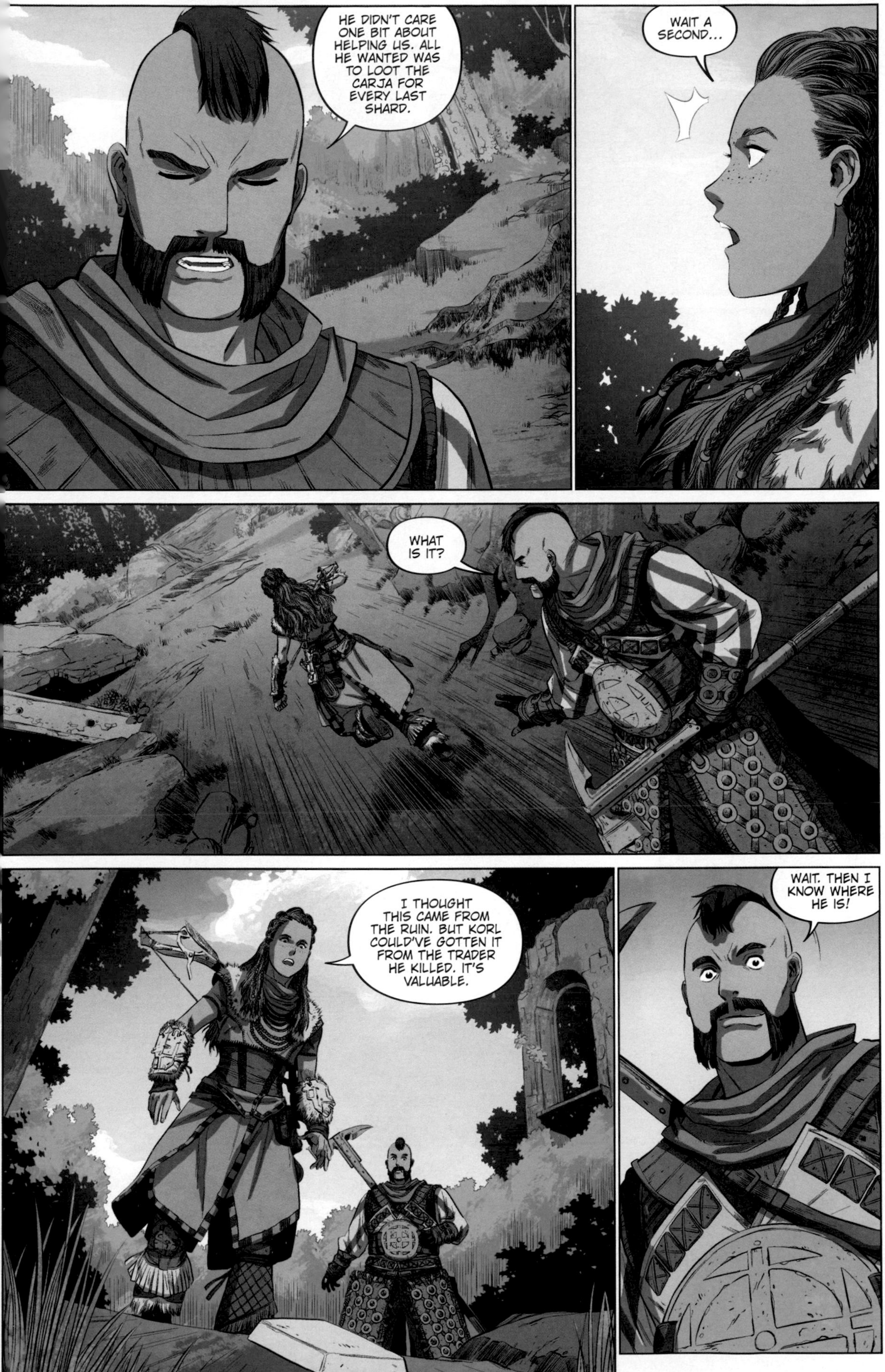
HE DIDN'T CARE ONE BIT ABOUT HELPING US. ALL HE WANTED WAS TO LOOT THE CARJA FOR EVERY LAST SHARD.
WAIT A SECOND...
WHAT IS IT?
I THOUGHT THIS CAME FROM THE RUIN. BUT KORL COULD'VE GOTTEN IT FROM THE TRADER HE KILLED. IT'S VALUABLE.
WAIT. THEN I KNOW WHERE HE IS!

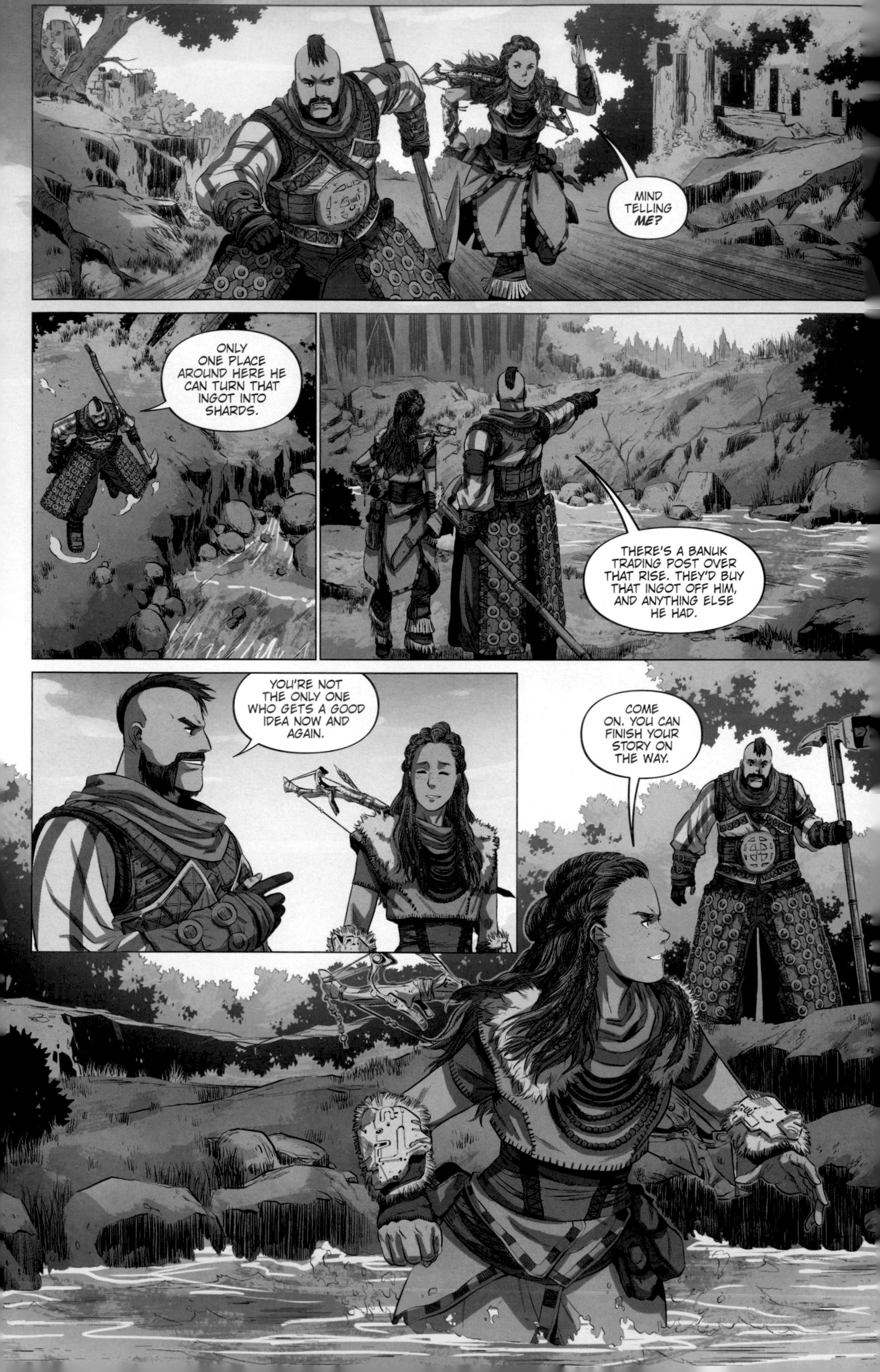
MIND TELLING *ME?*
ONLY ONE PLACE AROUND HERE HE CAN TURN THAT INGOT INTO SHARDS.
THERE'S A BANUK TRADING POST OVER THAT RISE. THEY'D BUY THAT INGOT OFF HIM, AND ANYTHING ELSE HE HAD.
YOU'RE NOT THE ONLY ONE WHO GETS A GOOD IDEA NOW AND AGAIN.
COME ON. YOU CAN FINISH YOUR STORY ON THE WAY.

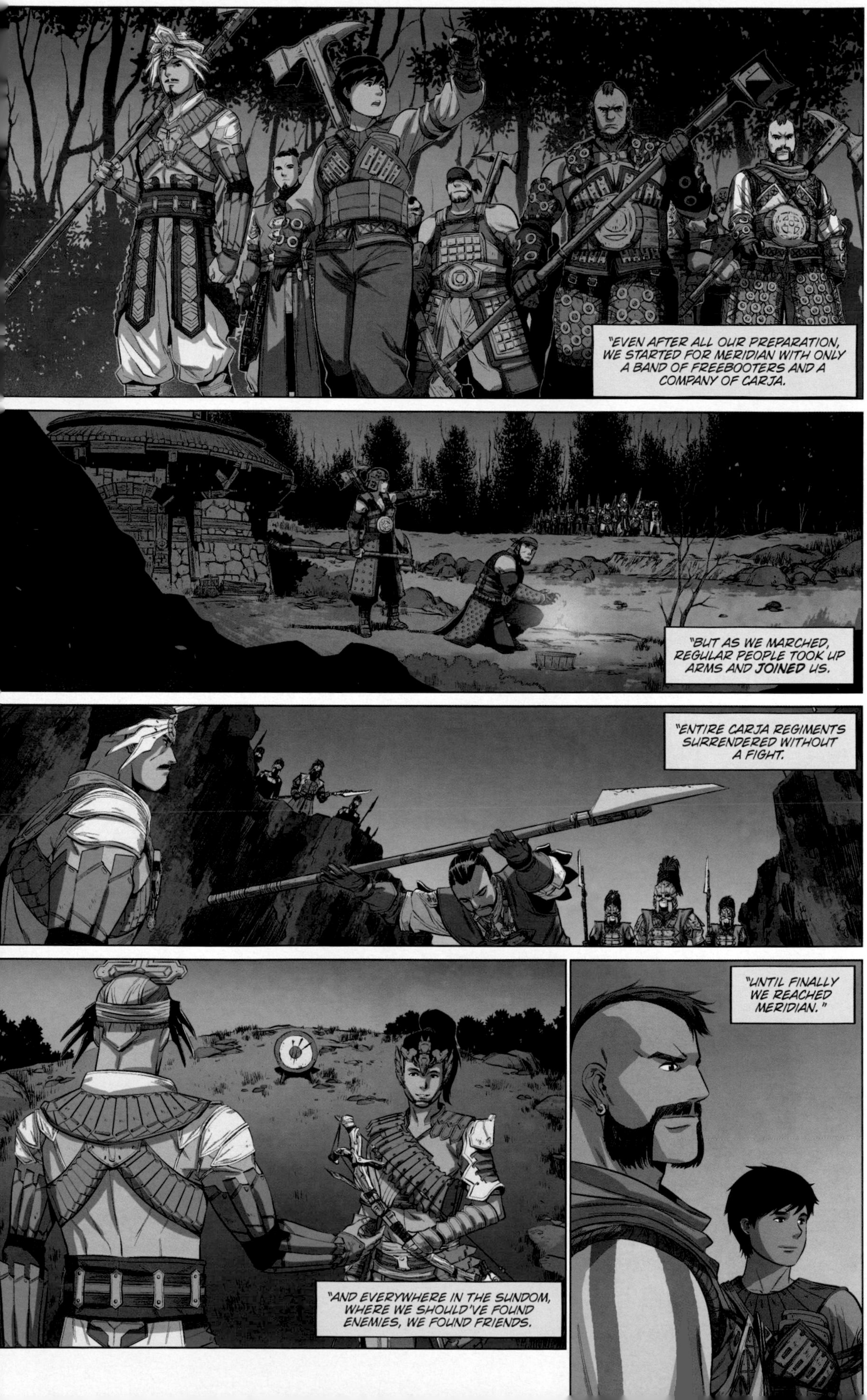
"EVEN AFTER ALL OUR PREPARATION, WE STARTED FOR MERIDIAN WITH ONLY A BAND OF FREEBOOTERS AND A COMPANY OF CARJA.
"BUT AS WE MARCHED, REGULAR PEOPLE TOOK UP ARMS AND JOINED US.
"ENTIRE CARJA REGIMENTS SURRENDERED WITHOUT A FIGHT.
"AND EVERYWHERE IN THE SUNDOM, WHERE WE SHOULD'VE FOUND ENEMIES, WE FOUND FRIENDS.
"UNTIL FINALLY WE REACHED MERIDIAN."

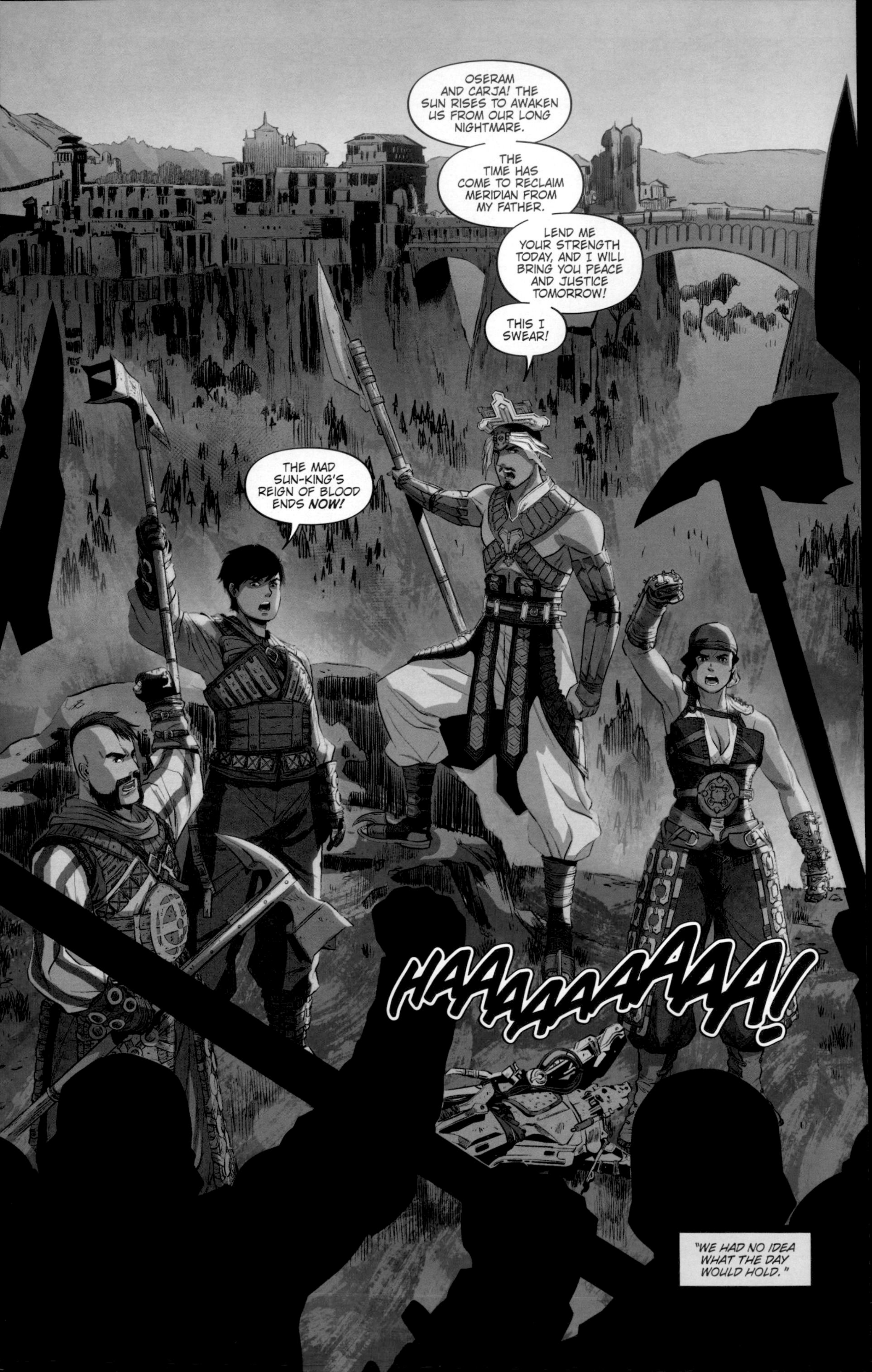
OSERAM AND CARJA! THE SUN RISES TO AWAKEN US FROM OUR LONG NIGHTMARE.
THE TIME HAS COME TO RECLAIM MERIDIAN FROM MY FATHER.
LEND ME YOUR STRENGTH TODAY, AND I WILL BRING YOU PEACE AND JUSTICE TOMORROW!
THIS I SWEAR!
THE MAD SUN-KING'S REIGN OF BLOOD ENDS **NOW!**
HAAAAAAAAA!
"WE HAD NO IDEA WHAT THE DAY WOULD HOLD."

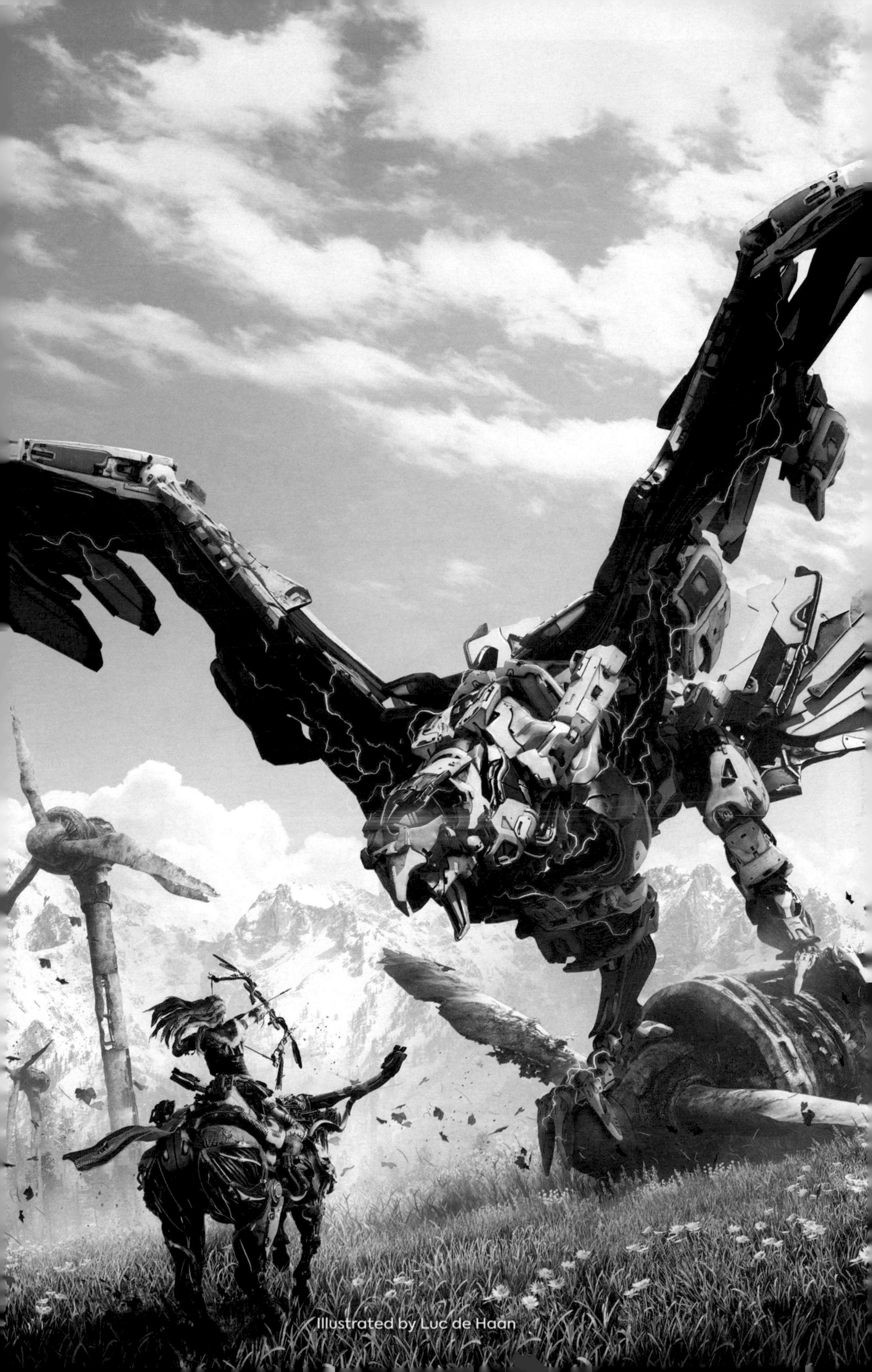

Illustrated by Luc de Haan

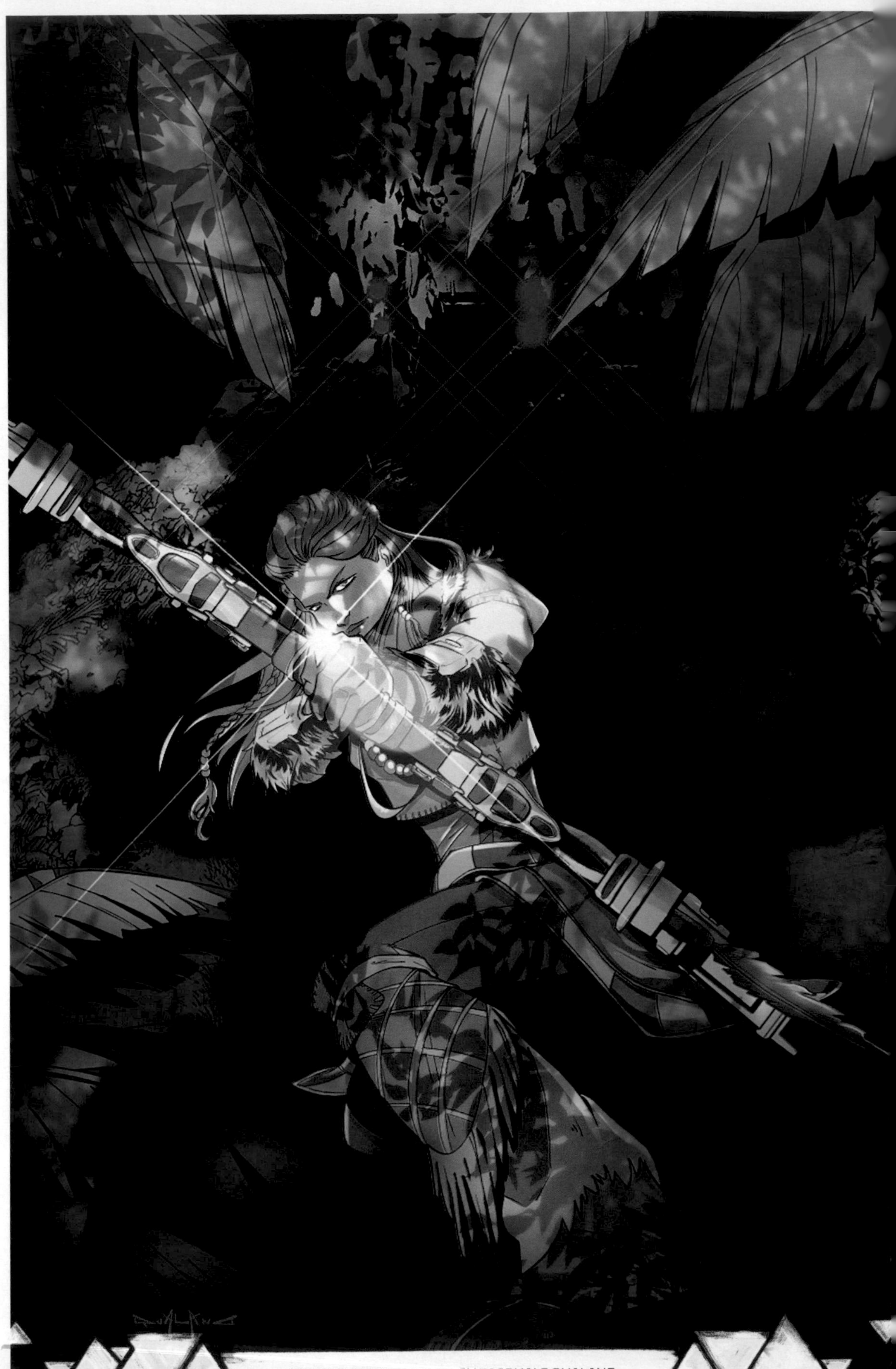

CHAPTER FOUR | COVER BY PASQUALE QUALANO

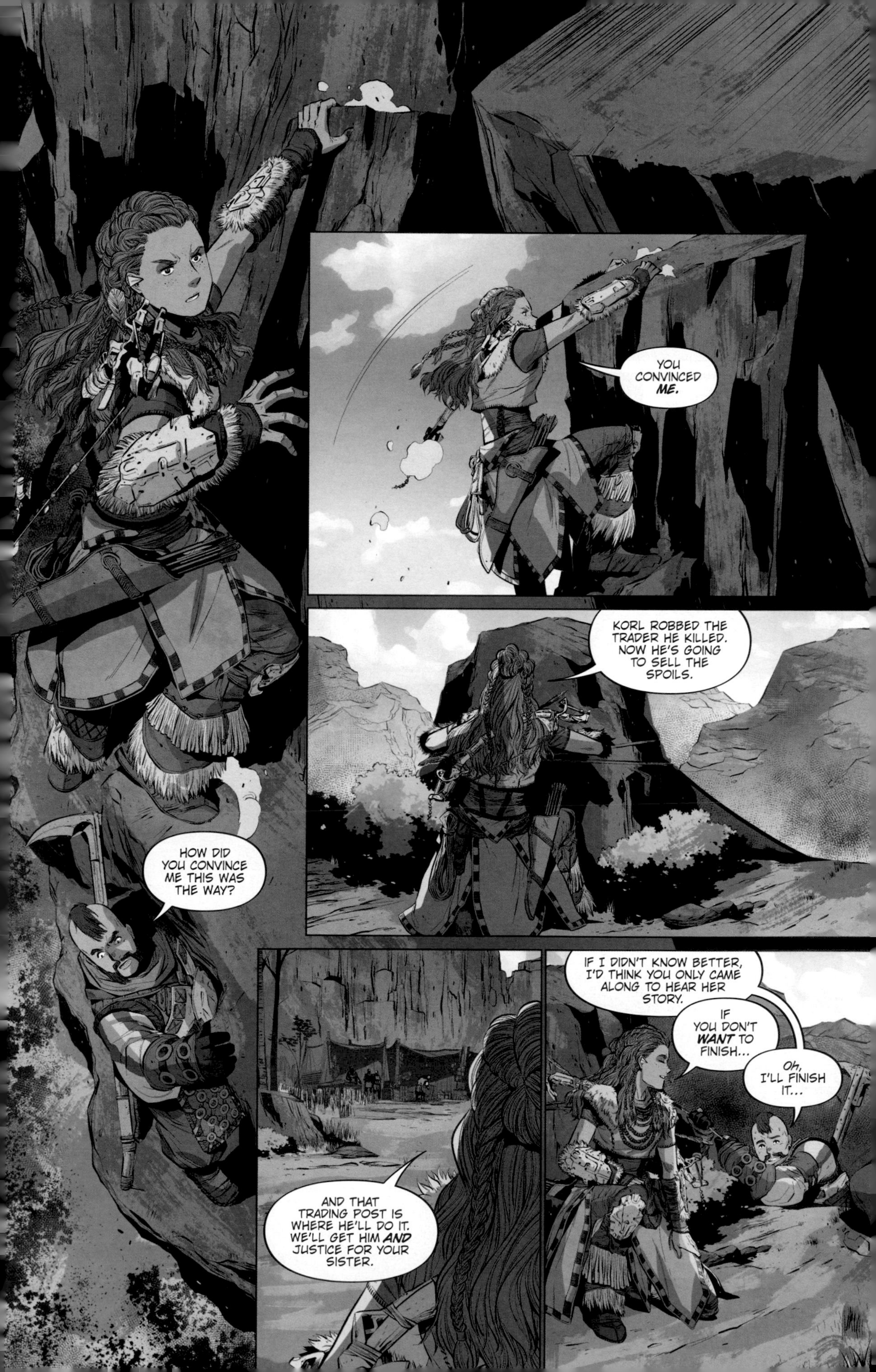
HOW DID YOU CONVINCE ME THIS WAS THE WAY?
YOU CONVINCED ***ME.***
KORL ROBBED THE TRADER HE KILLED. NOW HE'S GOING TO SELL THE SPOILS.
AND THAT TRADING POST IS WHERE HE'LL DO IT. WE'LL GET HIM ***AND*** JUSTICE FOR YOUR SISTER.
IF I DIDN'T KNOW BETTER, I'D THINK YOU ONLY CAME ALONG TO HEAR HER STORY.
IF YOU DON'T ***WANT*** TO FINISH...
Oh, I'LL FINISH IT...

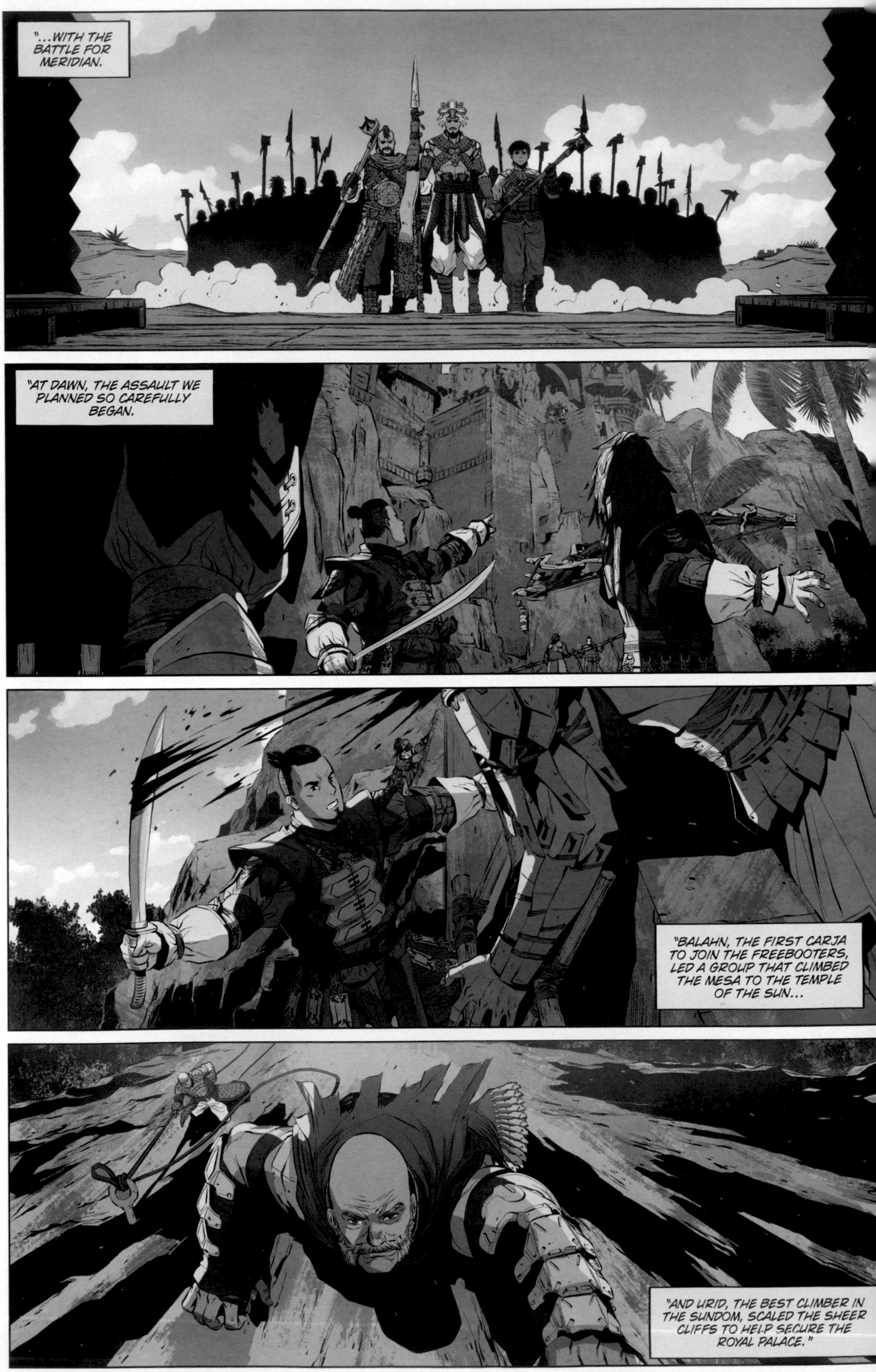
"...WITH THE BATTLE FOR MERIDIAN.
"AT DAWN, THE ASSAULT WE PLANNED SO CAREFULLY BEGAN.
"BALAHN, THE FIRST CARJA TO JOIN THE FREEBOOTERS, LED A GROUP THAT CLIMBED THE MESA TO THE TEMPLE OF THE SUN...
"AND URID, THE BEST CLIMBER IN THE SUNDOM, SCALED THE SHEER CLIFFS TO HELP SECURE THE ROYAL PALACE."

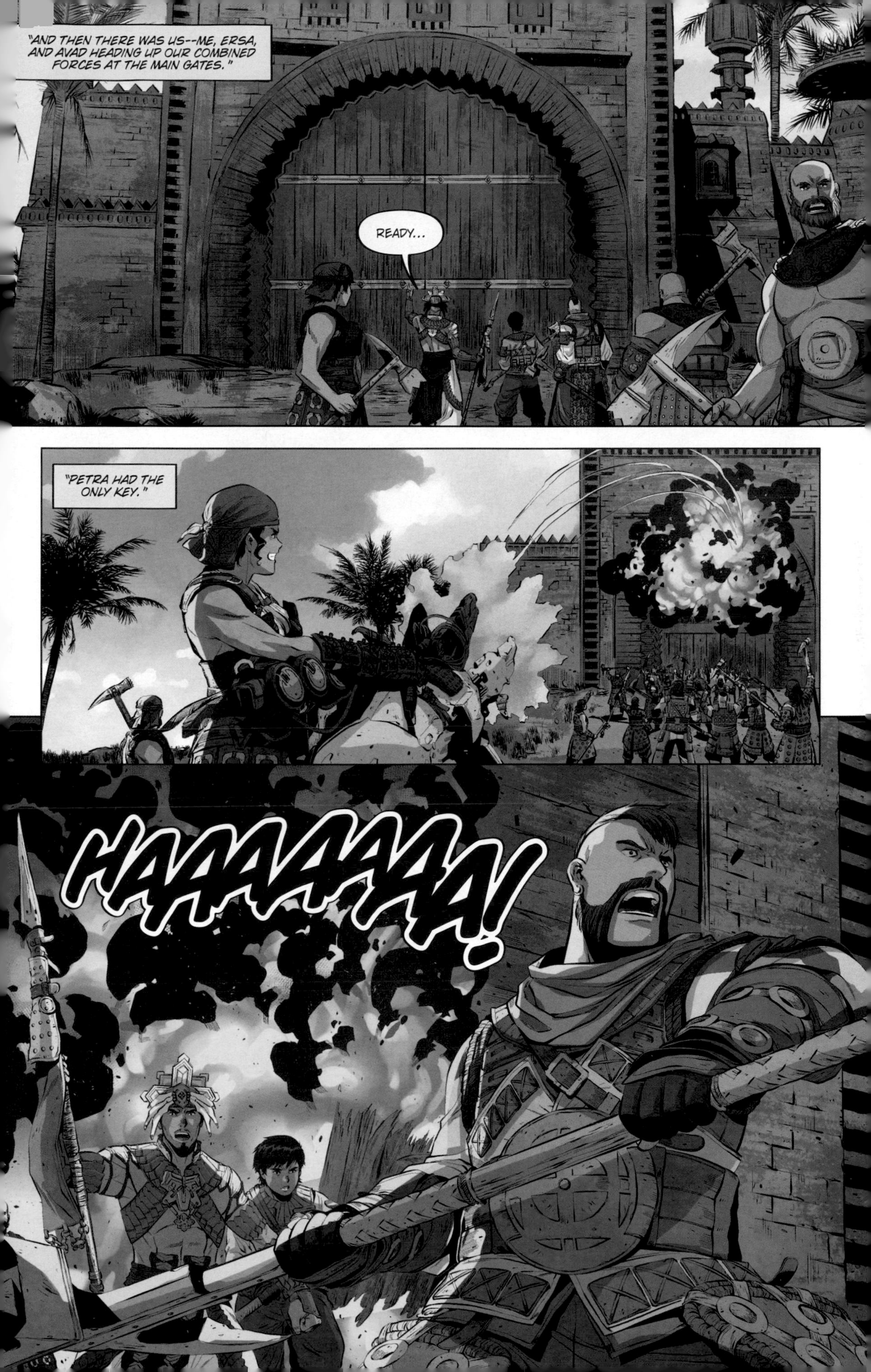
"AND THEN THERE WAS US--ME, ERSA, AND AVAD HEADING UP OUR COMBINED FORCES AT THE MAIN GATES."
READY...
"PETRA HAD THE ONLY KEY."
HAAAAAAA!

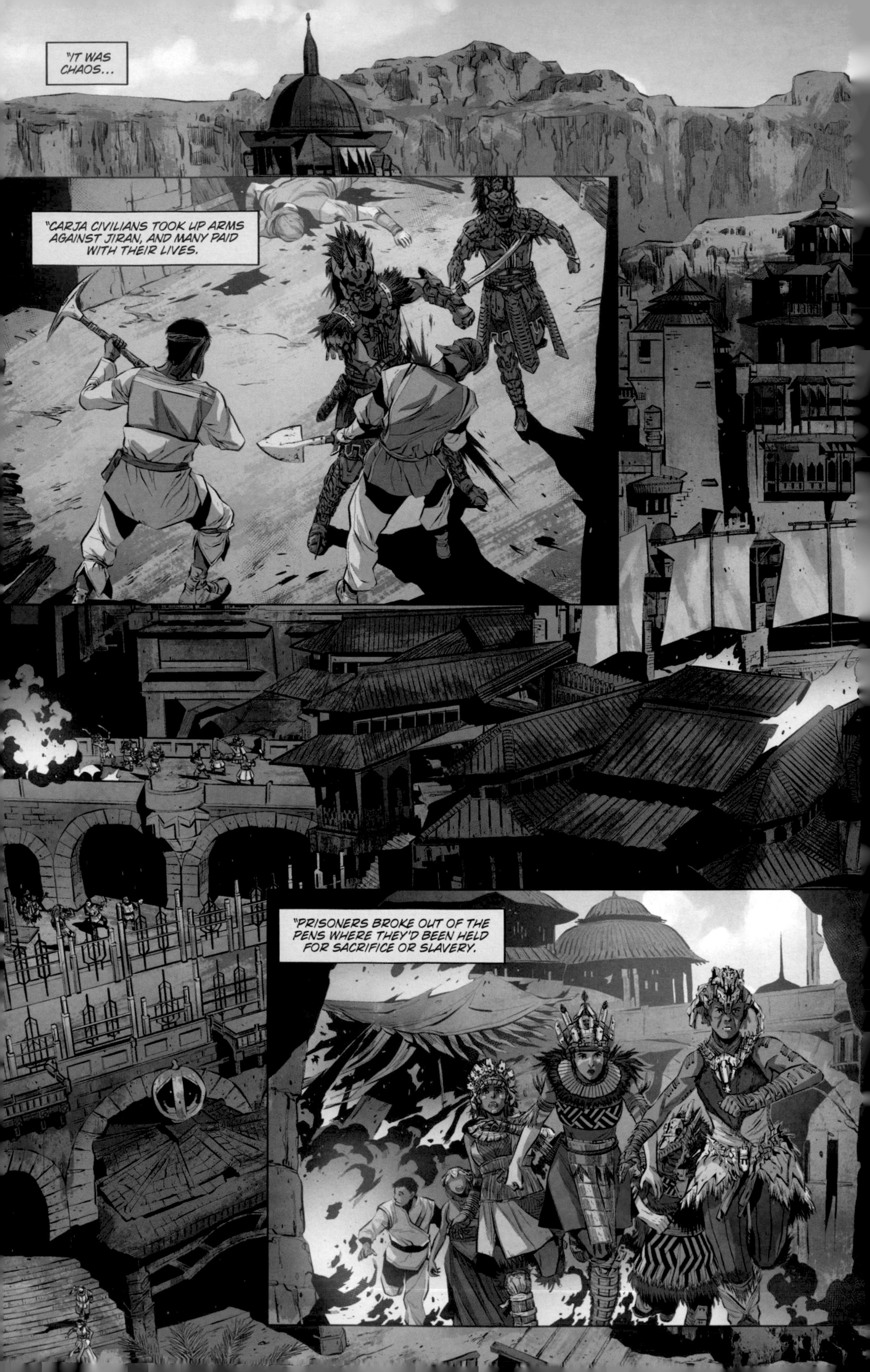
"IT WAS CHAOS...
"CARJA CIVILIANS TOOK UP ARMS AGAINST JIRAN, AND MANY PAID WITH THEIR LIVES.
"PRISONERS BROKE OUT OF THE PENS WHERE THEY'D BEEN HELD FOR SACRIFICE OR SLAVERY.

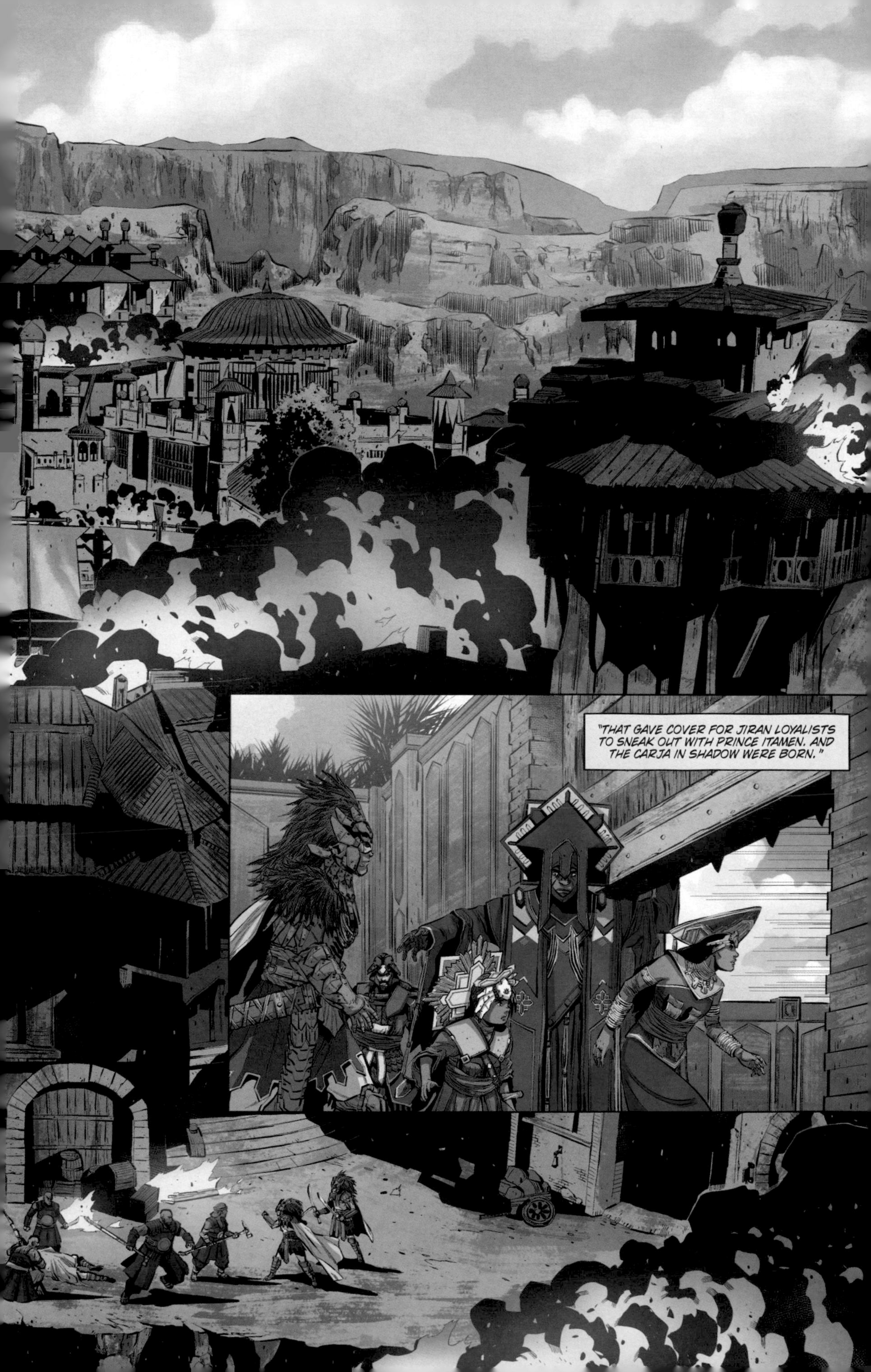
"THAT GAVE COVER FOR JIRAN LOYALISTS TO SNEAK OUT WITH PRINCE ITAMEN. AND THE CARJA IN SHADOW WERE BORN."

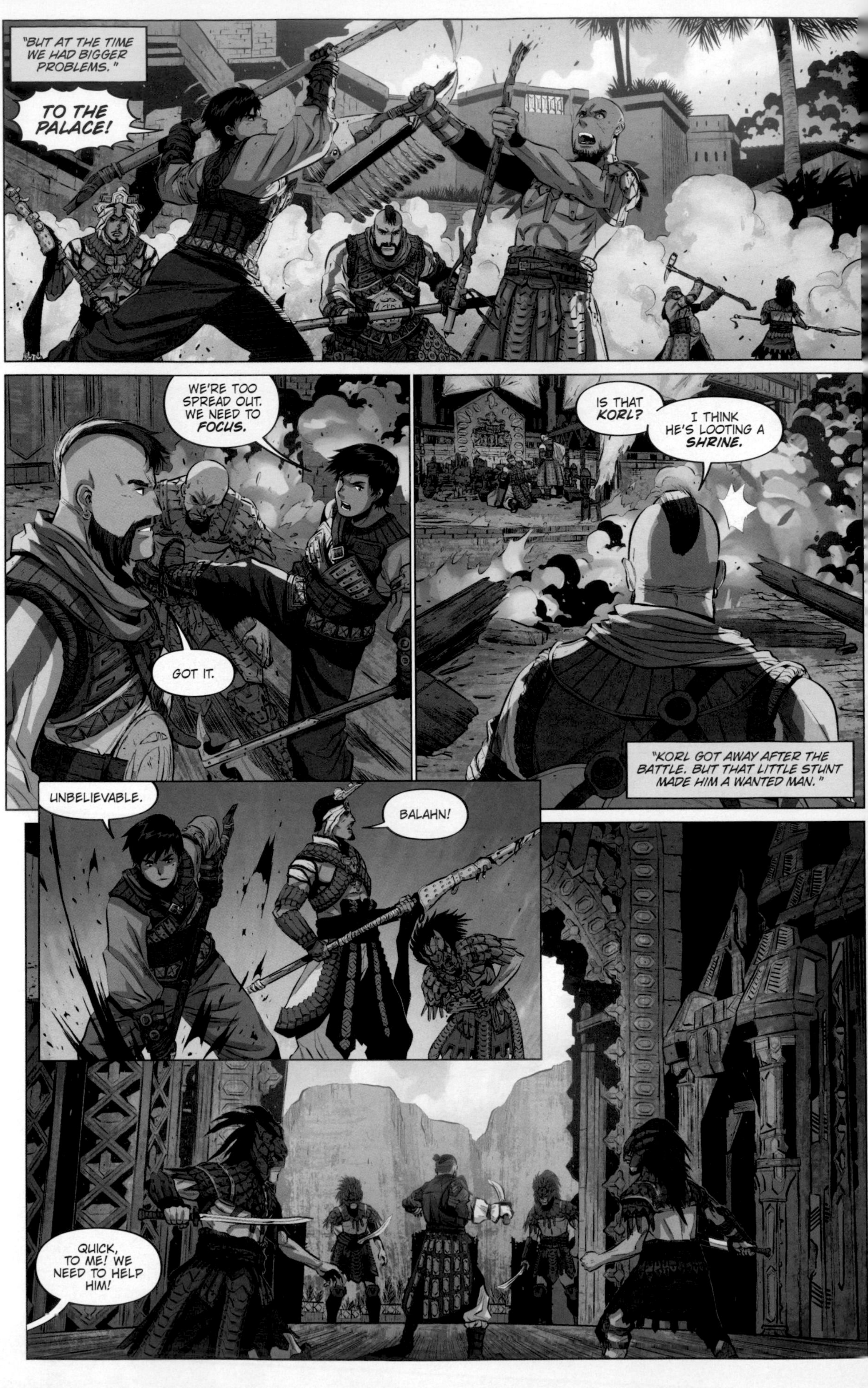
"BUT AT THE TIME WE HAD BIGGER PROBLEMS."
TO THE PALACE!
WE'RE TOO SPREAD OUT. WE NEED TO FOCUS.
GOT IT.
IS THAT KORL?
I THINK HE'S LOOTING A SHRINE.
"KORL GOT AWAY AFTER THE BATTLE. BUT THAT LITTLE STUNT MADE HIM A WANTED MAN."
UNBELIEVABLE.
BALAHN!
QUICK, TO ME! WE NEED TO HELP HIM!

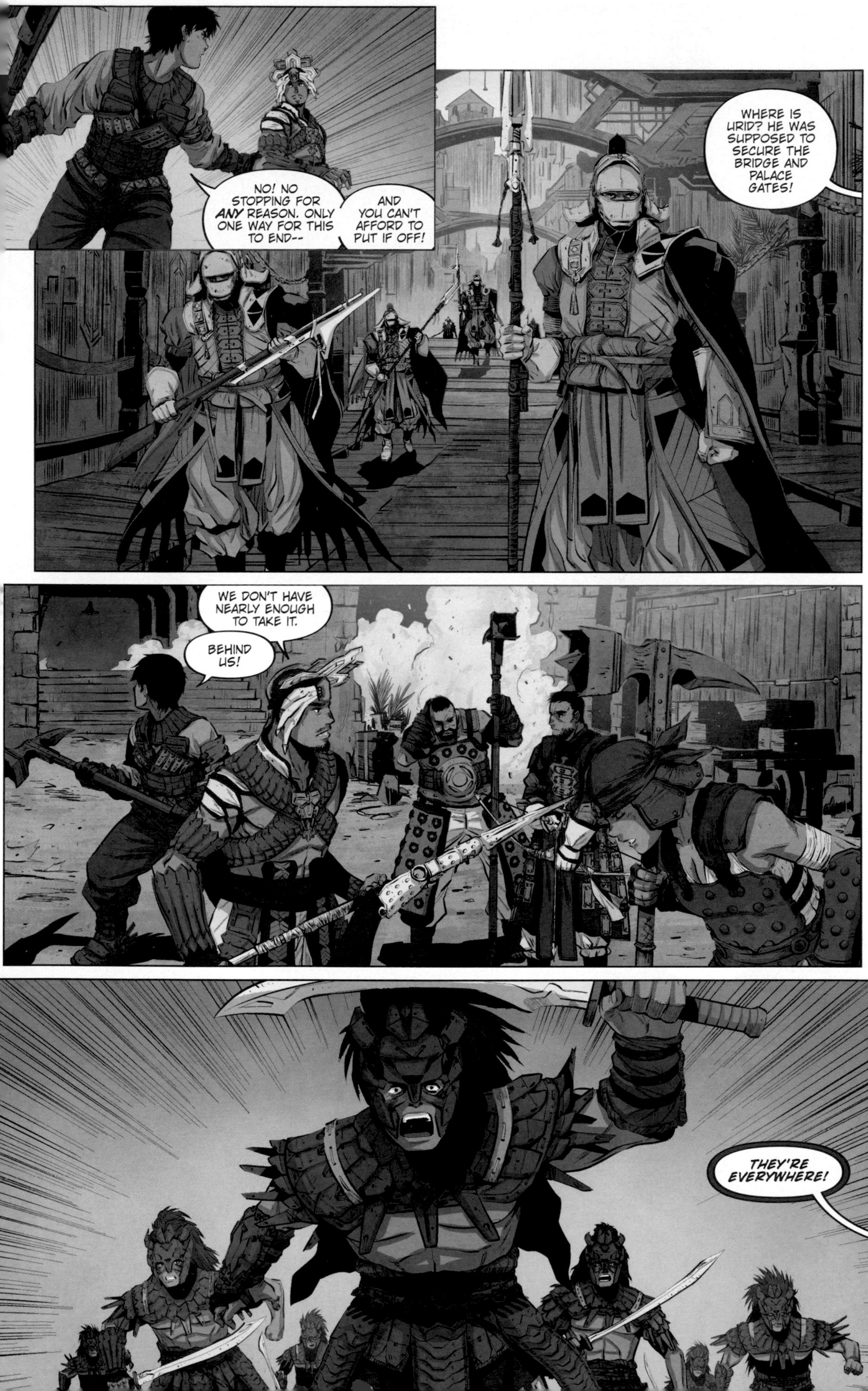
NO! NO STOPPING FOR ANY REASON. ONLY ONE WAY FOR THIS TO END--
AND YOU CAN'T AFFORD TO PUT IF OFF!
WHERE IS URID? HE WAS SUPPOSED TO SECURE THE BRIDGE AND PALACE GATES!
WE DON'T HAVE NEARLY ENOUGH TO TAKE IT.
BEHIND US!
THEY'RE EVERYWHERE!

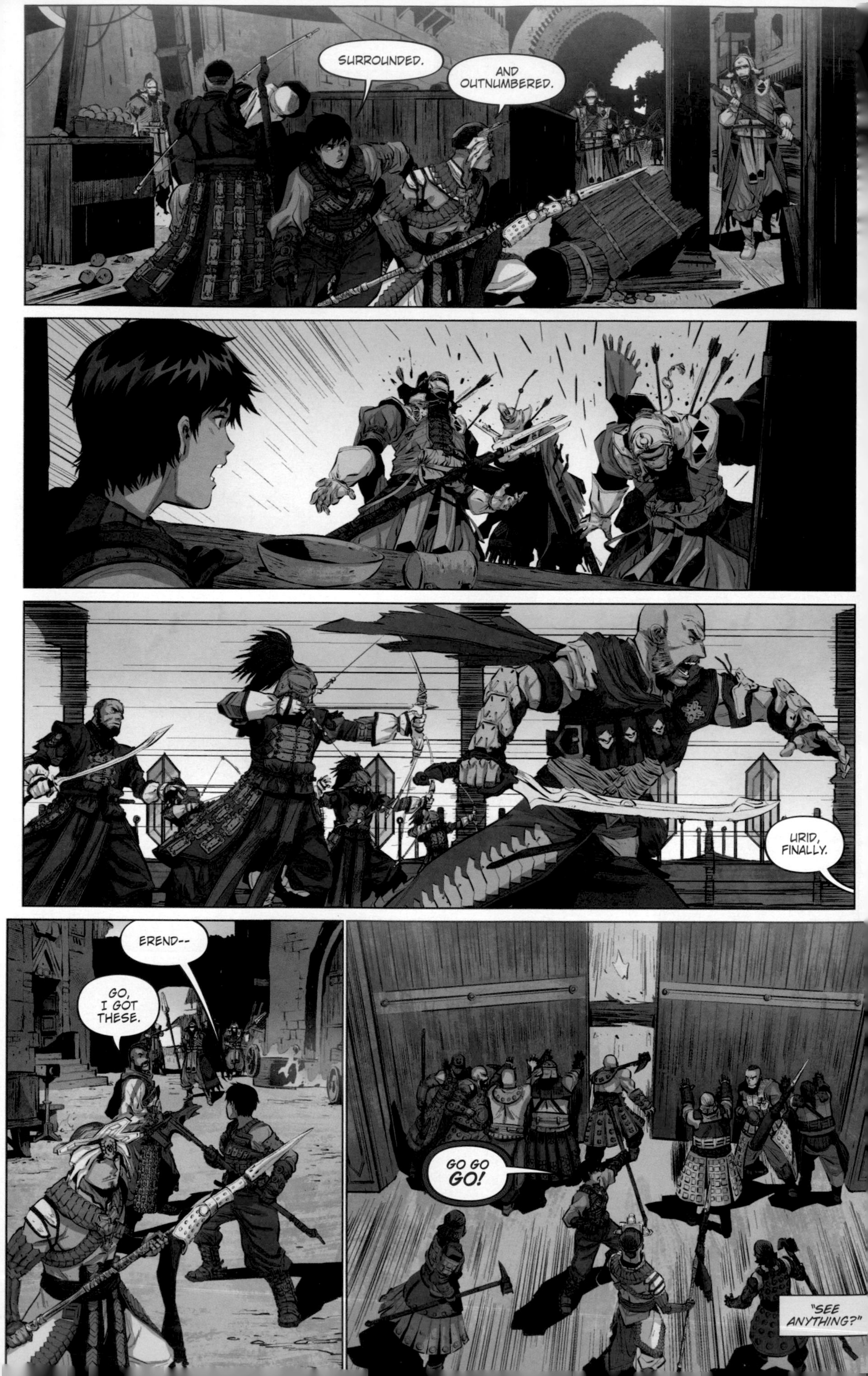
SURROUNDED.
AND OUTNUMBERED.
URID, FINALLY.
EREND--
GO, I GOT THESE.
GO GO GO!
"SEE ANYTHING?"

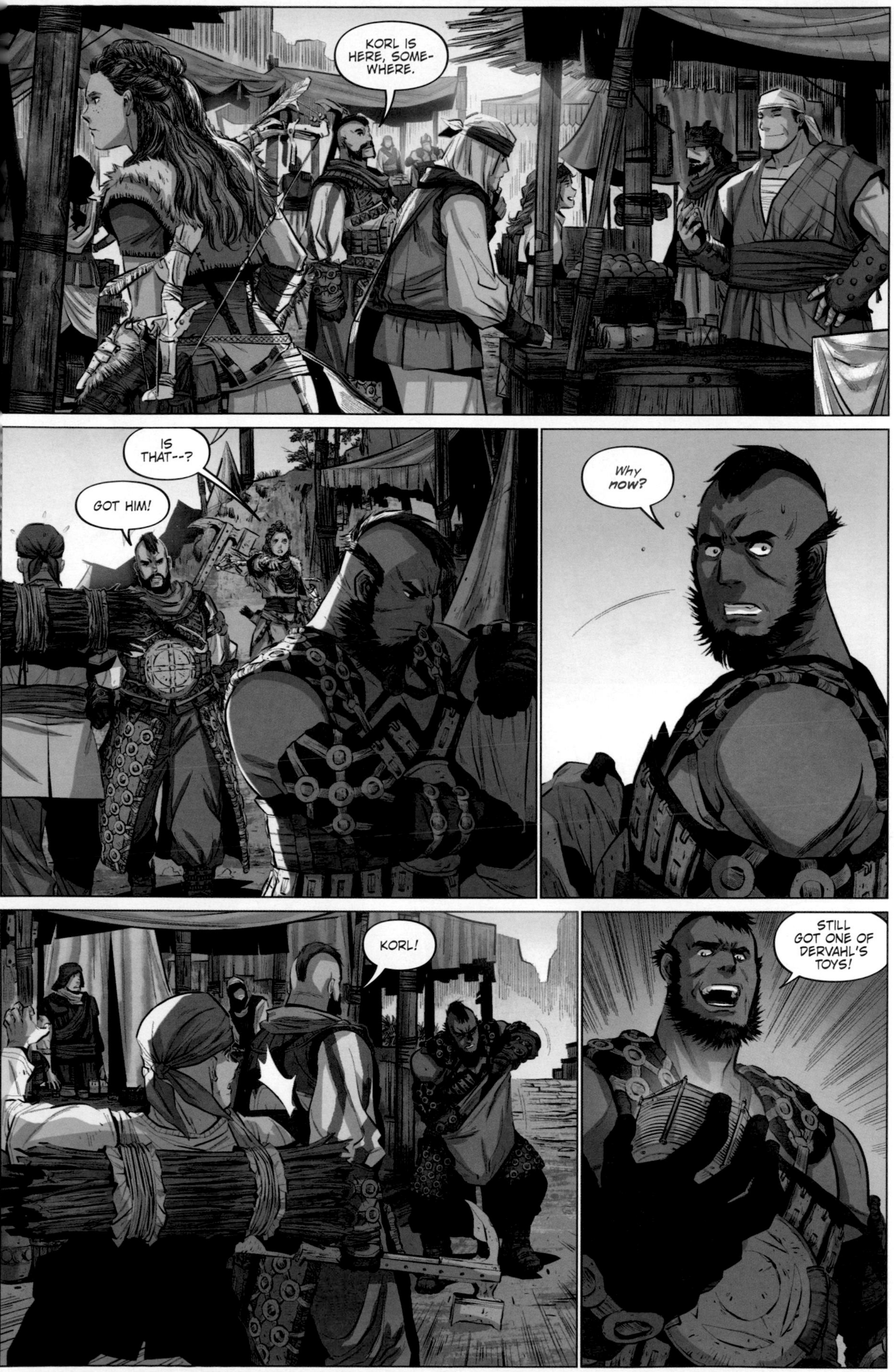
KORL IS HERE, SOME-WHERE.
IS THAT--?
GOT HIM!
Why now?
KORL!
STILL GOT ONE OF DERVAHL'S TOYS!

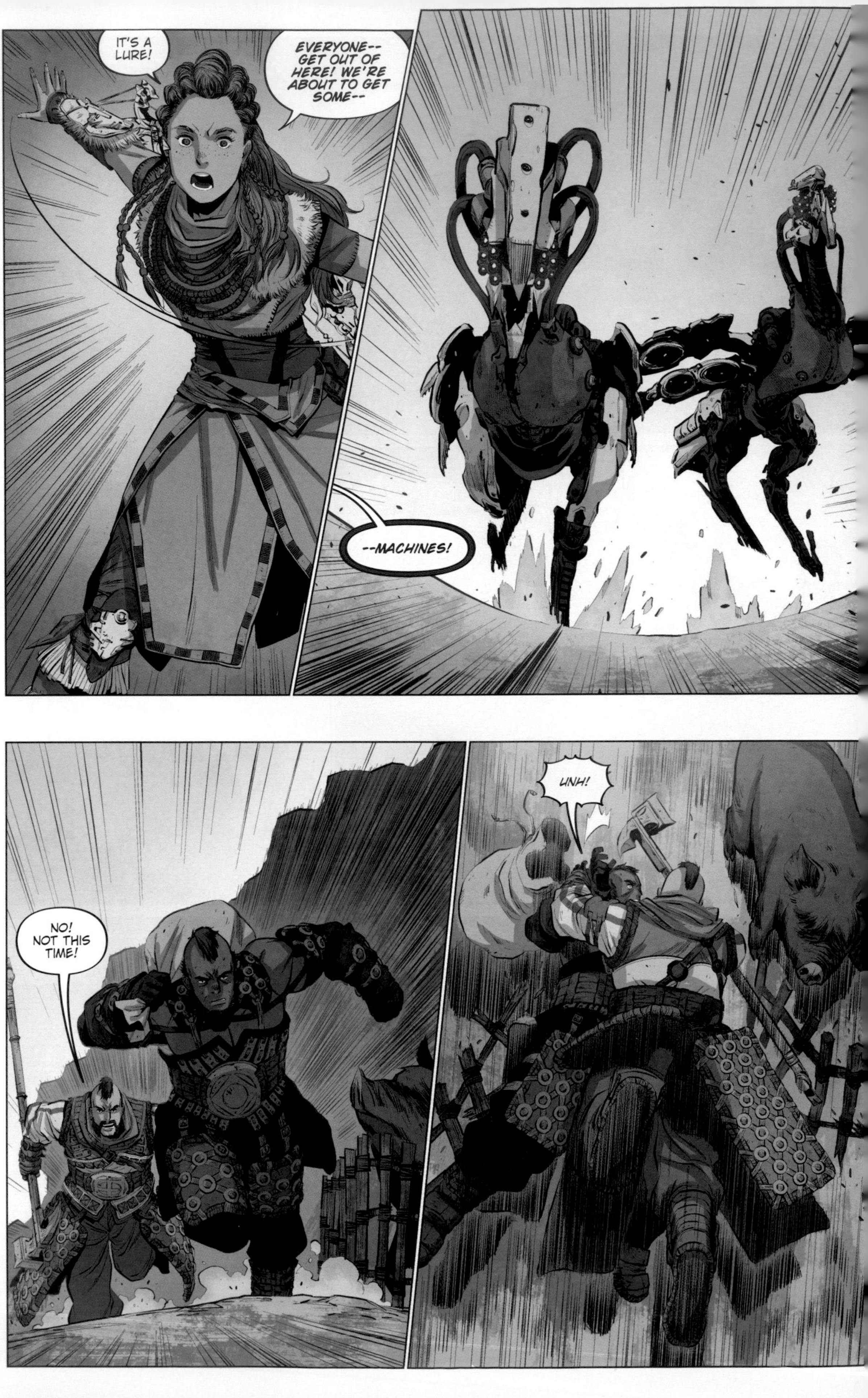
IT'S A LURE!
EVERYONE-- GET OUT OF HERE! WE'RE ABOUT TO GET SOME--
--MACHINES!
NO! NOT THIS TIME!
UNH!

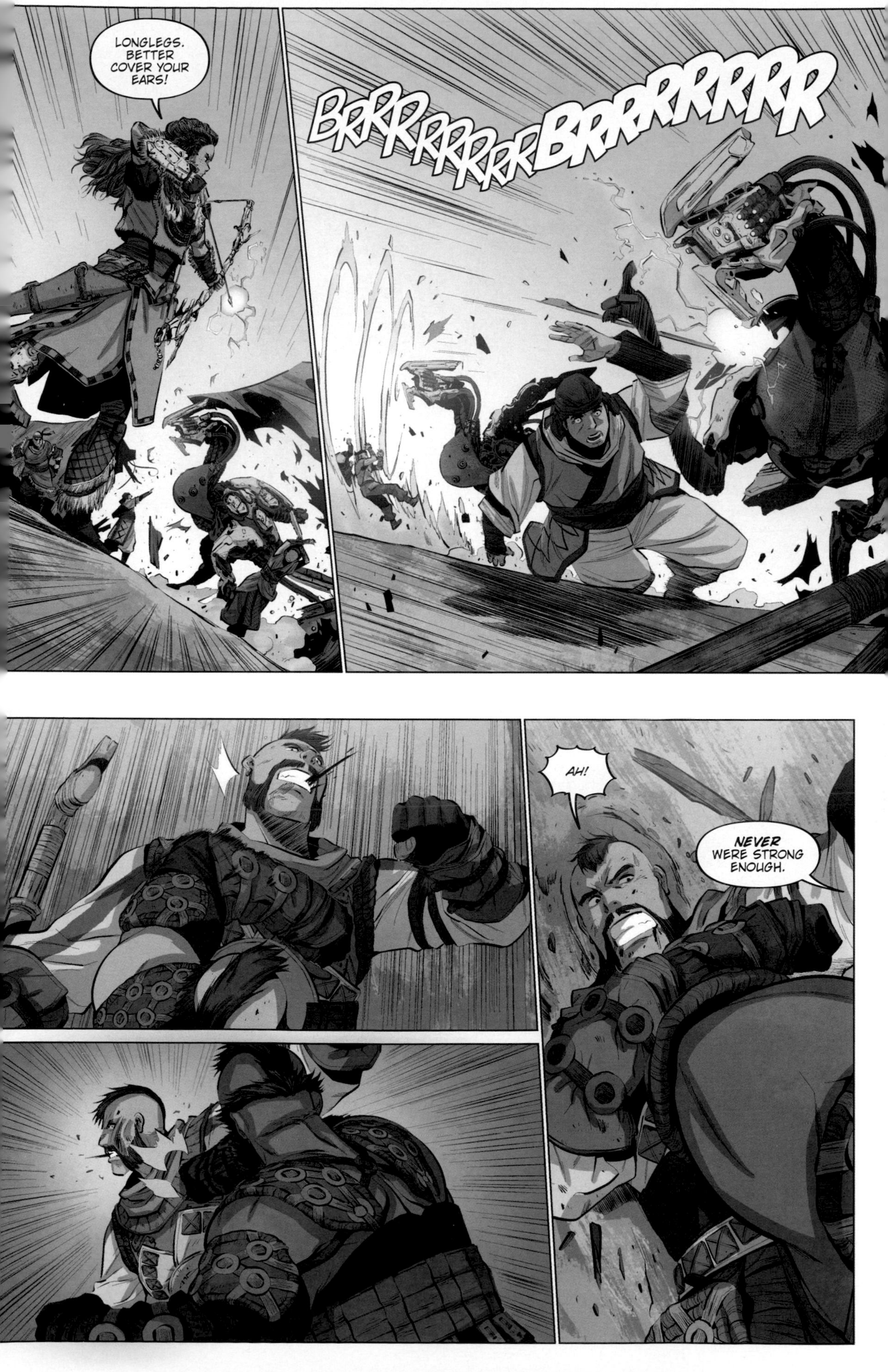
LONGLEGS. BETTER COVER YOUR EARS!
BRRRRRRRRRBRRRRRRRRR
AH!
NEVER WERE STRONG ENOUGH.

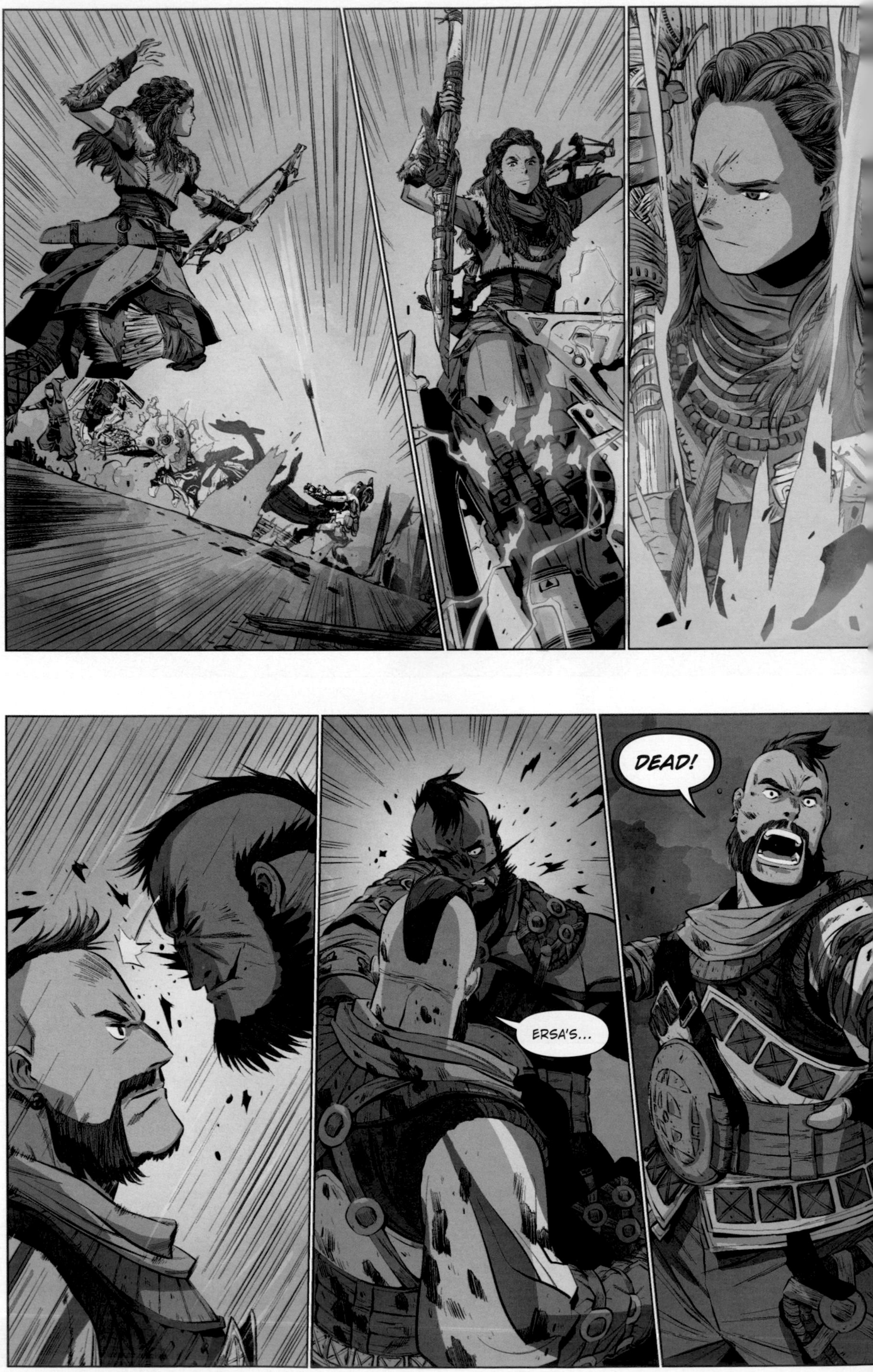
ERSA'S...
DEAD!

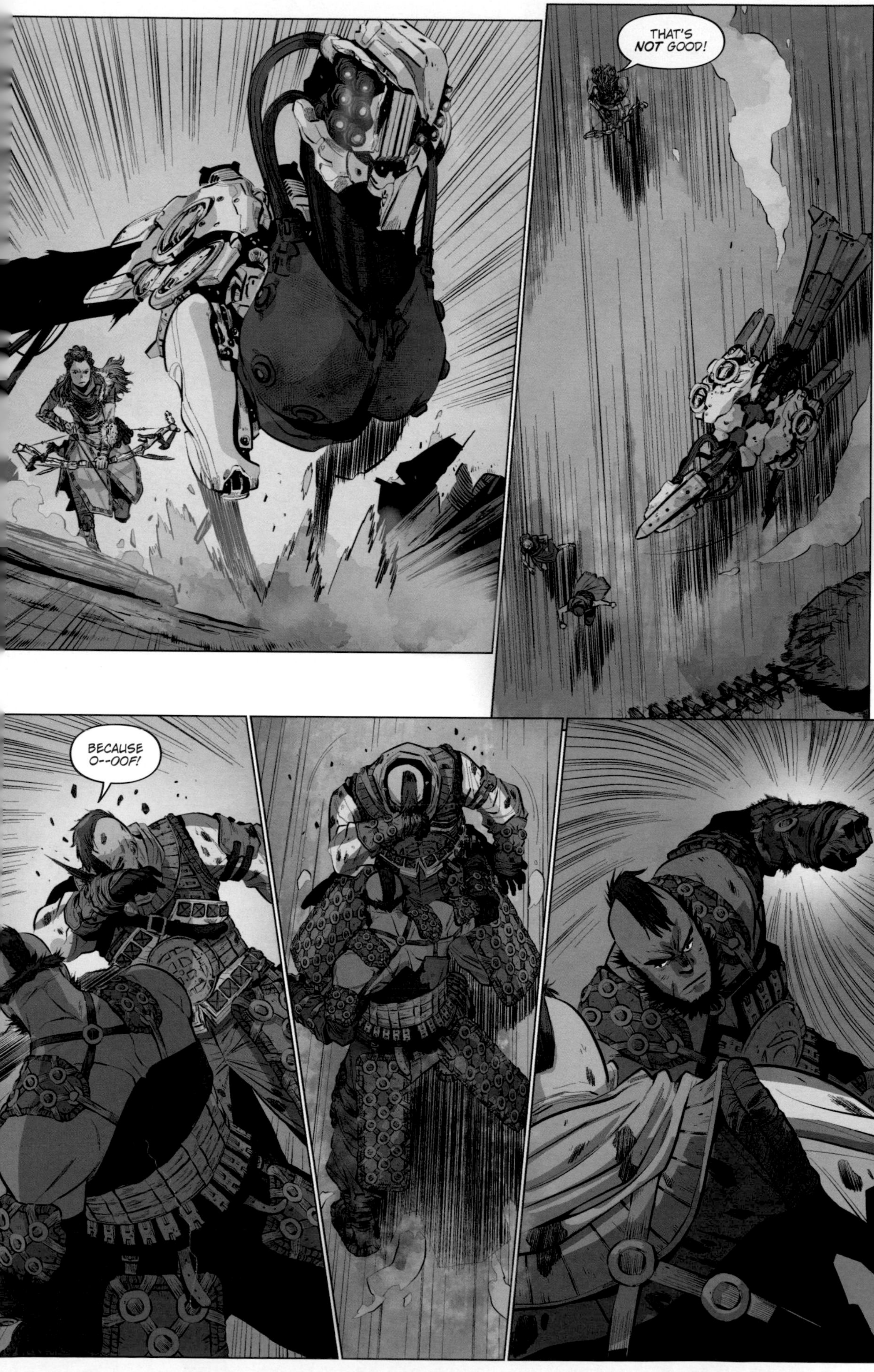
THAT'S NOT GOOD!
BECAUSE O--OOF!

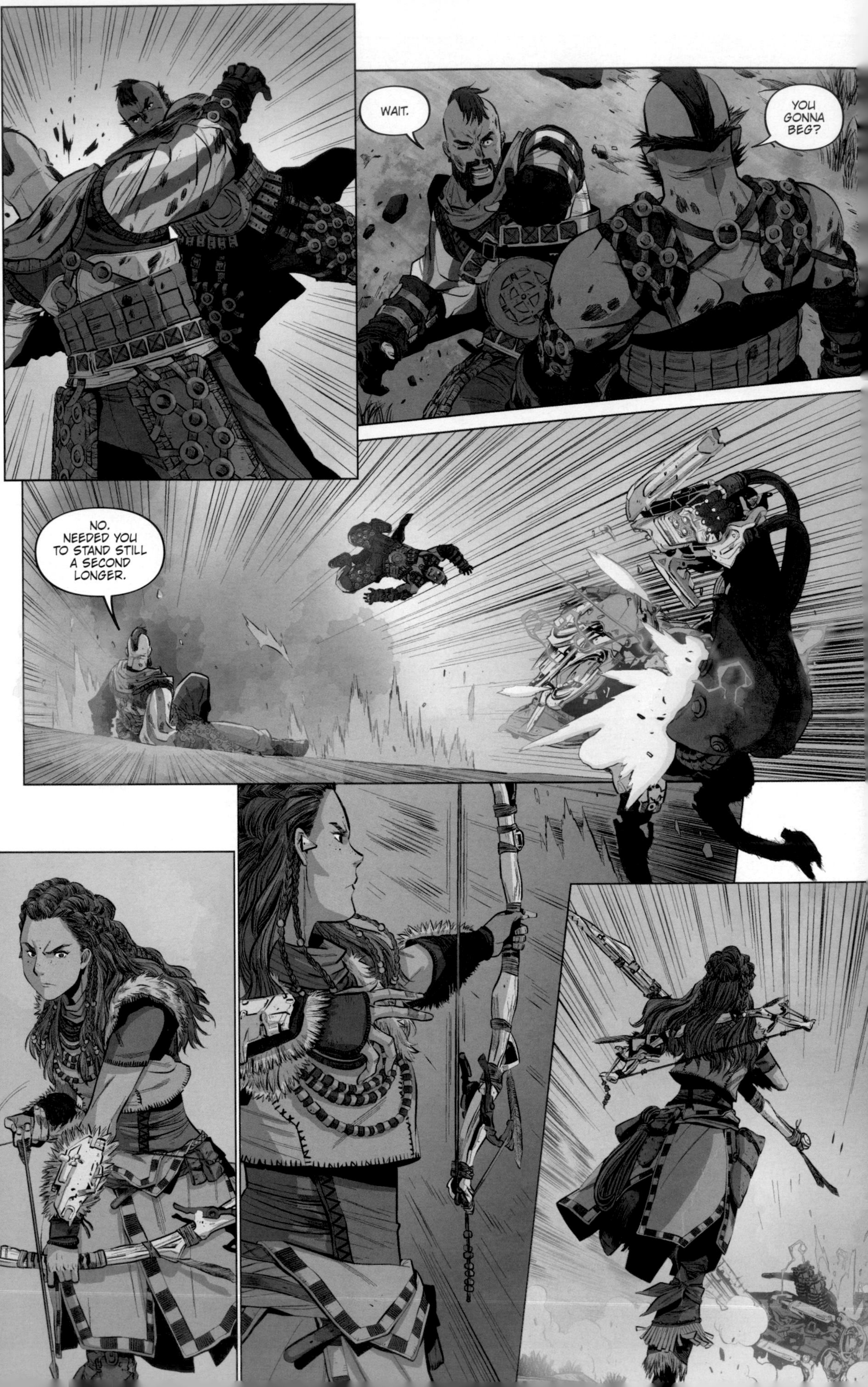
WAIT.
YOU GONNA BEG?
NO. NEEDED YOU TO STAND STILL A SECOND LONGER.

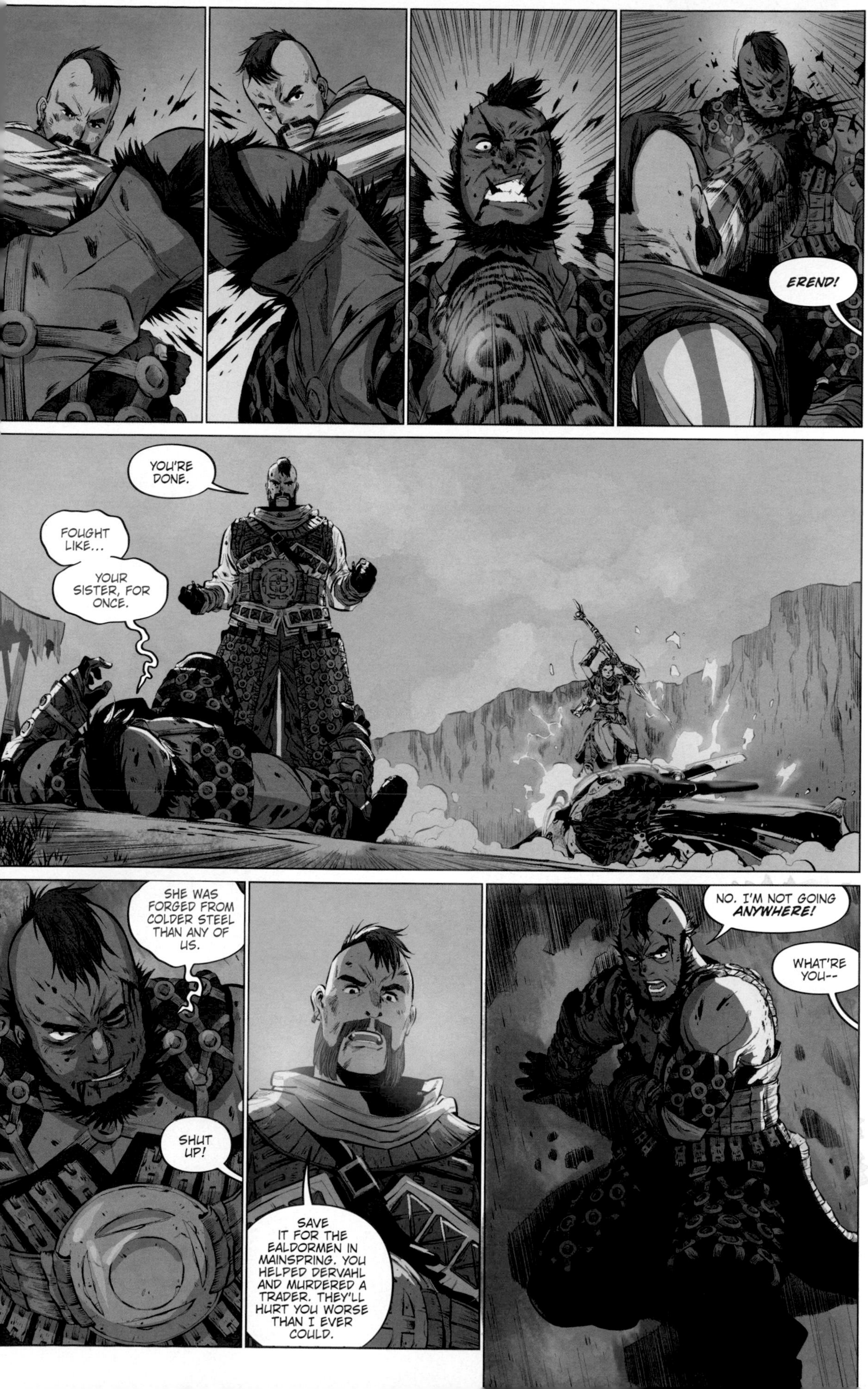
EREND!
YOU'RE DONE.
FOUGHT LIKE...
YOUR SISTER, FOR ONCE.
SHE WAS FORGED FROM COLDER STEEL THAN ANY OF US.
SHUT UP!
SAVE IT FOR THE EALDORMEN IN MAINSPRING. YOU HELPED DERVAHL AND MURDERED A TRADER. THEY'LL HURT YOU WORSE THAN I EVER COULD.
NO. I'M NOT GOING ANYWHERE!
WHAT'RE YOU--

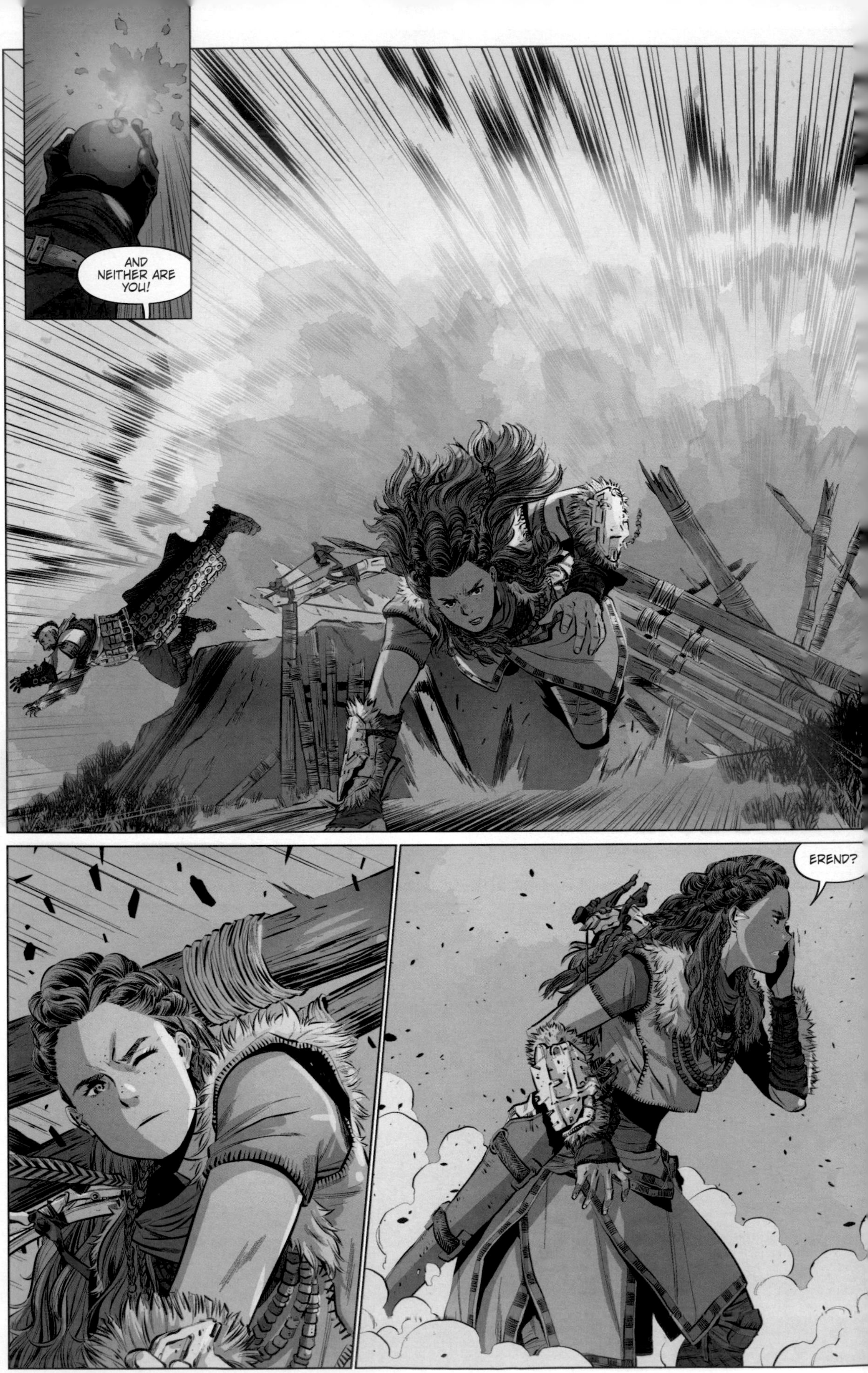
AND NEITHER ARE YOU!
EREND?

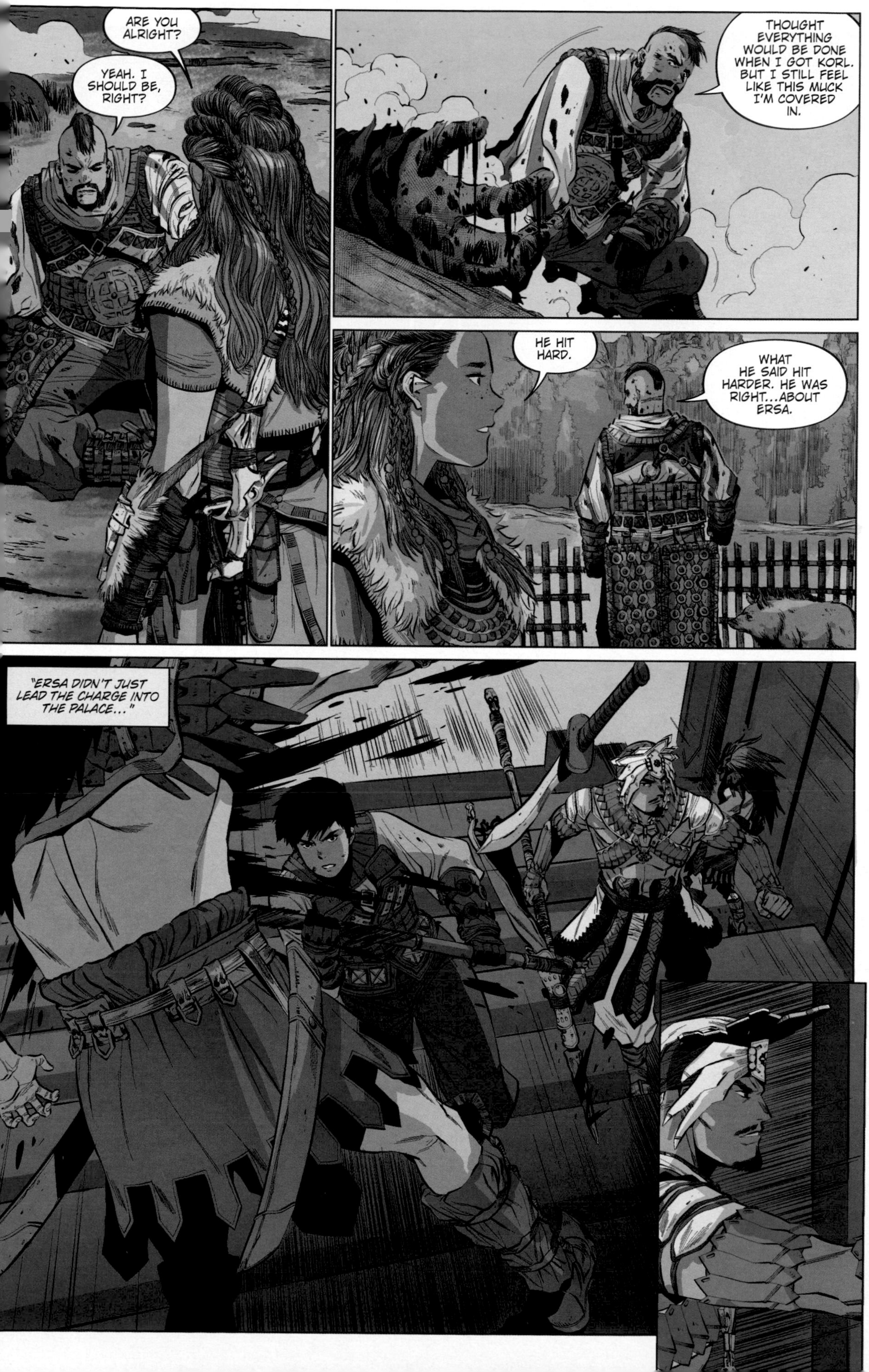
ARE YOU ALRIGHT?
YEAH. I SHOULD BE, RIGHT?
THOUGHT EVERYTHING WOULD BE DONE WHEN I GOT KORL. BUT I STILL FEEL LIKE THIS MUCK I'M COVERED IN.
HE HIT HARD.
WHAT HE SAID HIT HARDER. HE WAS RIGHT...ABOUT ERSA.
"ERSA DIDN'T JUST LEAD THE CHARGE INTO THE PALACE..."

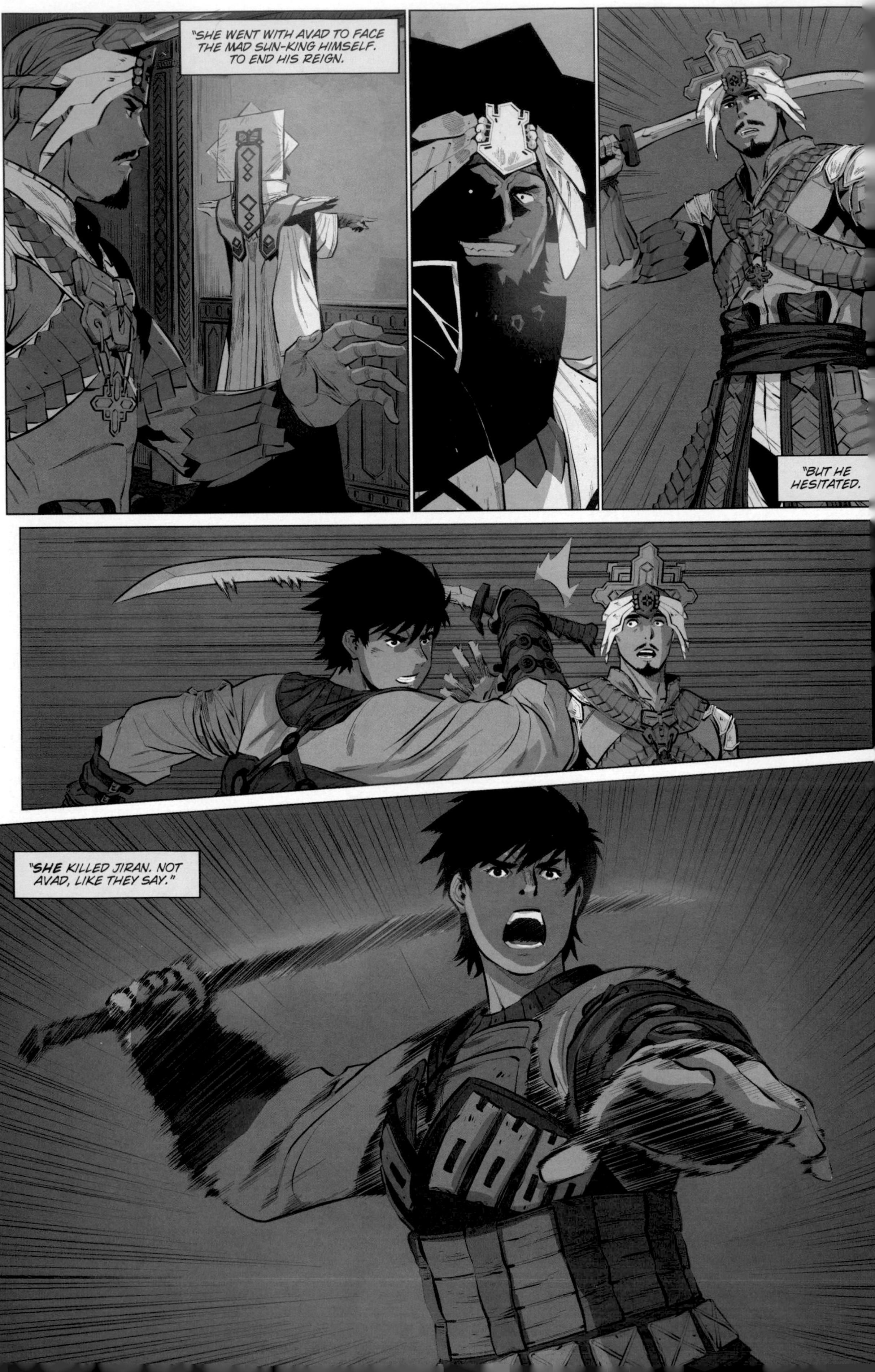
"SHE WENT WITH AVAD TO FACE THE MAD SUN-KING HIMSELF. TO END HIS REIGN.
"BUT HE HESITATED.
"SHE KILLED JIRAN. NOT AVAD, LIKE THEY SAY."

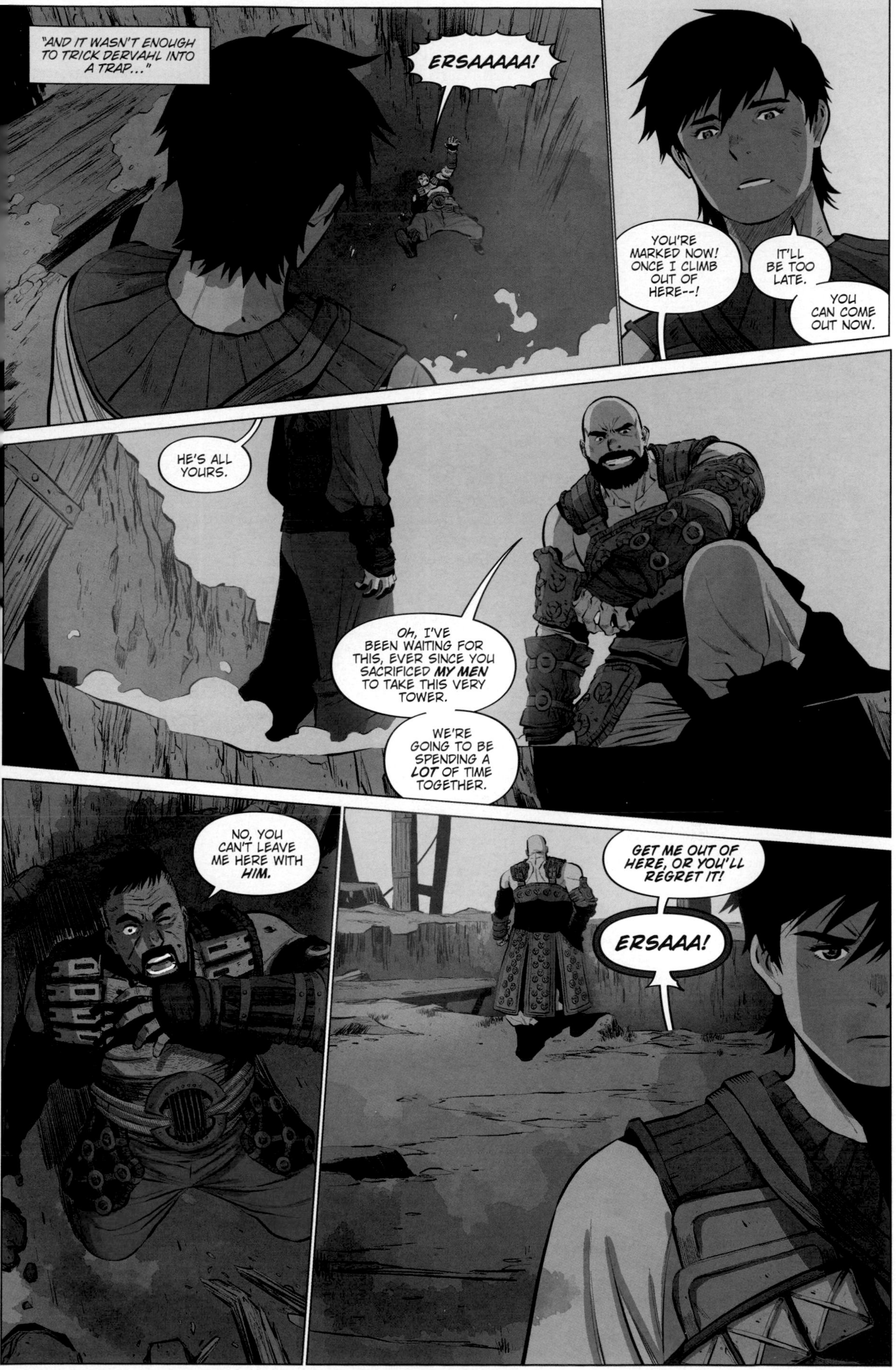
"AND IT WASN'T ENOUGH TO TRICK DERVAHL INTO A TRAP..."
ERSAAAAA!
YOU'RE MARKED NOW! ONCE I CLIMB OUT OF HERE--!
IT'LL BE TOO LATE.
YOU CAN COME OUT NOW.
HE'S ALL YOURS.
Oh, I'VE BEEN WAITING FOR THIS, EVER SINCE YOU SACRIFICED MY MEN TO TAKE THIS VERY TOWER.
WE'RE GOING TO BE SPENDING A LOT OF TIME TOGETHER.
NO, YOU CAN'T LEAVE ME HERE WITH HIM.
GET ME OUT OF HERE, OR YOU'LL REGRET IT!
ERSAAA!

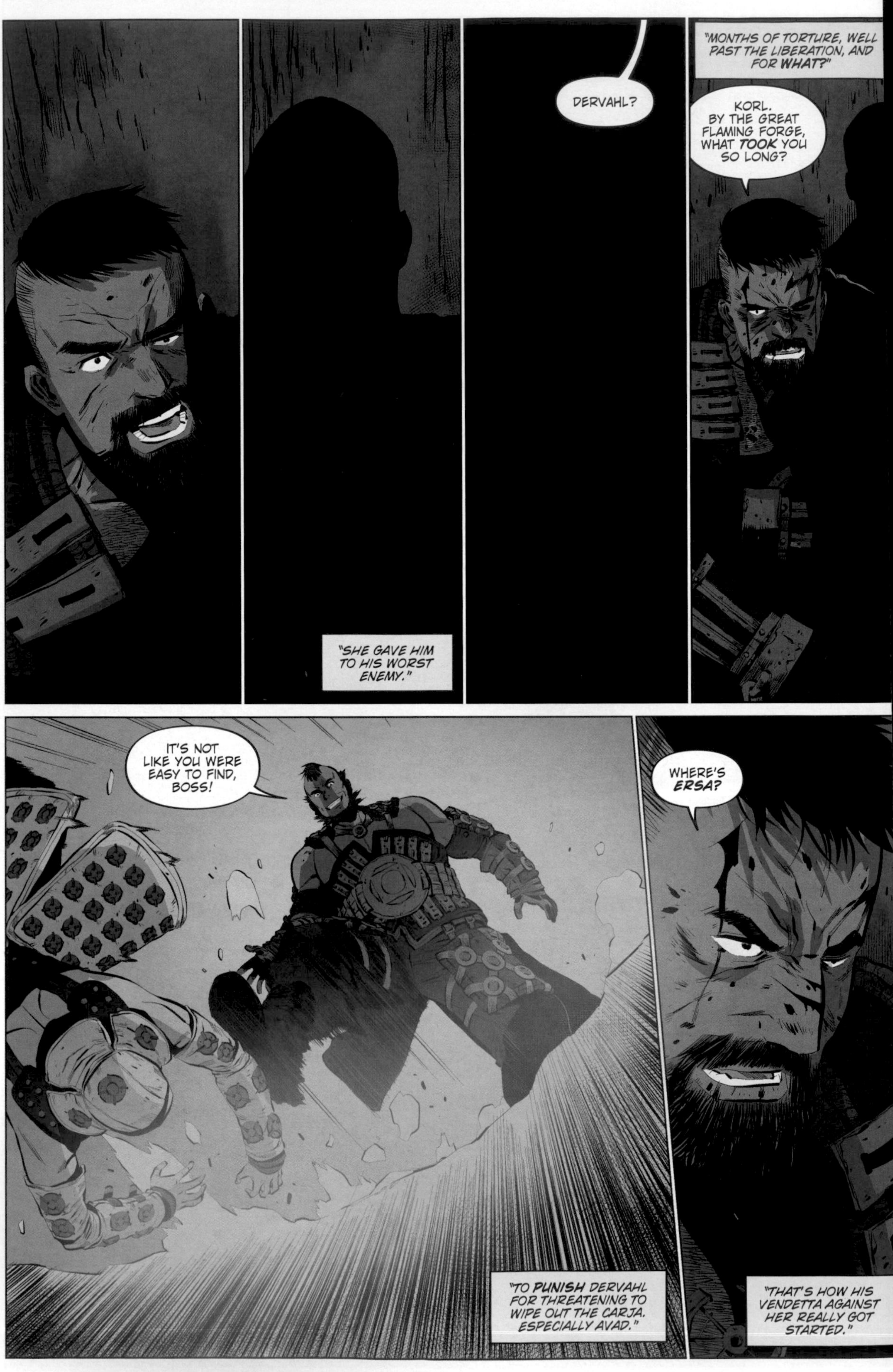
"SHE GAVE HIM TO HIS WORST ENEMY."
DERVAHL?
"MONTHS OF TORTURE, WELL PAST THE LIBERATION, AND FOR WHAT?"
KORL. BY THE GREAT FLAMING FORGE, WHAT TOOK YOU SO LONG?
IT'S NOT LIKE YOU WERE EASY TO FIND, BOSS!
"TO PUNISH DERVAHL FOR THREATENING TO WIPE OUT THE CARJA. ESPECIALLY AVAD."
WHERE'S ERSA?
"THAT'S HOW HIS VENDETTA AGAINST HER REALLY GOT STARTED."

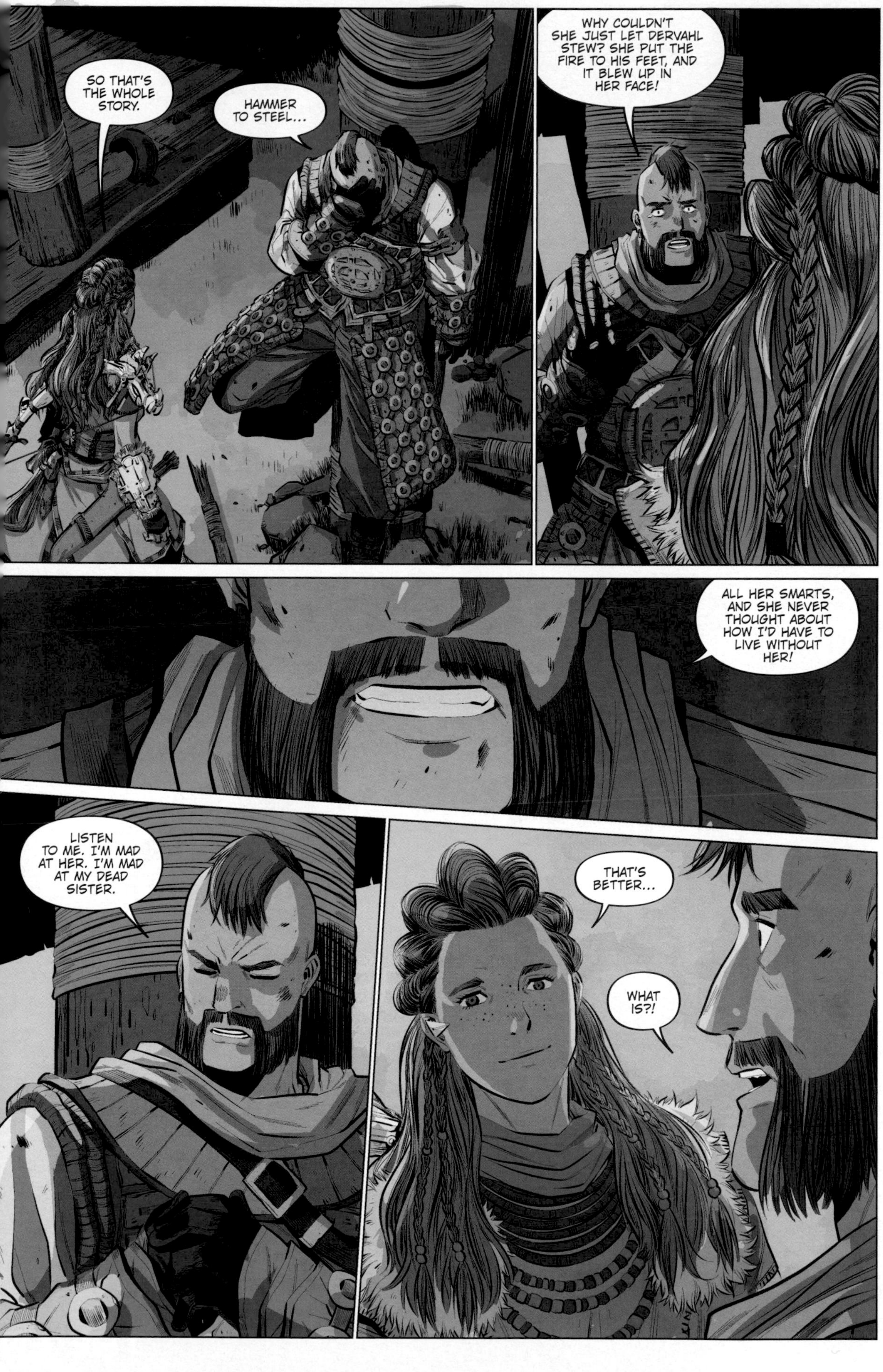
SO THAT'S THE WHOLE STORY.
HAMMER TO STEEL...
WHY COULDN'T SHE JUST LET DERVAHL STEW? SHE PUT THE FIRE TO HIS FEET, AND IT BLEW UP IN HER FACE!
ALL HER SMARTS, AND SHE NEVER THOUGHT ABOUT HOW I'D HAVE TO LIVE WITHOUT HER!
LISTEN TO ME. I'M MAD AT HER. I'M MAD AT MY DEAD SISTER.
THAT'S BETTER...
WHAT IS?!

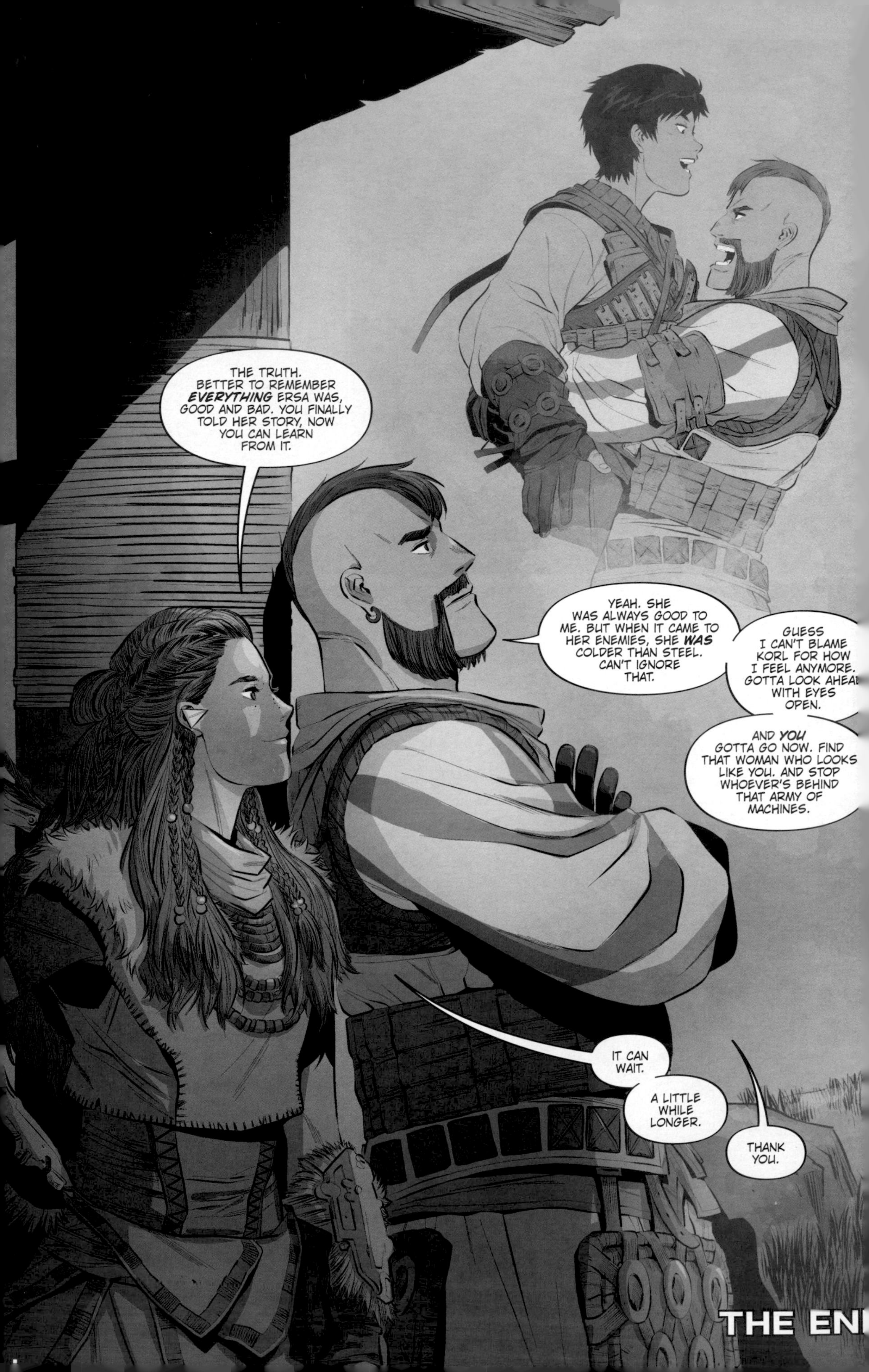
THE TRUTH. BETTER TO REMEMBER EVERYTHING ERSA WAS, GOOD AND BAD. YOU FINALLY TOLD HER STORY, NOW YOU CAN LEARN FROM IT.
YEAH. SHE WAS ALWAYS GOOD TO ME. BUT WHEN IT CAME TO HER ENEMIES, SHE WAS COLDER THAN STEEL. CAN'T IGNORE THAT.
GUESS I CAN'T BLAME KORL FOR HOW I FEEL ANYMORE. GOTTA LOOK AHEAD WITH EYES OPEN.
AND YOU GOTTA GO NOW. FIND THAT WOMAN WHO LOOKS LIKE YOU. AND STOP WHOEVER'S BEHIND THAT ARMY OF MACHINES.
IT CAN WAIT.
A LITTLE WHILE LONGER.
THANK YOU.
THE END

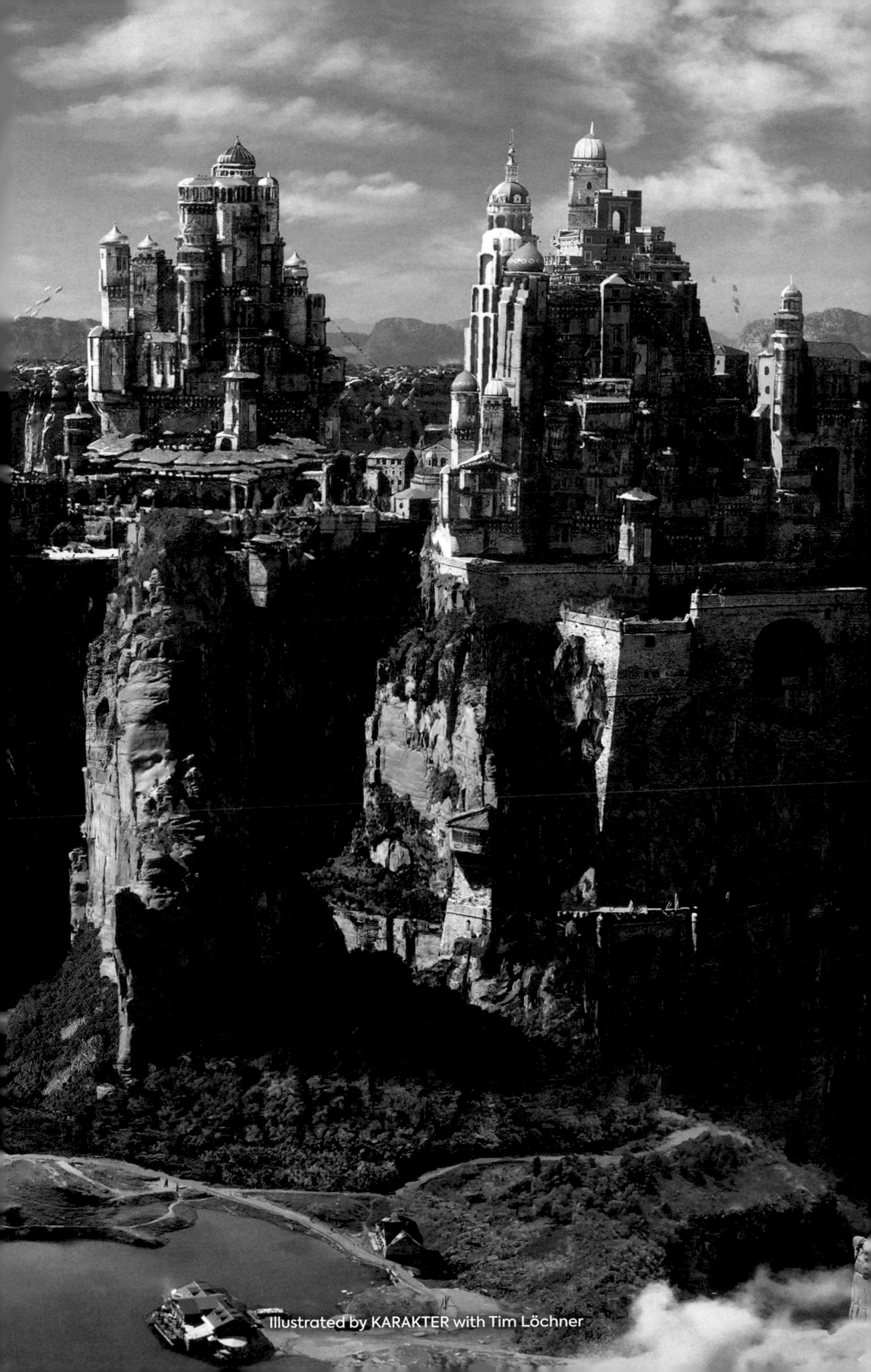

Illustrated by KARAKTER with Tim Löchner

SKETCHBOOK

We proudly present a mini gallery of Elmer Damaso's *Horizon Zero Dawn* sketches...

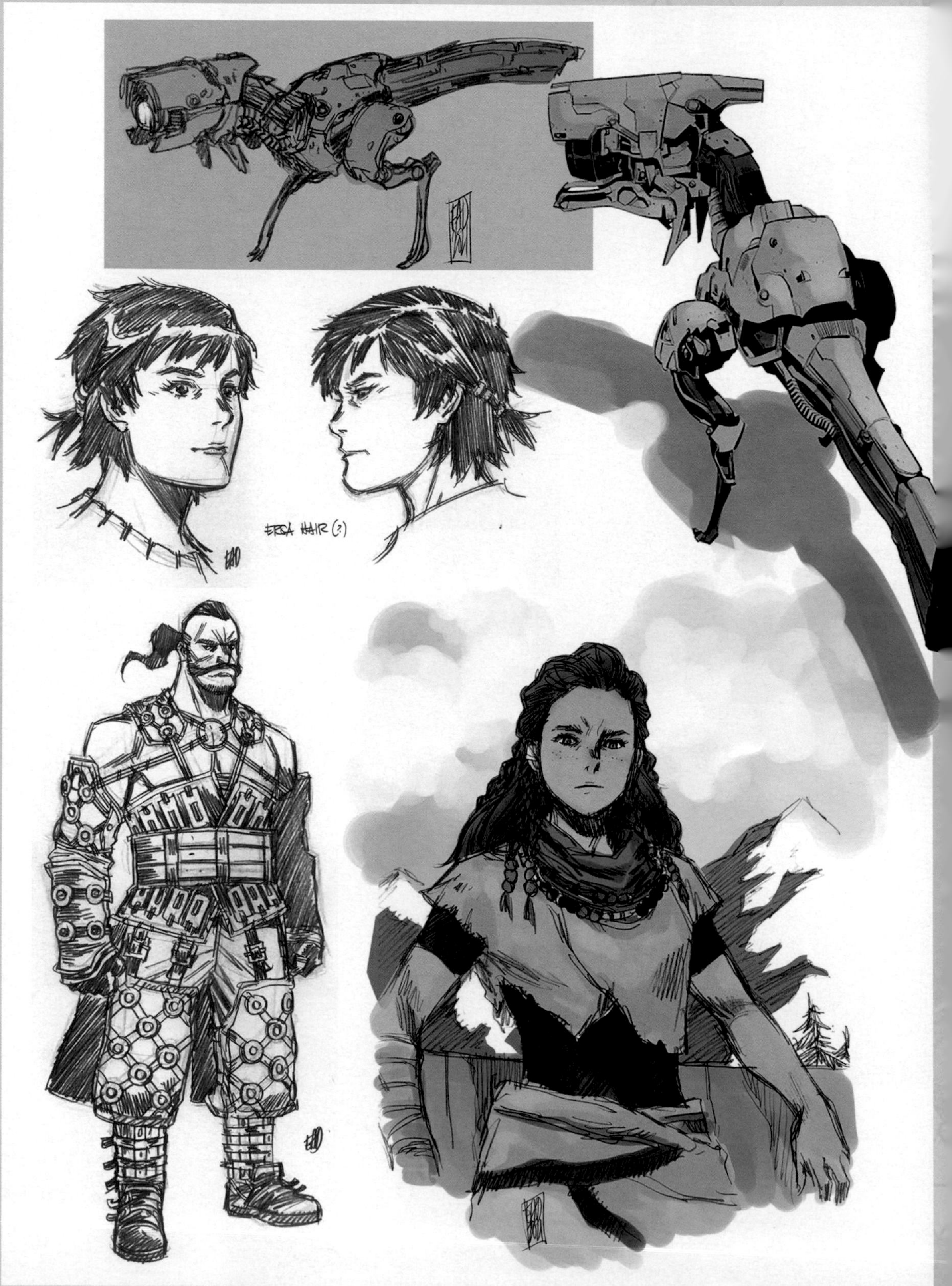
ERSA HAIR (?)

MACHINE TRADING CARDS

Ravager
Class: Combat Habitat: Found across all terrain types

Description | Like its Sawtooth brethren, the Ravager is a medium-sized combat machine with a lean, canine-like chassis. Its claws are well-suited for rapid melee attacks, and its back supports a mounted cannon for ranged engagement. It is frequently found guarding herds of acquisition-class machines like Grazers or Lancehorns.

Stormbird
Class: Combat
Habitat: Mountains and Skies

Description | These massive fliers were adapted from terraforming machines designed for atmospheric detoxification. Now outfitted with a devastating array of shock-based weapons, they strike terror in the hearts of even the most capable machine hunters. The best hope of defeating one is to tie it down with a Ropecaster and confront it on the ground.

Tallneck
Class: Communications
Habitat: Found across all terrain types

Description | Oblivious to interruption, these giants circle wide areas, monitoring local conditions. Their massive, disc-like heads contain communication hubs that send out signals to other machines. While completely peaceful, they are often guarded by packs of combat units like Ravagers or Stalkers.

Longleg
Class: Recon
Habitat: Found across all terrain types

Description | Longlegs are one of the fastest land-based reconnaissance machines. While they primarily scan for hidden threats and alert allies of danger, their powerful legs and disorienting sonic attacks turn them into formidable opponents in a fight. Every seasoned hunter knows their distinctive call can only mean one thing – trouble is on the way.

CONCEPT COVERS

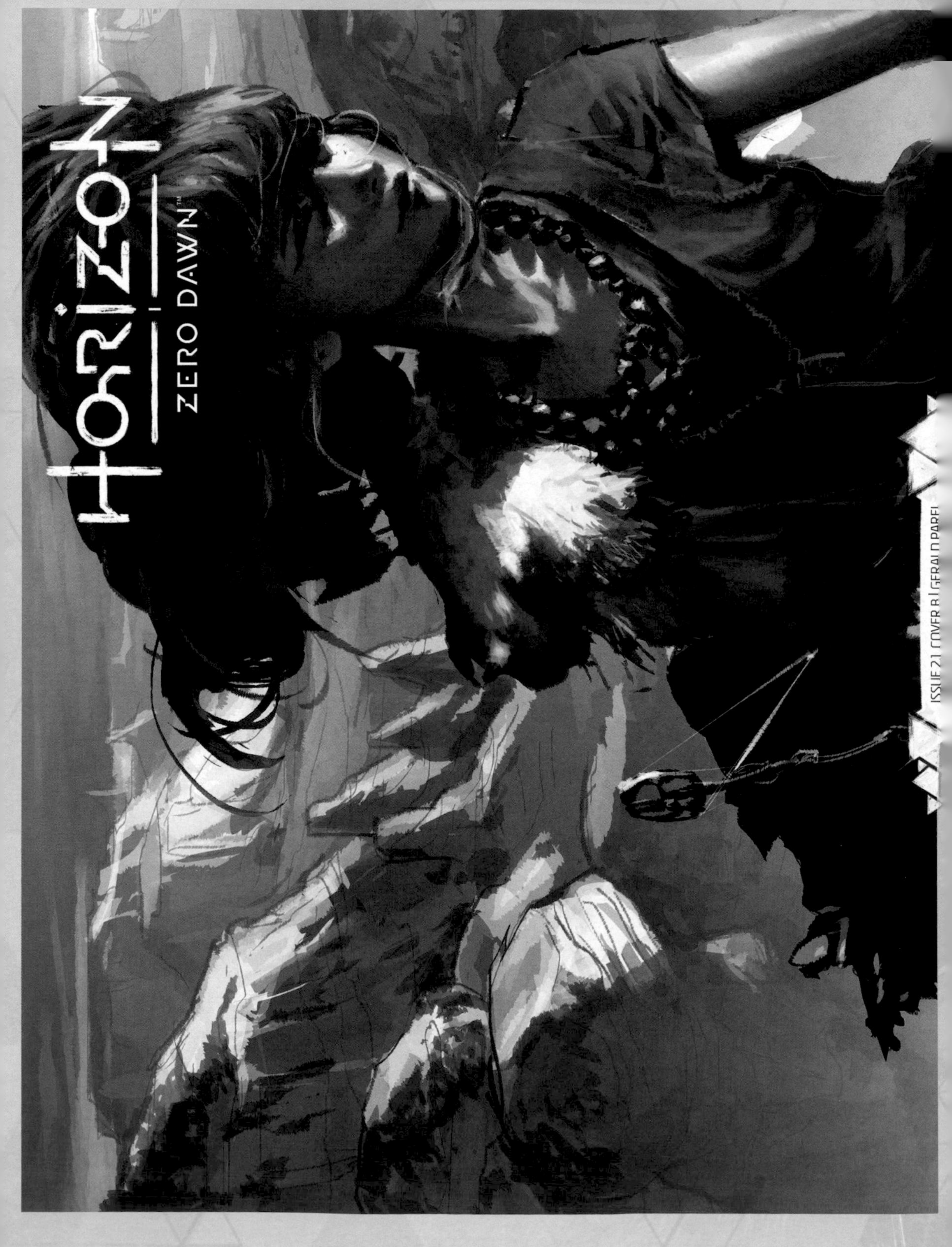
HORIZON
ZERO DAWN™
ISSUE 21 COVER B | GERALD PAREL

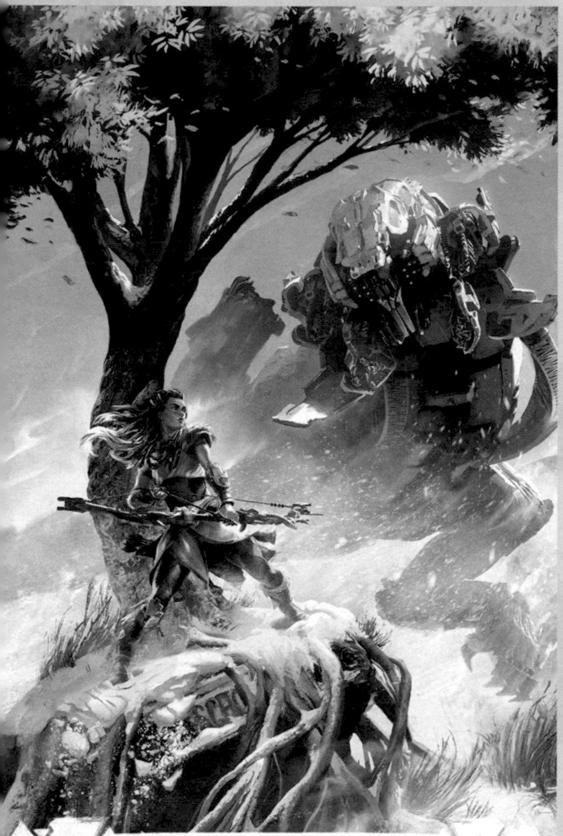

ISSUE 2.1 COVERS PACK EXCLUSIVE | LUC DE HAAN, ILYA GOLITSYN & ERIK VAN HELVOIRT

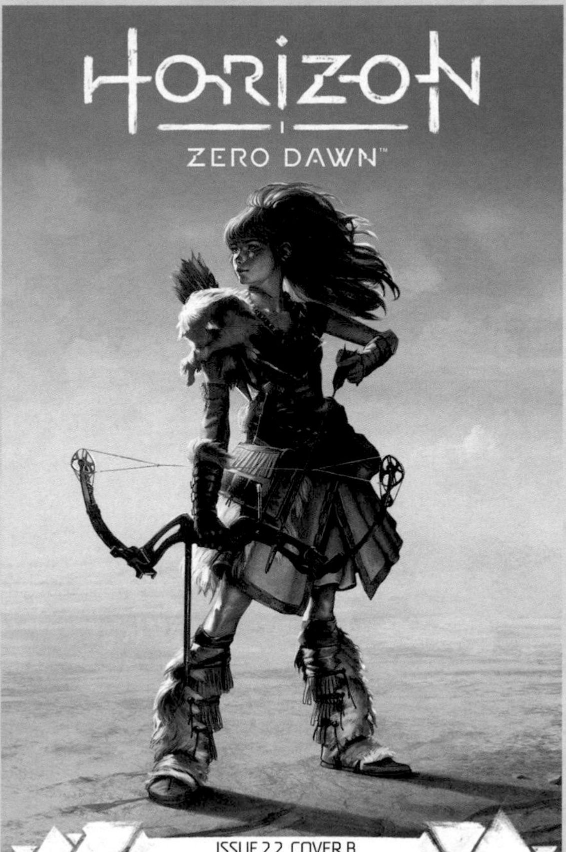
HORIZON
ZERO DAWN™

ISSUE 2.2 COVER B
JANA SCHIRMER & ILYA GOLITSYN

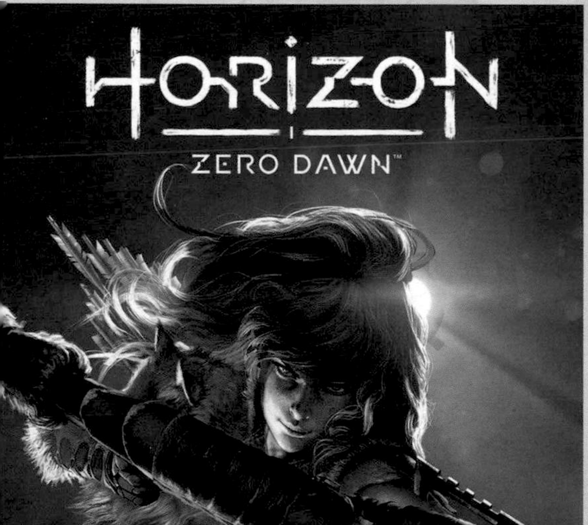
HORIZON
ZERO DAWN™

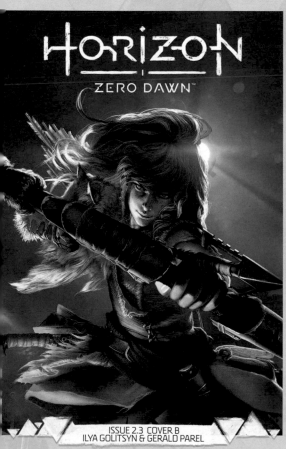

ISSUE 2.3 COVER B
ILYA GOLITSYN & GERALD PAREL

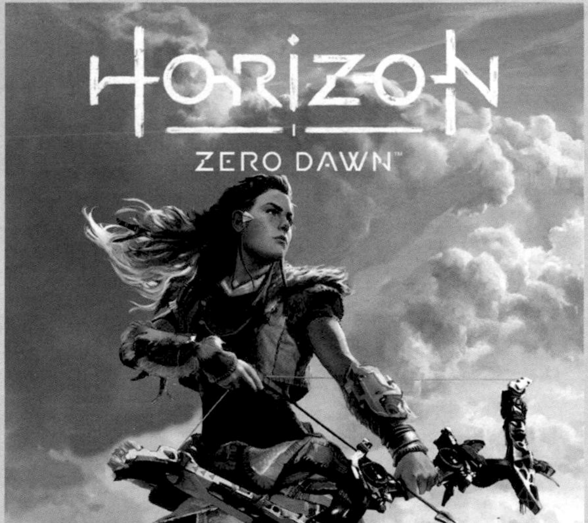
HORIZON
ZERO DAWN™

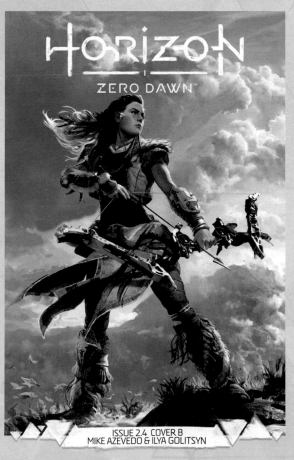

ISSUE 2.4 COVER B
MIKE AZEVEDO & ILYA GOLITSYN

COVERS GALLERY

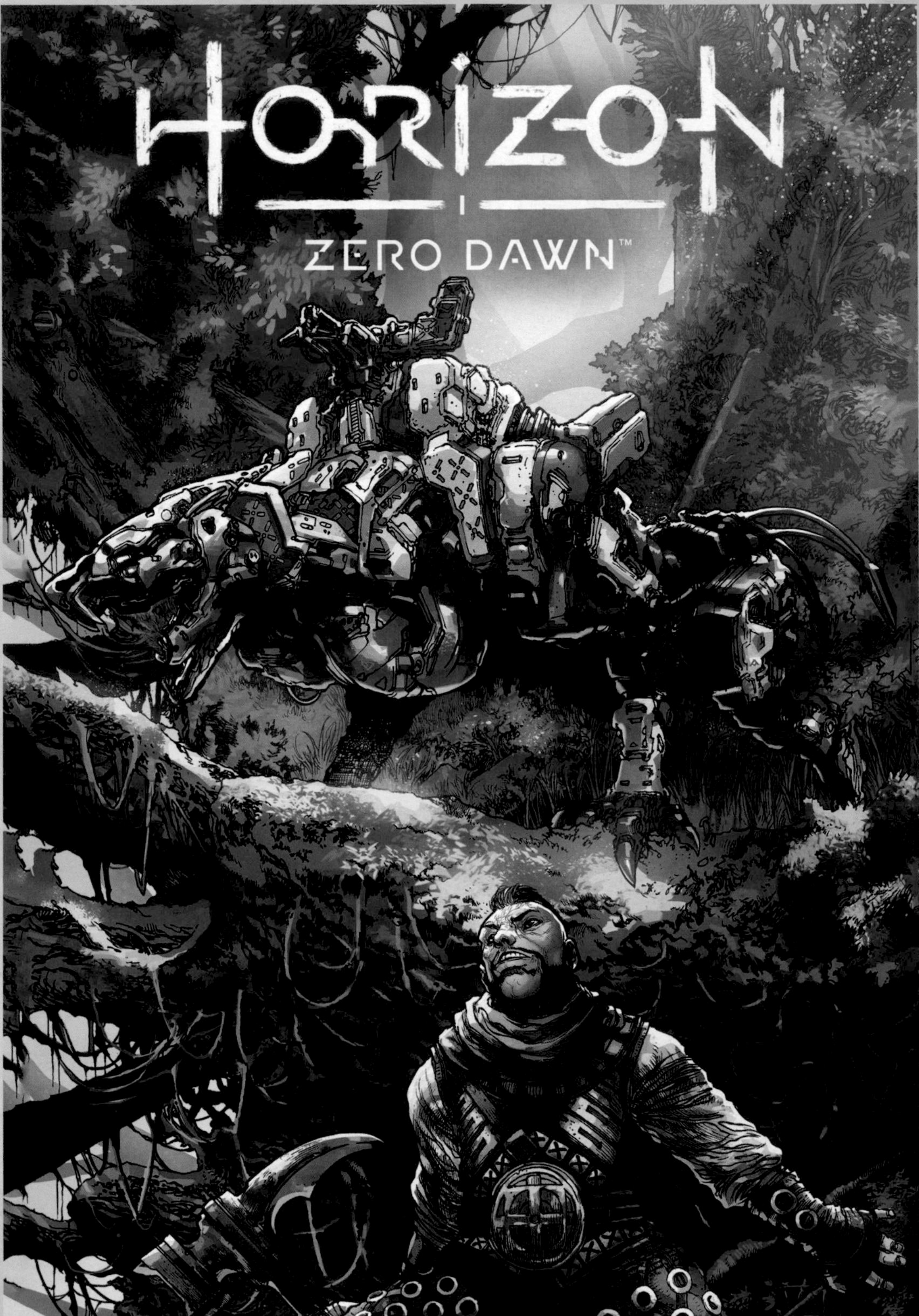
HORIZON
ZERO DAWN™

ISSUE 2.1 COVER C | HARVEY TOLIBAO OF MAGNUS ARTS
& KEVIN TOLIBAO OF HMT STUDIOS

COVERS GALLERY

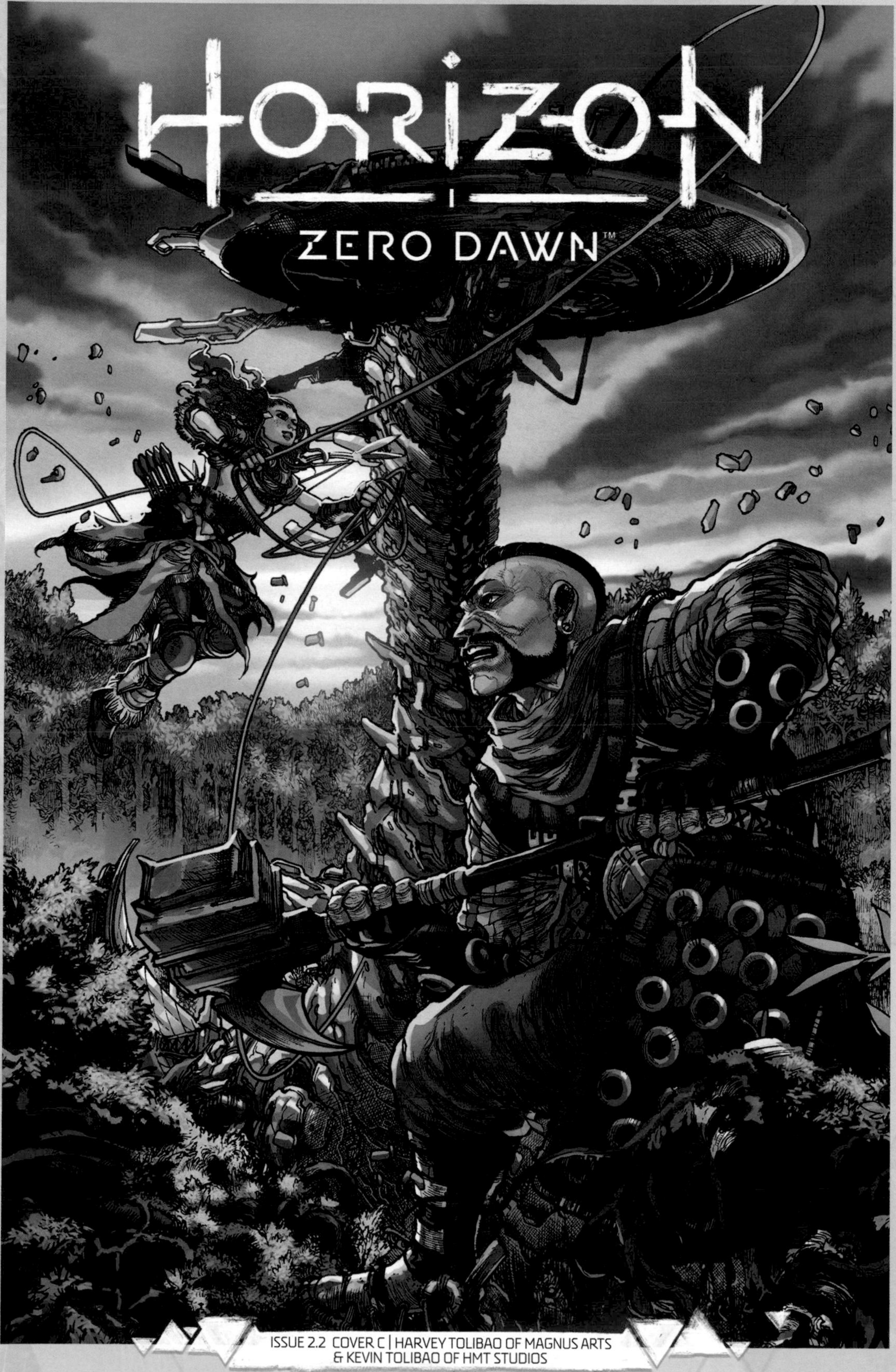
HORIZON
ZERO DAWN™

ISSUE 2.2 COVER C | HARVEY TOLIBAO OF MAGNUS ARTS
& KEVIN TOLIBAO OF HMT STUDIOS

COVERS GALLERY

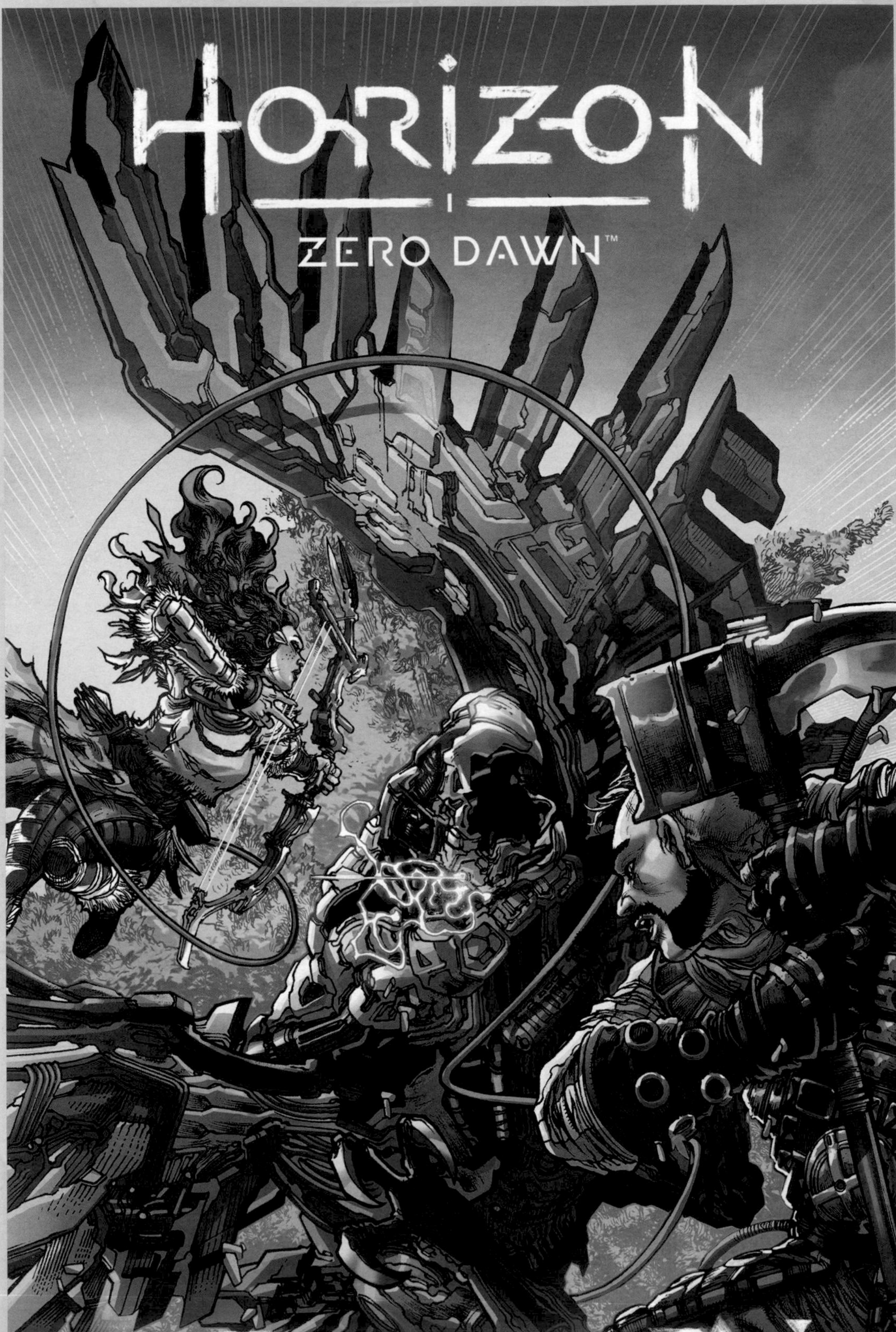
HORIZON
ZERO DAWN™

ISSUE 2.3 COVER C | HARVEY TOLIBAO OF MAGNUS ARTS
& KEVIN TOLIBAO OF HMT STUDIOS

COVERS GALLERY

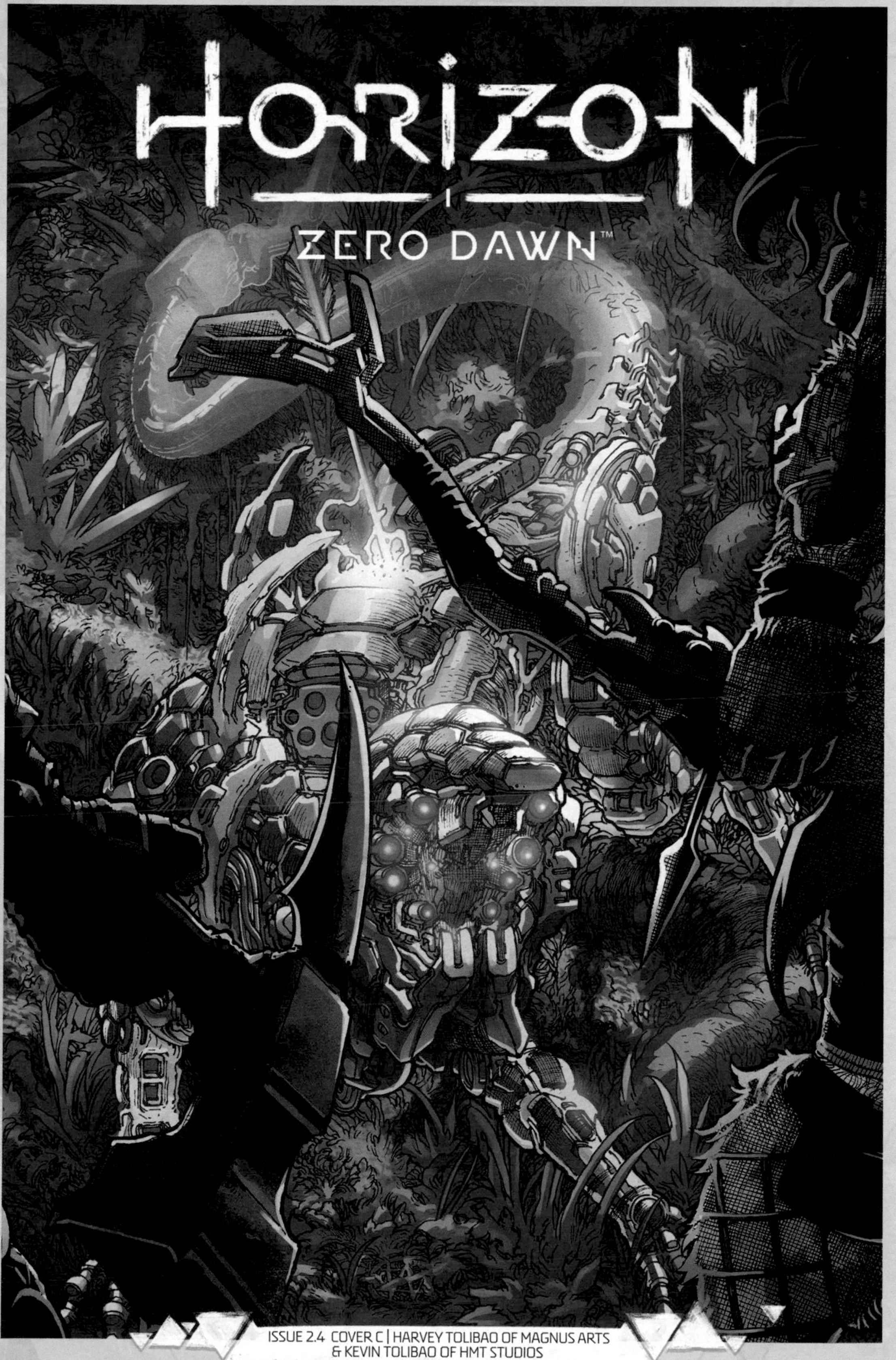
HORIZON
ZERO DAWN™

ISSUE 2.4 COVER C | HARVEY TOLIBAO OF MAGNUS ARTS
& KEVIN TOLIBAO OF HMT STUDIOS

HORIZON ZERO DAWN™

ART PROGRESS

Pencils and inks by Elmer Damaso and Colors by Bryan Valenza

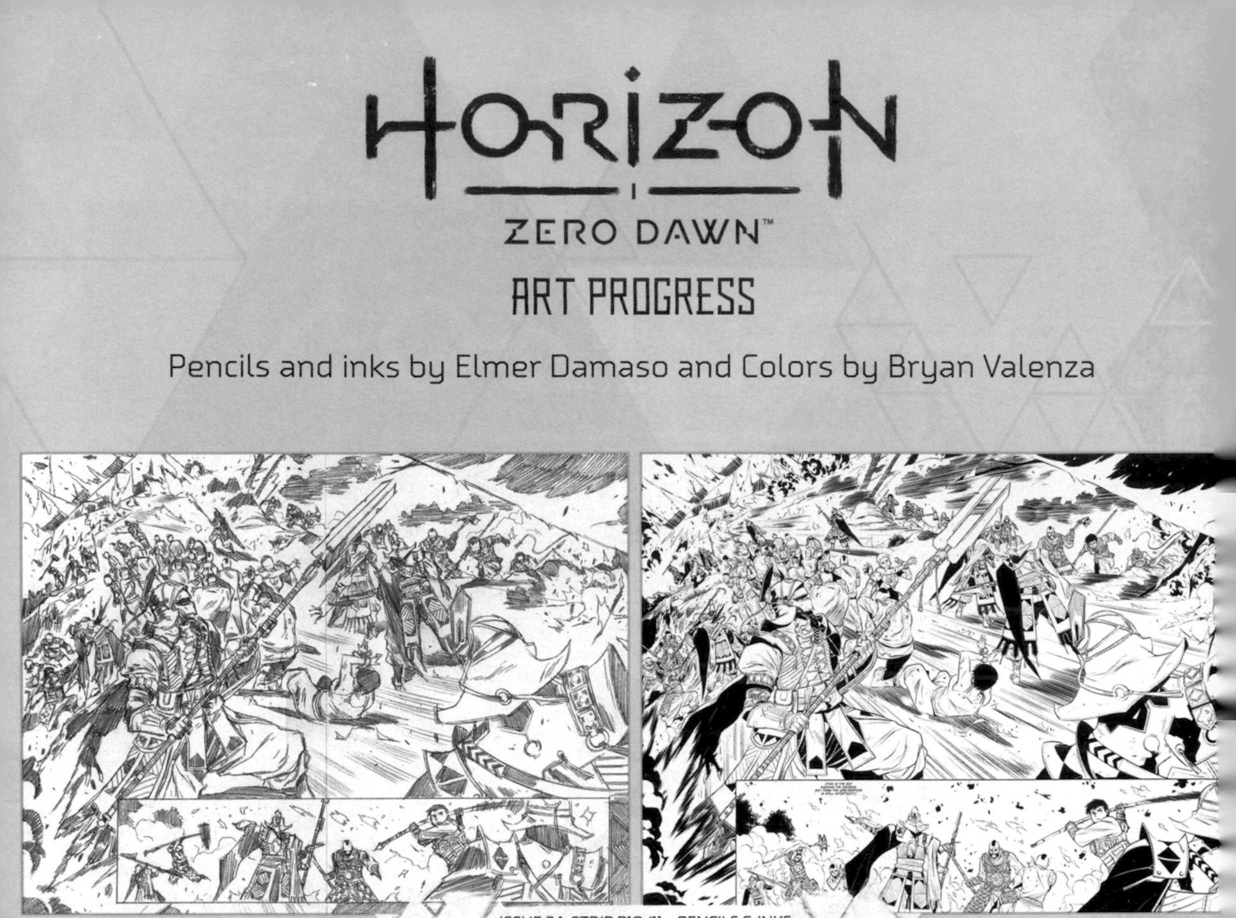

ISSUE 2.1 STRIP P10/11 - PENCILS & INKS

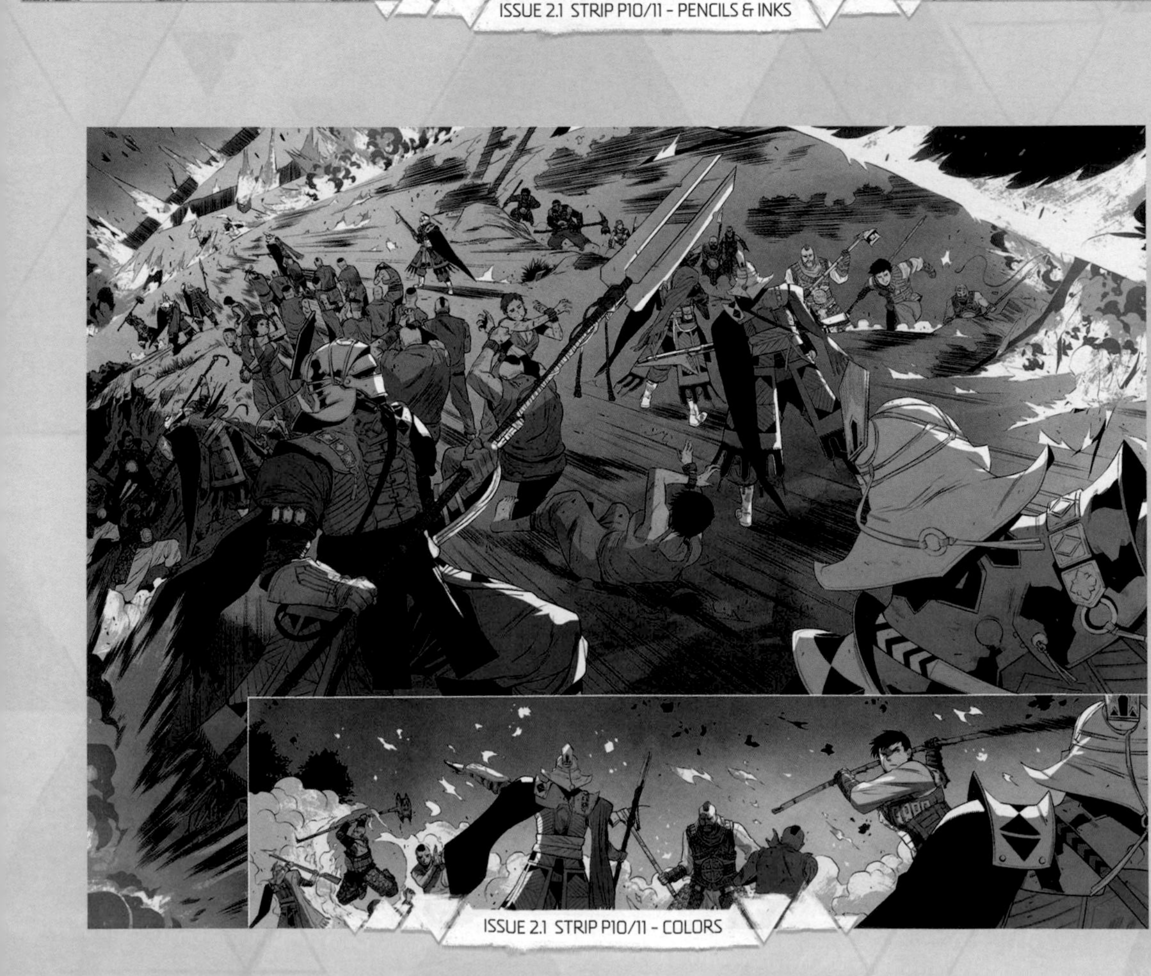

ISSUE 2.1 STRIP P10/11 - COLORS

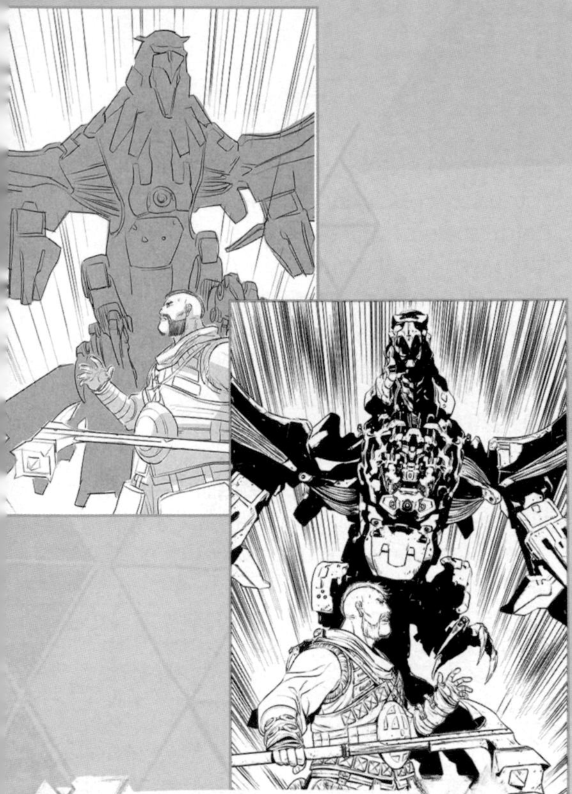

ISSUE 2.2 STRIP P26 - PENCILS & INKS

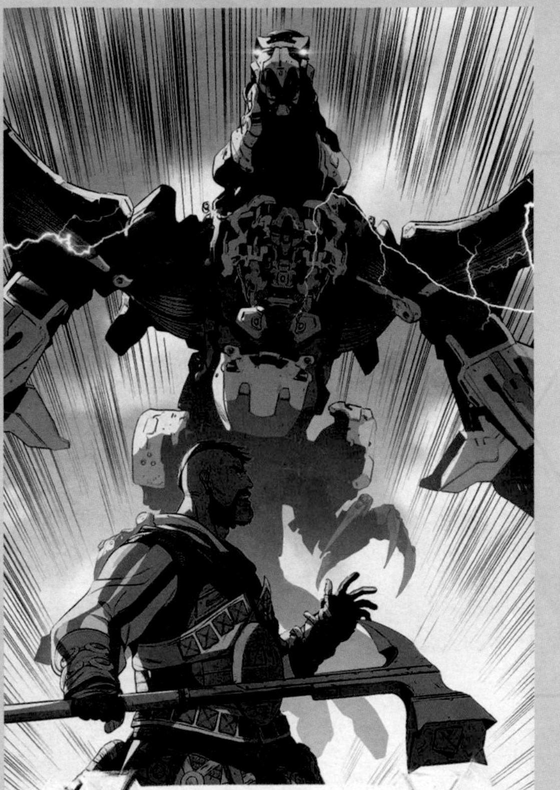

ISSUE 2.2 STRIP P26 - COLORS

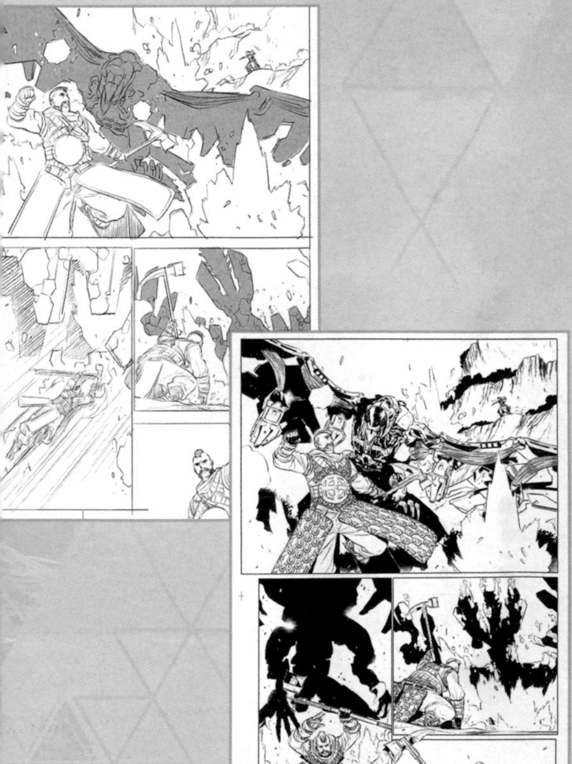

ISSUE 2.3 STRIP P6 - PENCILS & INKS

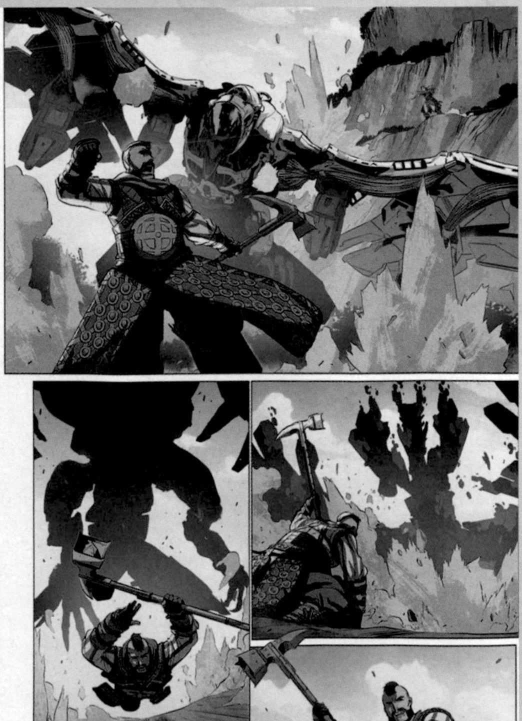

ISSUE 2.3 STRIP P6 - COLORS

BIOGRAPHIES

ANNE TOOLE has written for television, games, comics, digital series, animation and more. She most recently wrote for *Ghosts of Tsushima: Director's Cut*. A two-time Scribe Award nominee, her comics credits also include *Women of Marvel* #1 and *Halo: Lone Wolf*. She won a Writers Guild award for Best Video Game Writing for her work on the original *Horizon Zero Dawn* game.

ELMER DAMASO has been working as a manga and comic book artist for almost 20 years, and has previously worked on titles such as *Speed Racer*, *Hero Factory*, *Kingdom of Assassins*, and *Robotech/Voltron*.

BRYAN VALENZA is a comic book colourist and founder of the BEYOND Colorlab coloring studio, and he has been working in comics since 2012. His previous coloring work includes *Robotech*, *Witchblade*, *Red Sonja* and *Vampirella Meets Betty and Veronica*.

JIM CAMPBELL is a twice-Eisner-nominated comic book letterer with a long list of credits to his name, including *Blade Runner 2019*, *Robotech*, and *The Raid* from Titan Comics. When not working on bringing dialogue and SFX to life on the page, he runs a blog full of tips and advice for future letterers.

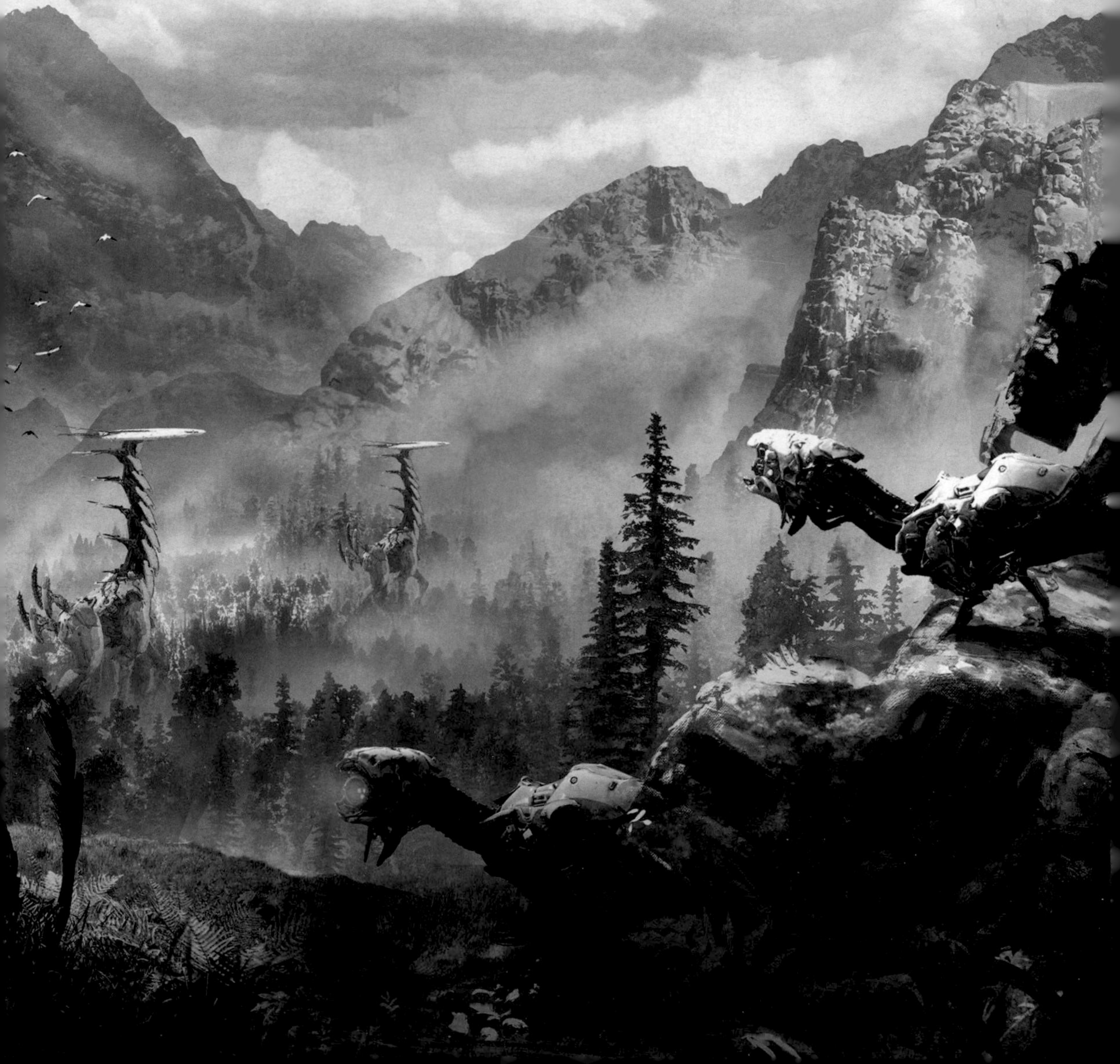